Run
East

Run East

Flight from the Holocaust

Jack Pomerantz and
Lyric Wallwork Winik

University of Illinois Press
Urbana and Chicago

This book is printed on acid-free paper.

Library of Congress Cataloging-in-Publication Data
Pomerantz, Jack, 1918–
Run east : flight from the Holocaust / Jack Pomerantz and Lyric Wallwork Winik.
p.   cm.
Includes bibliographical references and index.
ISBN 0-252-02325-0 (alk. paper)
1. Pomerantz, Jack, 1918–   . 2. World War, 1939–1945—Personal narratives, Jewish.
3. Jews—Poland—Radzyn Podlaski—Biography. 4. Refugees, Jewish—Soviet Union—
Biography. 5. Jewish soldiers—Soviet Union—Biography. 6. Holocaust, Jewish (1939–
1945)—Poland. I. Winik, Lyric Wallwork, 1966–   . II. Title.
SA135.P63P664   1997
940.53 18 092—dc21
[B]   96-51240
CIP

To Nina, who is everything to me
J.P.

For Jay, forever, for everything, with love
L.W.W.

Contents

Preface

This book is the product of a remarkable collaboration, spanning several years. It began with two people, a writer and a man with an extraordinary story to tell, a tape recorder, and hundreds of questions on yellow-lined pads. For over a year and a half, I interviewed Jack Pomerantz, covering the story of his life from his birth into grinding poverty in Poland, through his struggle to survive as a Jew in the Soviet Union, where he fled from the Germans during the savage years of World War II, and finally to his journey to the United States from a refugee camp after the war.

Jack Pomerantz's compelling story spans three continents, moving from Poland to Kiev, to Soviet Central Asia and Siberia, then to Moscow and Berlin, and finally to Austria and the United States. It captures a significant part of the Holocaust that to this day remains too little explored by historians and memoirs, namely the world of European Jews who fled into the Soviet Union and were used by the Soviets, sometimes as Siberian laborers, other times as soldiers fighting on the eastern front.

Jack Pomerantz survived these experiences and offers the rare perspective of a Jew discovering the horror of the Holocaust and the destruction of his family as he returns to eastern Europe, moving west through the Ukraine and Poland, all the way to Berlin. His story opens a different, yet critically important window into World War II, that of a refugee on the run in the Soviet Union, where Muslim, Christian, and Jewish worlds collide. It is a story that matters for history.

At the start of this project, I was faced with the challenging task of how best to recount and give shape to Jack Pomerantz's story. After considerable reflection I chose to write and present it in the first person. This choice had the benefit of preserving the authenticity of Jack Pomerantz's voice and his feelings and observations. It would also allow him to speak to the reader and for the historical record, at a time when each year more voices from this period are forever silenced.

After over a hundred hours of interviews, often combing a single incident repeatedly for details, I transcribed the material and then organized, arranged, and wrote it into a narrative, to tell the story of Jack Pomerantz's remarkable survival and the story of his family and, equally important, to give historical shape to the vanished world of Jewish struggle and survival on the eastern front.

Beyond the actual interviews, I also conducted extensive outside research to check facts, dates, events, and locations for accuracy and to examine the myriad facets of the subject. I used materials, some previously classified, from the Library of Congress and the National Archives, as well as documents and maps from the New York Public Library and YIVO, the Institute for Jewish Research, in New York, and also original war texts produced by the United States Military Academy at West Point, which detail Soviet and German military operations on the eastern front in World War II. I also consulted with leading Soviet scholars of the period. Finally, together, Jack Pomerantz and I reviewed each page of the manuscript drafts for accuracy and clarity.

As the reader can see, the task of writing this story presented special challenges. Yet to the extent that it was daunting, it was also rewarding for me as both a historian and a writer, for this book rests at the intersection of the large, historical events of the Holocaust and World War II and one man's poignant, distinctive story.

Ultimately, on a personal level, the resulting manuscript is both a labor of love and a product of faith and trust: trust that one person can share, understand, and value the life of another; and faith that there are no greater gifts a writer can give than not only to tell a story that otherwise might never have been told but also to help recover a missing history.

L.W.W.

Acknowledgments

A book is like a journey, and there are many people who provided sustenance and shelter to this project along the way.

During this process, Elie Wiesel and Debórah Dwork of Clark University provided vital words of encouragement. Doris Bergen of the University of Vermont offered a highly sensitive, thoughtful, and insightful reading of the manuscript. Her support was essential to its success. Alan Adelson, executive director of the Jewish Heritage Writing Project, was a caring, helpful reader, who had great understanding of the book and why it matters. Peter Berkowitz of Harvard University was a wonderful source of encouragement and information. Amos Perlmutter of American University was full of ideas and counsel. At Johns Hopkins University, Dorothy Ross, Ron Walters, and Lou Galambos provided invaluable advice and guidance. Jane Mohraz, associate editor at the University of Illinois Press, provided sensitive and thoughtful copyediting.

Finally, this book has been especially fortunate to receive wonderful care and support from Judy McCulloh, executive editor at the University of Illinois Press. It could not have received a more welcoming home.

In addition, we would like to offer our individual thanks.

A deep and profound thanks to Jim and Lark Wallwork, who have provided many years of friendship, who had such trust in me that we agreed to build a house on a handshake, and who have shared not just themselves but also their caring. And I thank them for their daughter, Lyric.

My children, Francine and Arlene, are two of the joys in my life. Francine and her husband, Keith Kasper, have also given me three other special joys, my grandchildren, Alexander, Shaina, and Hannah.

For thirty-five years, Betsy Miller, as well as her late husband, Bill, has been a true and lasting friend. Anthony and Dorothy Barone have also shared wonderful years of friendship with me, along with their children, Andrea and Paul Lanza and Lisa and Lenny Liotta. My thanks also go to my friends George and Georgine Brazer. Greta and Sheldon Skolnik, my sister-in-law and brother-in-law, have been a special family for me.

I want to thank my dear friend Dr. Marvin Soalt. I am also grateful to Dr. Stephen Guss, the cardiologist from Morristown, New Jersey, who has saved my life. Most of all, I want to thank my wife, Nina, who is my greatest love and my greatest joy. What I suffered during the war, the heartbreak and devastation, my wife has fixed. I have the most beautiful married life any man can have. Nina has given me a new life for forty-three precious years.

J.P.

Professionally and personally, I want to thank Sara Brzowsky, Larry Smith, and Walter Anderson, my editors at *Parade* magazine. There is not a finer group of people to write for and to learn from. It is an immense pleasure to work with them and to know them.

My thanks also to the teachers and friends who have inspired me, especially Pat Lionetti at Pingry and John Fleming, Julie Agoos, Paul Muldoon, and Carolyn Kizer at Princeton. I also owe a debt of gratitude to Burnie Bond; Veneeta Acson; Howard, Samantha, and Nicholas Streicher; Nancy Curby; Jon Karp; Sophie Rosenfeld; and Arabella Meyer, who have been great sources of encouragement and support. Finally, my lasting thanks to Dr. Ron Kurstin, for all that he has taught me about human compassion and kindness.

My special thanks as well to Norm and Elaine Winik, for their warm words of encouragement, and to Herb Winik and Lynn Abrams, my father-in-law and mother-in-law, for their support and belief in what I was doing. Thanks also to Frances Saunders for sharing her widsom and enthusiasm. Deep thanks to my parents, Jim and Lark Wallwork, who have always believed in this book and enthusiastically supported it. They have constantly and lovingly encouraged my mind and my dreams. My most enduring debt is to my husband, Jay Winik, for whom thanks are not enough. He has more faith in me than I have in myself. He is a talented writer and brilliant thinker, a remarkable person, with a wonderful kindness. He is the most special person I know, my love and inspiration, the half that makes me whole.

L.W.W.

Run
East

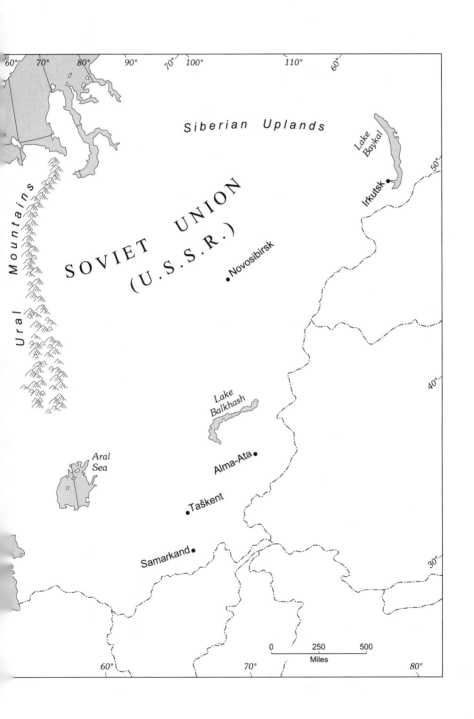

1

When the Planes Came

The German planes came in the morning.

We knew they were coming. We knew Poland was under attack, and the Germans were bombing towns. We knew the German army, in tanks and trucks, was racing across Poland with lightening speed. Only the day before, the Germans had reached Łuków, a town of seven thousand, east of Warsaw and less than fifteen miles from Radzyń, my home.

My mother's family was from Łuków. Her sister and brother-in-law still owned a bicycle shop there. We knew Łuków. We knew the people, the streets, the markets, the synagogue. But now the Łuków we knew was no more. For hours, people from Łuków, some riding on carts, some walking with bundles, some with nothing, had been streaming into Radzyń. Some families came with cows and horses, even cages of chickens, trying as they fled to haul everything they owned. Some of these people stopped and stayed, but many others simply kept moving.

We watched them pass through our streets in disbelief and did nothing. There were people in Radzyń who had never been to Łuków, who had never been beyond the fields that ringed the town. They watched and rolled their eyes, wondering what had made these people from Łuków set out for the unknown. That September morning, many of them and the rest of Radzyń's six thousand residents had awoken and begun the day much as they had any other.

We knew the Nazis and their planes were coming, and yet we didn't know, for most people in Radzyń had never seen a plane.

When the planes finally arrived, the panic was terrible. People ran, screaming and crying. Women covered their heads and wailed. Children stood dazed on the streets. Men ran from their shops as glass shattered and walls collapsed into piles of rubble. Some people tried to hide in bushes or ran from the town toward the woods, where they thought the planes couldn't spot them. But there was nowhere to hide.

The fire department siren sounded as the planes fired into the streets and into nearby fields. It was a pathetic, futile warning. There were no high buildings, no guns, nothing to stop these planes from coming in low.

I was on the streets when the planes attacked. I was twenty-one and had seen a few cars and some buses, but nothing like this, the noisy engines, the shiny metal, riding on air. In my wildest dreams, I could never have imagined a plane. I stared up in wonder, as their heavy humming echoed in my ears. Suddenly the slow, monotonous noise was pierced by a high-pitched squeal of diving wings. Then came a thunderous sound that rocked the earth. The first bombs had been released, whistling in an ever-faster arc through the air until they collided, violently, with the ground.

I remember the horror of feeling solid earth suddenly shake beneath my feet. I ran down an alley and flattened myself against the brick wall of a house, thinking that if I just pressed myself tight enough against the rough brick, maybe the planes would not see me, maybe a bomb would not catch me. My arms, my legs, my back, every part of me shook from fear. When I looked up, the planes were so close I could see the outlines of faces inside. I saw the smooth cheeks of a gunner, and then I wrenched my eyes away. If I could see this man, then almost certainly, he could see me.

The planes didn't just attack once, they left, and then they came again.

The first time the bombing stopped, I went looking for my family, for my brothers and sisters and my mother and my father. It seemed that everyone in Radzyń was looking. The terrifying hum of engines and thunderous explosions had been replaced by crying—mothers in search of their children, children rushing terrified through the streets—and the frenzied, breathless running of people who only moments ago had been pinned in houses and cellars and courtyards. People ran up and down the same streets, not knowing where to go.

Jews, Poles, everyone was just trying to survive. It was chaos.

At first, I couldn't find anyone in my family. I ran through the market, past overturned carts and baskets of broken eggs, their yolks seeping along the ground. The main streets were littered with broken glass, thousands of shards glinting in the sun. I turned down my street, where houses were wedged one against the other and only a thin strip of sidewalk separated their gray wooden fronts from the road. I called out names. Finally, I saw my mother coming out of a doorway, where she had hidden near our home. I grabbed her by the arm, and we raced away from the town into the countryside. We didn't try to take anything with us. We would come back after the bombing stopped. At that moment, I only thought to run, not to look back. It would be almost five years before I saw Radzyń again.

My mother and I headed toward a farm village called Branica, where my father knew several farmers. In the event of trouble, my whole family had planned to gather there. I knew the route by heart, beginning with a wooden bridge that stretched across a fast-moving brook on the outskirts of Radzyń. A little ways upstream was a flour mill, and nearby was a sunny bank where young people would go on summer holidays to picnic and drench themselves in the cool water. On that morning though, the usually green banks smelled of singed grass, and the bridge I had always crossed, which throughout my life had borne up under the weight of carts and horses, was now bombed wreckage, battering against the rocks downstream. Since the bridge was gone and the brook was about twenty-five feet wide, the situation seemed hopeless. Neither my mother nor I knew how to swim.

But we had no choice. The last few weeks had been dry and the brook was low. I slid down the bank. The water rose quickly, soaking me up to my hips. It was cold. Trying to balance in the current, I reached out my hands to help my mother. She was tall for a woman and did not hesitate. Gripping my arm, she stepped into the flow. Quickly, the water came up toward her waist. Her skirt grew heavy and matted, and I had to drag her across the soft mud bottom. Rocks and pebbles poked through my worn shoes. With each step, I envisioned the bottom suddenly dropping away and the water rushing up over us. But the bottom did not drop. It stayed flat and muddy, with slick sharp rocks. I pushed my mother onto the opposite bank, and we clawed our way up the grass. We stood for a moment, wringing our heavy clothes, and rested. And then I heard it, a soft hum.

Looking up, I saw the planes in the distance. I grabbed my mother's arm, practically pulling her along the road. She was panting for breath, but I would not let her rest. We had to keep going.

As we watched the planes move toward us across the sky, I could feel my mother's heart beating. I could almost hear her heart. I was her youngest child. When I was growing up, she saved scraps of food for me, so I would have a bit extra to eat. When I was two years old and very ill for days with a high fever and chills, she bundled me up, boarded a bus, and traveled almost eighty miles to Warsaw so I could be examined by a skilled doctor. She had raised eight children, barely having food for their stomachs and clothes for their backs. Yet she was still a gentle, beautiful woman, and I loved her.

I gripped her hand as we walked along the road. I did not know this was the last morning I would ever feel her touch.

Within minutes, the planes were in front of us, swooping down on the fields, shooting at the cows, at anything that moved.

The land outside Radzyń was rich and flat, with pastures and fields covered with crops and flowers. Clumps of thick, leafy bushes were scattered across the fields and near the road. As the planes converged above, I pushed my mother under one bush whose branches fanned out wildly on all sides, and I crawled in after her.

We huddled against the ground, completely silent. My pants and shoes felt heavy and clammy. Cool dirt pressed against my flushed cheeks and through my shirt, like a salve on my skin. As each bomb fell or a spray of bullets hit, the earth shuddered. I kept moving my feet and my arms, sliding them back and forth to make sure I was still alive. I reached out to shake my mother's limbs to see if they still moved, to see if we had been shot.

Bombs and bullets were falling everywhere. I kept imagining that I had been hit, even though all the while I was moving my legs and my arms. When the bombing stopped, we stayed under the bush, slowly looking through the tangled branches and leaves, feeling all along the ground around us for blood.

We waited, but the planes did not return. All we heard were the low-pitched moans of cows. I crawled out first. Whichever way I turned, there were bomb craters, on the road, in the fields. Nothing but craters and dead cattle, their bellies ripped open by gunshots. Then, a little way off, I saw someone walking.

My heart began to pound faster, and I froze with fear. But, as the figure came closer, I could see that he was wearing a *tallis,* a Jewish prayer shawl. He had pulled the shawl over his head, so that it completely covered his eyes, his mouth, his entire face.

I said to my mother, "Look at this man walking, how does he see to walk? His face is covered." To myself, I thought, "How can I be scared? A person who wears a prayer shawl like that wouldn't harm anyone."

He kept coming closer along the crater-covered road, and I called out, again and again, "Who is it? Who is it?"

Finally, as the figure neared us, he lifted the shawl. It was my father.

At first, I could say nothing. I wanted to speak, but no words would come. I simply stood there, shaking. In the midst of mangled land and livestock, my father was alive. We stared at one another in silence. Then I asked him, "How did you see to walk with the tallis over your head?"

He stood facing me, his fingertips touching the tallis, and answered, "God was in the front of me, leading me."

2

Radzyń
Remembered

I was born on May 5, 1918, in a barn on a bed of straw. My mother was hiding in the barn when I was born. Outside, a pogrom was raging. Homes were being raided and people attacked, beaten, tortured, even killed. Families were stripped of their possessions and sometimes forced to watch as their things were smashed, burned, or otherwise destroyed. The violence was unpredictable. Sometimes, it would move across an entire region like a storm rumbling across an open plain. Other times, it was local, contained within a city or town. Sparked by a single incident, an unkind word, a bad business transaction, a simple rumor, the violence would flare for days. Only one thing was certain about a pogrom: its targets were Jews.

This time, the pogrom was probably launched by Cossacks escaping Russia and the Bolshevik revolution. But, during this period, Poles began pogroms as well. The history of pogroms against the Jews stretches back to the Middle Ages. Nineteen eighteen and 1919 were, however, years of rampant savagery and destruction, of wild bursts of rage. My mother had sought shelter in barns during earlier attacks. Now, once again, she tried to lie quietly, wrapping me in rags, amid the animals and straw.

I grew up sleeping on straw, one brother on either side of me, two facing me. We barely had room to roll over, and almost every night I was kicked in the mouth as I slept. The layer of straw was so thin that I could usually feel the rough wooden floor underneath. In the summer, the straw grew matted from the heat of our bodies and damp from our sweat. In the winter, we huddled together on the floor for warmth against the biting cold.

Ten of us, five sons, Moshe, Ytzel, Luza, Srulke, and me, Yankel, three daughters, Serke, Esther, and Genia, and our parents, Abish and Freida Pomeranice, lived in three rooms, the largest of which was ten feet by ten feet. My father, a tall, slender man with a long, flowing beard, worked as a peddler in Radzyń, my mother came from a family of peddlers in Łuków. My father was a poor man, but he had a good name and was respected in the community. My mother was a striking woman, even though her clothes were simple and her wig, worn by all Orthodox women, was plain.

Abish and Freida's marriage had been arranged by a matchmaker and approved by their families. In Radzyń, matchmakers rarely selected someone from another town, and I never knew why my mother had been chosen for my father. Perhaps it had to do with her dowry or even religious titles and bloodlines. I don't know, I only remember that every bit of money my mother saved, she put aside for my sisters' dowries, for their weddings.

Most of Radzyń's three thousand Jews were poor. Families lived in rented rooms scattered across one section of the town. We were the poorest of the poor. Our home was actually a shed in the backyard of a Polish family's home. We had nothing, not even a table so we could sit down to eat. Our water had to be carried in buckets from a brook more than a thousand feet away. Our bathroom was a covered hole in the ground behind the shed. The poverty was oppressive and unrelenting. We were often cold. Frequently, during the winter, my brothers and I would sneak out at midnight to break the slats off of neighborhood fences. We burned the slats for heat because we couldn't afford even the cheapest wood or coal. But cold was nothing compared with hunger.

We were constantly hungry. There were weeks when we would go for two, even three days without any solid food before my mother had enough money to buy a loaf of bread. When she returned with the bread, all eight children would be waiting by the door, and everyone would try to grab a piece of the loaf. Several times, when we were all very young, we ripped my mother's dress in our frenzy to get to the heavy, crusty bread.

My mother tried to make do. Night after night, she chopped potatoes and onions into fine slices, so fine that a couple of potatoes could feed the ten of us. She fried them up and we washed them down with sour milk. My mother always tried to have a meal for Shabbat, the Friday night Sabbath. Sometimes, it was a slice of Challah bread or fish or chicken soup. Many times, however, we didn't have anything.

Even tea was a luxury. As a rule, we drank it only when my sister Genia visited a doctor's family who lived a few blocks away. Sometimes, without a word, they would press a handful of the fragrant leaves into her palm as she left. If they had no fresh leaves, they often gave her wet ones, which they would otherwise use again.

On the Jewish holidays, it was particularly painful to be so poor. We could smell the rich aroma of our neighbors' cooking, feel steam come in our windows from their boiling pots. We, however, often had nothing to cook. During those times, my mother would not say a word. She would simply stoke the fire, her face turning red from heat, her eyes watering from the rush of smoke. Then she would fill her own pots with water and boil rags to make our neighbors think that we were also cooking.

I can remember a few instances when we did have a little spare money, and my mother would start preparing for a holiday. She would get out the candles, and we would have soup and Challah. At those moments, the house came alive. Even my father allowed himself to smile.

Around Passover, we often received a special treat—a package from the United States. My mother's brother and two of her sisters had emigrated to the United States around 1920, after the pogroms at the end of World War I. Each year, our aunts and uncle sent us a package with five U.S. dollars and some clothes. My mother would not use even one of the American dollars to buy food. Instead she put the American money aside for Serke's, Esther's, and Genia's dowries.

Once our aunts and uncle sent all the children shoes. They were stiff and shiny and very narrow. I forced my feet to fit into those shoes, causing terrible pains and big, red blisters. Every step hurt, but I wore those shoes because I had nothing else. We all wore those stiff, narrow shoes because otherwise we'd be barefoot in the frost. Eventually, I slit the sides of the shoes and made them last for years. Clothes were the same way, we wore them year after year.

No matter how little we had, my mother insisted that our home always be clean. Each day, she and Genia washed the floors and spread fresh cut pine branches to leave a fresh smell. Several times each day, too, someone would walk over a quarter of a mile to draw water and carry it back. Genia usually went, although sometimes my mother would carry the buckets, which swung from a wooden yoke on her shoulders. But the moment Genia noticed my mother and the buckets missing, she would run after her and insist on lugging back the heavy, sloppy buckets herself. Carrying water was a thankless task, and years of it hunched women's backs and gnarled their hands.

My mother tried to make do, but she could never be sure from one day to the next whether she would be able to buy food. Neither could my father.

Peddling was very unsteady work. Sometimes my father would make a little bit of money, but often he would come home with nothing after a long day.

Farming was the best way to make money around Radzyń, but no Jews farmed because, for all practical purposes, Jews in the region could not own land. In the first decades of the century, a few Jews had owned farms, but vandals destroyed their crops, barns, and livestock and, house by house, drove them off the land. When I was young, no one was left to teach Jewish children how to farm, so children were brought up to work in the towns or as day laborers. Boys followed their fathers into various trades. A few were profitable, but many more were not.

In Radzyń, as in other Polish towns, successful Jews worked as tradesmen, as tailors or shoemakers, as blacksmiths or butchers. One very lucky Jew owned a mill that made flour. Others worked as small vendors, including one man who sold ice cream. He made it right on the sidewalk, in a wooden barrel that rested inside a metal can. He would pack ice and salt around the barrel and then crank the handle, around and around, thickening the eggs and sweet, sugary cream. Sometimes, I would hang around the barrel, hoping he would ask me to crank the handle. My reward was an ice cream, a scoop of the thick, sweet cream inside a chewy waffle. I loved each bite. For me, ice cream was one of the rarest and most delicious things on earth. But, like with many other vendors and store owners, he struggled. In the 1930s, a boycott of Jewish-owned stores spread across Poland. Times were even worse for Jews who did not own stores or were not skilled in a trade.

One of our neighbors, the Graboevitz family, used to "rent" sections of fields in which Polish farmers had planted potatoes. Each harvest season, the family would pay money in return for being allowed to dig up a potato field. They paid for digging privileges without knowing how many potatoes were in the ground. If the field contained a good crop of potatoes, the family would make money. If there were only a few, then they would lose. They never knew until they started digging.

Peddling was not much more secure. Each morning, before dawn, my father would leave the house, carrying a large basket, and head toward farm villages, five, even ten or more, miles away from Radzyń. My father would buy chickens, geese, calves, ducklings, eggs, onions, potatoes, wheat, flax, anything that farmers had for sale, even sweet-water fish from ponds. He would either pay for his purchases or buy on credit and then leave the items behind while he went on to the next farm. After he made all his purchases, if he could not carry everything in his basket, he would rent a horse and wagon from one of the farmers to transport the goods back to town. He could not afford his own wagon.

My father did not sell his merchandise on the streets. He had a regular clientele of shop owners and cooks who bought from him. But they did not buy all the time. Sometimes my father managed to sell what he had purchased, but not always. Then he would lose what little money he had or, worse, be in debt to a farmer. Radzyń had many peddlers competing against each other. One family even bought chickens and shipped them in crates to Warsaw for sale.

The uncertainty took a toll on my father. He was frequently upset because he never knew from one day to the next whether we'd have money for food. He had to sell many chickens just to make enough profit to buy some chicken lungs and livers. Our family could not afford to buy those simple items my father sold. All we could hope for was that he would make enough profit to be able to buy a loaf of bread.

Sometimes, my father would leave the house with a hundred zloty and return with fifty, and then everyone suffered. He would yell at my mother and sometimes also take out his frustrations on my brothers and me.

When I was eight, my father started to take me with him to the farms. If we were going to purchase chickens, we would leave before dawn. We had to arrive before the chickens woke and scattered across the yard. They could be caught only when they were still asleep, inside the coop. The road to the chicken farmers ran past an old cemetery. Each morning, I was convinced that, as I passed, one of the dead would rise up from the graveyard and follow me down the road. Going to the farmers, I had my father to protect me. But I had to carry the chickens back home by myself. Each time, before I ever reached the cemetery, my heart began to race. As I passed by the stones, I would turn around and begin to walk backwards, so I could see the cemetery after I passed, to make sure no one was following me. I always turned around and looked, never knowing if this time one of the dead would come after me. The only thing worse than my fear when I passed by the graves was the punishment my father would give me if I refused to go with him for the chickens.

By the time I was twelve, I could go alone to the local farmers' places to peddle or to work as a laborer. If they offered me any food, it was usually ham. I was always hungry, so it didn't take much for them to convince me to eat the ham, although pork is not kosher, and I was breaking the rules of my religion. Sometimes, the farmers would tell me that they were doing "a great thing for Christ" by giving me ham. Once, my father discovered I had eaten ham. He became furious and punished me very harshly.

In Radzyń, however, pork was only a small part of the problem.

Radzyń was one town but two worlds: Jews and Poles. Founded in 1768, it was the district capital in the province of Lublin. Radzyń was a beautiful place. There were flowers and small gardens, a park and a river with a special place along its banks for picnicking and swimming. On Saturdays, young people in Radzyń put on their finest clothes and promenaded down the main street. If you had a new tie, you showed it off on a Saturday. The proudest people out walking were those with shiny, new boots.

An old Polish czar's summer palace and lush grounds stood in one section of Radzyń, and at the very center of town was a white stucco church, surrounded by a richly decorated wall. Horses and wagons rolled down Radzyń's paved streets, and poppies grew in the fields ringing the city. There was beauty, but there was also poverty. And there were divisions.

Jews in Radzyń had a separate community and culture. Even outwardly, Jews looked different from Poles. While Poles tended to be very fair-skinned, Jews were generally darker. Jews spoke Yiddish rather than Polish, and most older Jews dressed in long black clothes, quite different from the white shirts, butternut brown pants, and narrow-brimmed hats worn by Poles.

Throughout Poland, Jews and Poles lived in a kind of constant tension, and Radzyń was no different. About half of Radzyń's population was Jewish. The Jews were very close. They worked together, spoke Yiddish together, worshipped together. Nearly everyone was related to everyone else. Most Jews in the community had nicknames, something to describe their appearance or profession. Of course, there were differences. Jewish Zionists would argue bitterly with Jewish communists. Butchers, peddlers, and other tradespeople competed with one another. But overall, we were very close. We had to be.

Many of Radzyń's residents were fiercely anti-Semitic. Jewish families had to keep their shutters closed because Polish children constantly threw rocks at the glass. On the streets, Poles would jab Jews in the ribs with their elbows or stick out a foot so a Jew would trip and fall. Sometimes, you were lucky if all you did was fall.

Once, a group of Polish boys began beating one of my friends because he was Jewish. I went to help him, and a Pole slit my cheek with a knife, cutting right through the skin and flesh, into my mouth.

The police in Radzyń were even worse. They carried thick night sticks and swung them menacingly as they walked. They threatened to make arrests for minor, often dubious, infractions. When a policeman walked toward a Jew, the Jew had to step off the sidewalk, into the gutter, and walk in the filth until the policeman had passed by in his shiny boots.

Jews in Radzyń lived with anti-Semitism every day, with people who said they hated Jews because we "killed Christ." We heard horrible slurs and tales of hatred against Jews. Some Catholic priests even told their congregations that Jews had killed Catholic babies and used the babies' blood to make Passover matzos.

But the greatest irony of all was that both Jews and Catholics in Radzyń were deeply religious. Religion was an integral part of nearly everyone's daily life.

My father was a religious man. His lineage made him a *kohen,* who, according to Jewish tradition, is someone specially selected to bless and redeem a family's firstborn son. My father blessed many children, after birth and during illness. He placed great faith in God. Every Friday, my father would take my brothers and me to the *mikvah,* the Jewish baths, to be cleansed before we went to temple.

Our synagogue was a one-story, plain stone building, constructed at the beginning of the nineteenth century. Men went to the synagogue every day to pray. They sat in long rows with their prayer shawls draped over their heads, covering their faces. When women came for special services, they sat in a closed gallery, set off to one side. But my father did not just worship in temple. Each day, as he walked to neighboring villages and farms, he would wear his tallis and pray. He was, however, always careful to remove the shawl before he arrived in the villages, where Catholic farmers might feel uneasy at the sight of the prayer shawl.

My father prayed and accepted his fate, but my two older brothers did not. My brothers did not become peddlers, going farm to farm with a basket. Like my father, Moshe and Ytzel bought animals and produce from farmers, but they did not buy just a few eggs, chickens, or fish. They bought everything in quantity and had the farmers themselves transport the goods to the town. Over time, my brothers managed to make a good living. They could feed their wives, and they also helped provide for my parents, making life easier for my mother.

Luza, the middle brother, left for Warsaw when he was eighteen. There, he found work as a tailor and tried to save every bit of money he made. He ate bread and drank tea or coffee, but he did not allow himself the luxury of eating meat. When he came home to Radzyń for a holiday, he always brought something for everyone, a dress for my mother, a thin coat for my father, gifts purchased with the few zloty he'd saved.

Luza suffered during his final years in Radzyń because, as a teenager, he had joined the local Communist party. Regularly, the Polish authorities arrested him for communist activities and threw him in jail. Once I watched Luza being led from the prison to the courthouse for a trial. As he walked past me, he quickly brushed his hand across his head to show where the police had pulled out tufts of his hair. Several times, the police stuck needles under his nails, trying to get him to name other Communist party members. Luza said nothing. He joined the Communists because he believed the capitalists in Poland were denying hungry people food. Under communism, he told me, everything would be equitable, everyone would eat. Luza was a gentle person who would help any living being. He would do without food or heat so others could be full or warm. Throughout his entire life, he remained a soft, caring soul. To me, he was what God would want a human being to be.

By the late 1930s, my three eldest brothers, Luza, Moshe, and Ytzel had their own families and their own lives. For my sisters, the main concern was who they would marry. My oldest sister, Serke, married very well, becoming the wife of a leader of the temple in the neighboring town of Myekov. Esther, the middle sister, was a good businesswoman. She instinctively seemed to know all about buying and selling. She married a peddler in 1937, and after that, she even did a little matchmaking on the side. After Esther married, only my youngest sister, Genia, my brother Srulke, and I still lived at home. Genia was much more like my mother. She was a wonderful cook. She was even asked by several officials in the town to cook for them. But Genia preferred to stay at home with my mother.

Even with fewer children, life at home was not always easy. Because Luza belonged to the Communist party and my brother Moshe supported the party, Polish authorities forbade anyone in my family to attend local Polish schools. For a while, I went to Hebrew school, but, like many Jews in Radzyń, I never learned how to read or write Polish. Nor was I a very good student, although I was a good worker. By the time I was thirteen, I was working full time. The boycott of Jewish businesses led by Polish anti-Semites hurt my father's customers and thus hurt my father. He worked harder but made less. Food was so scarce that many nights I would lie in bed, listening to my stomach growl.

In the beginning, I did some peddling and a variety of odd jobs, mainly working as a field hand for Polish farmers, but eventually, I found a good job with a Polish casket maker, finishing wood on the caskets.

I didn't know it then, but my life in Radzyń was very safe. There were fights on the streets between Christians and Jews, between radical Communists and the Bund party, the Zionists, and other political parties. I was hungry, I was elbowed on the street, but I was also able to raise a couple of pigeons as pets in an attic above our home and climb a fence to pick flowers for a pretty girl who belonged to a youth group that prepared Jews to go to Palestine. On my street, boys played ball with one another on the sidewalks. Neighbors talked. I was poor, but no one minded. I was not looked down on because of poverty. I had my family and my friends. And then it began.

From the time I was very young, I had been singled out and abused for my religion. But when I was seventeen, I began to hear something new, something even more frightening. My family's landlord, a wiry, coarse man named Yashik Obremski, belonged to a fascist group in Radzyń. He began to talk about a man in Germany and about how he, Obremski, was going to help Hitler kill all the Jews. Obremski liked me, and many times he would call me over, smile, and say, "I'll kill all the Jews, but you, Yankel. I'll kill them all, but you, you I'll save."

Obremski scared me. He planted a seed of fear in my heart. By 1939, when I turned twenty-one, I was thinking almost daily about Obremski, about Germany, and about being a Jew.

In Radzyń, we heard news most often from people traveling, particularly from a few Jews fleeing Germany who passed through the town. First there were the stories of Hitler's election to power, then about *Kristallnacht*, the night of broken glass, unleashed against the German Jewish community on November 10, 1938. The Nazi SS (short for *Schutzstaffel*, an elite German guard) ordered synagogues, Jewish homes, and Jewish shops to be lit with flaming torches and burned to the ground. Jews running out of the flames were shot. Jewish property not destroyed by the fires was vandalized, and Jews were randomly arrested. The next month, members of the Polish Parliament cried out for the expulsion of all Jews from Poland. Jewish elders huddled together, speaking in low voices, but no one knew for sure who the real enemy was. Four months later, in March 1939, Hitler entered Prague, and Germany annexed Czechoslovakia. Jews and Poles, everyone in Radzyń grew afraid. Not knowing what would happen next, they were ravenous for any scrap of news.

In the summer of 1939, the town radio, which hung in front of the bicycle shop, blared all day long. Both Jews and Poles swarmed around the radio. As the weeks passed, more and more people gathered to listen to the broadcasts. It got so that the first thing people did in the morning was run to the radio and then rush back with the news. As the summer progressed, the news got worse. But people didn't leave. They just stood, several hundred deep, cupping their hands to their ears and listening solemnly to staticky voices broadcasting from places with unfamiliar names.

On September 1, the Germans attacked Poland. The Polish army sent cavalry brigades to fight against squads of German tanks. With their lances outstretched, the soldiers rode into the sights of the German gunners. The Germans fired, and it was over. By September 6, the Germans were closing in on Warsaw. Poles in Radzyń believed the Germans only wanted to control Poland, and once they had taken over the country, life would return to normal, and there would be peace.

But Jews in Radzyń heard different stories, from people fleeing from cities and towns to our west. They came through on foot and in wagons, alone and in caravans. Some carried only a single sack, others had tried to leave with all of their possessions, only later, out of exhaustion or fear or the simple breaking of a wheel, to abandon everything along a road. From these people, we heard that the Germans routinely rounded up local residents and forced them to work as laborers, fixing roads, bridges, or whatever else needed repair. Some spread rumors that people died because the Germans denied them food while they worked. But there was much that we did not know.

We did not hear that some laborers were lined up and shot after a day's work. The next day, the Germans simply collected a fresh group of Jews or Poles and forced them to work in the September dust and mud so that the German army could move ever deeper and faster into Poland. We did not yet know what it meant to live in a German Poland.

On September 9, 1939, we finally glimpsed the beginning of what was to come. That morning, the Germans bombed the Jewish section of Radzyń and the surrounding roads and fields. By month's end, German troops occupied Radzyń.

Jack Pomerantz in 1948, age thirty. (All photos courtesy of
Jack and Nina Pomerantz.)

Abish Pomerantz, Jack Pomerantz's father, in Radzyń, Poland, in 1938 (from a photograph located after the war).

Genia Pomerantz Orenbach (Jack's sister) and her husband, Chaskiel Orenbach, with their baby daughter, Yona, in 1947. Both Genia and Chaskiel survived the war by hiding in the sewers beneath the city of Lvov.

Moshe Pomerantz (Jack's older brother, seated first on the left) and his wife, Bransha (next to him), after World War II. Moshe spent the war in Soviet Central Asia and Siberia separated from his family.

Two friends of Jack Pomerantz during his second internment in Siberia.

Jack, far left, with other soldiers near Moscow in late 1943.

3

All I Could Think Was to Run

Together, on that September afternoon, my father, mother, and I began to walk toward Branica. The skies were silent and strangely empty. The German planes had vanished. Only the harsh smell of burning fuel and smoke lingered in the air. Somewhere else, undoubtedly, another town was being struck, other farmland pitted and scarred. But we could not hear it or see it.

We kept walking.

We moved very slowly, because my mother was weak and frequently needed to stop and rest. We followed the road from Radzyń past fields and small stretches of woods, which separated acres of flat pasture and farms. Along the way, we entered a wooded area to rest under the cool, safe branches. My father reached into his pocket and pulled out a tiny piece of hard sugar to give to my mother. It was all he had left.

It was not quite dusk when we reached Branica, a collection of farmhouses, storehouses, and barns. Each week, my father bought animals and produce from farmers in the area. We knocked on the door of one farmer who had always been honest in his prices and fair to my father. My father trusted this man, and without a moment's hesitation, he let us in. As we sat down, I felt a wave of relief. I also knew the farmer and liked him. I had worked for him in his fields several times, and he, too, had fed me ham.

That night, the farmer fed all of us. He gave us shelter in a small barn, amid eggs and butter, bags of wheat and corn, jugs of linseed oil, and strands of flax. We had straw to sleep on, and we could sleep knowing that this farmer would protect us.

In the early evening, my father left the barn to search for my brothers and sisters. While he looked for them under cover of darkness, my mother and I stayed inside and waited. Anxious, we jumped at the slightest sound. But when my father returned, he had Moshe and his wife, Ytzel and his wife and daughter, Srulke, and Genia with him. My mother looked from face to face, as if she were memorizing the sight of each child. I knew she must also be thinking about Serke, Esther, and Luza, all of whom lived beyond Radzyń. When I looked at her eyes, I saw she was just seconds away from tears.

My brothers, my father, and I talked and argued, trying to decide what to do. We had no radio, no way to know what was happening. Outside, there were only the quiet sounds of night, the steady hum of crickets, a breeze moving over the ripening crops in the fields. Still, I felt afraid. I had visions of hundreds of these German planes swooping back over Radzyń. I believed the Nazis would return. I wanted us to leave Branica, to keep running. My father and brothers did not agree. The bombing had ended, they argued, the worst was over.

But as they spoke, Mr. Obremski's words, "I'm going to kill all the Jews," kept echoing in my mind. I remembered him proudly telling me about Hitler, about Hitler's book, *Mein Kampf*. He would rap on his chest when he spoke about ridding the world of the Jews. I decided then that Obremski would never save me. He would never save any of us. I fell silent as everyone continued to talk. I kept thinking, "What is my next move?" All I could think was to run.

Once again, I tried to explain my fear to my family, but they did not share it. They did not want to leave their homes, their communities, everything they had ever known. "We don't want you to go, to gamble with your life, to take chances," my brother Moshe told me.

"You are the youngest," he said. "To leave would not be safe, it would be wrong."

I listened to my brother, but lying on the straw that night, I listened even harder to my fear.

In the middle of the night, I got up, very quietly. I took a piece of leftover bread and put on a short black jacket. Clutching my shoes in my hands, I tiptoed across the floor. I woke no one, said good-bye to no one. I was afraid my brothers and sisters or my mother and father would try to stop me. Almost too scared to breathe, I nudged open the rough barn door.

I don't know when they realized I was gone. Maybe someone woke up in the night and realized my spot was empty or maybe it took them until dawn to discover I had fled from the barn. There would be no way to contact me, no way for my family to know where I was or where I was heading. They would not even be able to know if I was still alive.

My parents never knew. At the end of September, in the final moments before the German army entered Radzyń, several hundred Jews, mostly young men and women fled east into Soviet-occupied territory. My brothers and sisters were among them. My mother and father chose to stay behind.

When I left that barn, I left my parents forever. I had no photos, nothing to remind me of how they looked. I know that my mother was beautiful, that my father stood straight and was strong, but time dulls the recollection of their individual features and expressions, of how they appeared day to day. I left with nothing to record that we had ever been a family together, nothing except for memories.

My parents never knew that any of their children survived.

My parents stayed, and the Germans came. And soon after that, the Germans came for the Jews. In December of 1939, nearly all of Radzyń's Jews were trucked to the neighboring towns of Sławatycze and Miedzyrzec to register as Jews. There, some were also assigned to labor brigades. But the Germans had not yet begun wide-scale deportations and liquidations in Poland, and, after a few months, most Jews returned to Radzyń. Again, they thought the worst was over.

In the summer of 1940, an open ghetto was established in Radzyń. Groups of Jews organized resistance activities, but the Nazis were not deterred. In August of 1942, many of Radzyń's Jews were deported to the Nazi death camp Treblinka. A second deportation occurred in December. That same month, according to Nazi records, Radzyń's Jewish ghetto was "liquidated."

My parents were not sent to Treblinka.

One afternoon, sometime before the deportations, several German soldiers loaded my mother and father onto a Polish man's horsecart. The Polish man drove the cart to a field and watched as the Germans drew their guns and ordered my father to dig a grave for my mother, to dig her grave while she was still alive.

My father refused. He refused to take the shovel. He faced the Germans, and he defied them.

One soldier pressed his gun against my father's mouth and pulled the trigger. Then the soldier turned to my mother and fired again.

The soldiers drove off, leaving my mother's and father's crumpled bodies to rot in the field.

Having watched the entire incident, the Polish man turned his empty horsecart around and headed back to Radzyń.

This man was Mr. Obremski's nephew Vladec. When I was a boy, twelve or thirteen and very hungry, he had sneaked food from his family's table and shared it with me. When I returned to Radzyń several years later, he told me what had happened to my parents as if it had been a regular event on any ordinary afternoon.

That mid-September night in 1939, the barn and my sleeping family quickly receded into the darkness. Within minutes I could no longer see the cluster of farmhouses that marked Branica. Now, there were just fields laden with crops on either side of me and the moon and the stars above. The world looked the same in every direction. I had no maps, but I kept walking, trying to avoid the ruts in the road. I was not alone. Other people were also walking.

They emerged like apparitions from the night shadows, sometimes with bundles under their arms or strapped to their backs, sometimes with nothing. They would appear as shoulders and backs in front of me or as silhouettes, stepping out from side roads. I would ask them, "Where are you going?" and, almost always, they were going in the same direction, east, toward Russia. With the German army bearing down from the west, only the vast expanse of Soviet territory to the east offered any real refuge. Although I wanted to go east, I had no idea which way was east. Except for one trip to Warsaw when I was two, I had never been more than fifteen miles away from Radzyń.

My only hope was to follow people on the road. I followed them and walked. I walked over half the night. Finally, I had to rest. I lay down in a field and slept for an hour. Then I got up and began to walk again.

I walked almost the whole next day. I had finished my bread. I had no other food, and I was afraid to ask the farmers whom I passed for anything. I was afraid because I was Jewish. I didn't know how many of them might feel as Obremski did, that the Jews had caused everyone's problems, that Poland should be rid of the Jews. Every figure in the fields made me uneasy. I grew tense at the sound of someone else coming down the road. But hunger and exhaustion were slowly overtaking me. By late afternoon, I could not take another step without food. Quietly, I turned off the road and began walking toward a lone house sitting on acres of land. With each step, my weary muscles tightened. If anyone approached me, I was prepared to run. I drew closer to a house. I peered in the windows. Empty.

Softly, I pushed open the door, stepped inside and looked around for a scrap of food. It seemed as though I spent ages looking. I tried to take small breaths, thinking small breaths would make less noise. Then I spied a lump of bread under a clean cloth. I seized the loaf and ran. I clutched the bread and let my heart and my legs carry me away from that house to a nearby woods. Once I reached the safety of the trees, I slowed to walk, still panting, until I was lost among the trunks and branches. I listened for the sound of footsteps but heard nothing. I sat down and ate, my hands tearing at the loaf. Not far away, I found a small brook, and, bending down, I cupped one hand and drank the cold water.

And, then, I began to walk again. I walked along the edges of the roads, sometimes cutting across paths in the fields or the woods. The German army was already ahead of me, and it was rapidly encircling the area from behind, enveloping the land in a large arc, ready to close and cut like two sharp scissors blades. I did not know where the German troops were. I only knew that the planes, trucks, and hoards of soldiers were out there, lurking somewhere just over the horizon.

The days faded one into another. I had no meals, no temple, no work, nothing to give shape or form to my time. I just kept walking, in a kind of stupor. As long as there were refugees on the road, I knew I had to keep walking. Sometimes I would walk with them, sometimes I would walk alone. It made little difference. I was too shy and afraid to say much of anything to anyone, except to ask if I was going the right way. I had never spent so many days away from home.

Each day, I also had to search for food. I would spend hours hiding, watching a house to see if it was empty. Then I would slip inside and hunt for bread or for any left-over scraps. I even ate food right out the fields. Using sticks or my bare hands, I dug in the ground for potatoes and ate them raw until my stomach churned. Sometimes I was too hungry to look for water to wash them, so I would just spit on their brown skins and rub away the roughest dirt. Often, as I walked, I chewed on kernels of wheat until my jaw ached.

Usually, I stopped to rest at dusk. When I could, I looked for a field with haystacks, found one large stack, made a hole in the hay, and crawled in to sleep. Other times, I waited until after dark and then slept among stalks of grain planted in a field or hid myself in the woods, spreading leaves over myself for warmth and resting on the mossy, fragrant ground.

Finally, one morning, I reached the Bug River. Tens of thousand of Jews fleeing Poland had already made it to the Bug. They descended on the river, which marked the border between German and Soviet forces, and Jews in the small towns along the shore helped ferry them across the water. On the other side was Brest-Litovsk, a large commercial and transportation center, some thirty-five miles northeast of Radzyń.

I crossed the Bug on a low, wooden boat. After nearly two weeks of sleeping outside, of walking, of scavenging for food, nearly two weeks of constant fear, I too had reached Brest. As I drew closer to city, I believed that if I could just pass inside, everything would be all right. In Brest, I could find work. I knew the name of a woman from Radzyń who now lived there. In a city, I could be one in a crowd, not just a lone boy, walking in split shoes along unfamiliar roads.

4

A Respite in Brest

I reached Brest-Litovsk right after the Soviet army did. In slightly over one week, the city had fallen from Polish control into German and then into Soviet. The Germans held Brest for seven days, September 15 to 22. During those days, they looted homes and businesses, leaving blocks of broken windows and ransacked buildings. They kidnapped Jews for forced labor. Then, suddenly, the German army withdrew.

Jews and other residents of Brest lined up to watch them go. Shaken, angry, they hurled rocks and bottles at the departing troops and army convoys. The Germans did nothing, but they remembered. Exactly twenty-one months later, the German army swept back across the Bug River. Then, the real destruction began.

During those intervening twenty-one months, Brest-Litovsk was occupied by Soviet forces and marked the western edge of Soviet territory. Under Hitler and Stalin's nonaggression pact, Brest, the site where Lenin's Bolsheviks had made peace with the Kaiser's Germans in 1918, became the dividing line for a new alliance between the Soviet Empire and the German Third Reich. The two powers had split Poland. To the west, it was swallowed by Hitler's Greater Germany, to the east, it lay under the mantle of the U.S.S.R.

What happened to Brest in a week and a half in September of 1939 mirrored Poland's fate of the past 150 years. Three different times during the late 1700s, the Germans and Russians carved up Polish territory, laying claim over entire regions of Poland, crippling, if not destroying the sovereign country. Both neighbors sent their armies into Poland during World War I, and Russian troops returned during the Polish-Russian war of 1919–20.

Now, in 1939, the troops were back.

As soon as I arrived in Brest, I starting asking for the Jewish quarter. I knew the name of a Jewish woman from Radzyń who had married a man from Brest and moved to the city. In the Jewish quarter, I started knocking on doors, asking for the family. I found her house in a cluster of five attached houses, with a courtyard in the back. I had nowhere else to go, and so, without hesitating, I rapped on her door.

I told her who I was. I told her about running away and leaving my family, about sleeping in the forest and in haystacks, about my fear of the Germans. She nodded. Her door opened wide. She tried to help anyone escaping from Radzyń, offering refugees food, clothes, money, and shelter. She did even more for me. She offered me a home.

The woman and her husband fed and housed me as if I had been their own son. "Whatever we have to eat, you're going to eat," she said. "You will eat with us." I spent over a year and a half in the safety and comfort of their walls.

After a day or two resting in the house, I began to venture out in the streets. In many ways, I was savvy and smart. I had learned something about survival from stepping down to walk in the gutters of Radzyń. But in many ways, at twenty-one, I was still a child, wild-eyed, curious, enthralled by all that stretched before me. Even under occupation, Brest was a bustling place. A big city, with wide, lively streets, Brest still brimmed with markets, merchants, and traders in the early weeks. There were rows of shops, Polish delis with kielbassa and ham hanging in the windows, Jewish butchers, egg vendors, even stores selling only liquor. With its crowds, restaurants, buildings, and homes, Brest was a new world, unlike anything I had ever seen or imagined in the tiny realm of Radzyń.

In those early autumn days, Brest also swelled with Soviet soldiers, dressed in green uniforms adorned with shiny red stars. The soldiers were awed by the well-stocked shops and harvest markets, and they bought whatever they could find, handing out ruble notes in exchange for bundles, big and small, flat and round. Besides the Soviets, an endless stream of refugees descended on the city from the west. Those who could stayed with relatives or acquaintances. Others, more well-to-do, rented rooms. Many, however, had nowhere to go. Dirty, tired, homeless, they filled the rail station and public buildings. Schools were transformed into barracks. People slept on the floor or even on the bare ground. The refugees congealed into a human mass, and the stench from soiled clothes and sweat was overwhelming. Yet, for now, in Brest-Litovsk, no planes flew overhead, no gunners fired, no bombs fell. Many people believed the war on this front had ended.

Even once the fighting in Poland subsided in late September, refugees continued to arrive. Residents and refugees alike would collect in restaurants to drink, eat, and share stories at long tables, over steaming bowls of cabbage and potatoes and loaves of dark bread. But these were also places where people searched for family and friends, hoping those they had left behind had made it safely across. Like these others, I too began asking and searching. I went from restaurant to shop to restaurant and back again.

Then, finally, in mid-October, I found Esther, Ytzel, Srulke, Moshe, Serke, and Genia. Suddenly, as if in a dream, we were together again. I was overjoyed just at the sight of them, standing before me, alive. I reached out to touch each one, scarcely able to believe they were real. I wanted to hear every piece of news.

Luza and his wife had managed to flee to Radzyń from Warsaw, and all of my brothers and sisters had left Radzyń just as the German army closed in. Believing the old would be spared and not wanting to hold back their fleeing children, my parents had stayed behind. But at least, I thought, now my brothers and sisters and I would all be together in Brest. It was not to be. Just as I had decided on my own to run from the barn in Branica, they had already made very different plans, plans without me.

Luza and his wife, along with two old friends from Radzyń, had already left the city. They wanted to see Moscow and to live in the heart of the Communist world. Within a day or two, Ytzel, Srulke, Esther, and Genia had planned to head south, into another part of Soviet-occupied Poland. Esther's husband and Ytzel's wife had distant relatives there, relatives who could give them a place to stay and help them until they could return home. In Brest, they could not find work, and they had almost run out of money for food. They had to sleep on the floor of a warehouse and wash at public baths, like beggars or stray animals. They were sure that life would be better outside of Brest. In the confusion, no one stopped to think that if people from the north of Poland were fleeing east, people from the south of Poland were also likely doing the same.

I could have traveled south, but I already had a place to live and food to eat. Ytzel, Esther, Srulke, and Genia told me they planned to return to Poland in a matter of months. They did not believe these new borders would last. I should wait in Brest, they said. It would not be long before everyone would return home. Moshe and Serke, however, had even more faith that everything would return to the way it was before. With the fighting over, they were heading back to Poland. Neither wanted to stay in the squalor and chaos of Brest. They believed we would all be reunited before the year was out. This war, they said, was over.

I was stunned. I had found my brothers and sisters only to lose them again. But this was what happened in war. Mothers and fathers sent off sons and daughters, the married sent off the single, the weak sent off the strong, people fleeing for their lives were wrenched from those they loved. I had only to look at the streets of Brest and see the swarms of refugees who had already left everything behind. I had only to look at myself.

But then, too, no one believed this chaos would last. Perhaps that was why we were all so willing to separate or, like me on that first night, to run.

When the Russians published a decree promising to repatriate all Jewish refugees from German-controlled Poland if the Jews registered, Moshe and his wife, Bransha, and their daughter, Bella, promptly signed up to return to what remained of Poland, as did my sister Serke and her family. They promised to write and let the rest of us know when we could return as well. Now, it was only a matter of waiting for the trains. A few days later, they boarded those trains, supposedly bound for Poland.

For weeks after, I waited for a letter from Moshe or Serke, but none came. Once all the trainloads left, rumors spread about their destination. We heard that the Soviets thought anyone who wanted to return to Poland was anticommunist. Instead of traveling west, the trains headed east, carrying the refugees into Siberia, to Soviet labor camps and collective farms. Although I had no news about Moshe and Serke, in my heart, I believed that they and their families were now deep inside the Soviet Union. Ytzel wrote that he, Esther, and Srulke were safely settled in the south. Genia , however, had left them to live in the city of Lvov. Another refugee might have asked her to come with her to a big city, where there were more jobs. Or perhaps, like me, it was instinct that drove her to run off alone. No one mentioned returning home.

From the end of October through the deepening cold of November, thousands of new refugees from Poland arrived, telling of Jewish homes being confiscated by the Germans, of groups of Jews being rounded up, of Jews being forced to register in order to work and eat. Then the news stopped. The Soviets shut the border. People trying to cross, in either direction, were shot. But instead of instilling a new fear, it was as if the city had been wrapped in a protective cocoon when it was closed off. The stories of atrocities that had gripped us all fall seemed to evaporate from the collective consciousness under the immediate threat of a brutally cold winter and dwindling supplies of food and housing. Some argued convincingly that the stories had largely been exaggerations. Residents continued about their business, newcomers tried to fit in. The present became indistinguishable from the future, the past seemed distant and gradually an abstraction.

Like many refugees, I was busy adjusting to Brest and to my new life. There were moments when a deep anxiety welled up inside me, a longing for my family and my old, familiar world. I had days when I felt weak, as if an uncertainty were eroding me from within. Some nights, I would fall asleep only to wake suddenly, feeling terribly alone. I felt the pull of wanting to be near my family, but now I had food to eat and my own space to sleep. My life was far better than it had ever been in Radzyń. Rather than risk the unknown, I decided to remain in the safety of those five attached houses and small court-yard in Brest, which had become my home.

I found work with the Soviets on a project to widen the Bug River. The Soviets had taken over factories, businesses, and even apartment buildings. Some private traders had stayed in business, but now almost everything be-longed to the Soviets, and only they needed laborers. They needed thousands of people to widen the Bug, which ran alongside the city. I registered to work on the widening project, to make money and also to protect myself. It soon became clear that those who didn't register could be conscripted. It was safer to volunteer. I went to work a couple of days a week, joining hundreds of oth-ers, some of whom were prisoners from labor camps. Soviet guards kept them separate and subdued. The workers were given shovels and hoes, and a few men operated big noisy machines. We spent our days scraping away at the riverbank. I hauled wheelbarrows full of soil and pitched dirt onto trucks. At the time, I didn't think to ask why were we widening the river, but now I would guess that the Soviets wanted to put a little more distance between them and the Germans, watching on the opposite shore.

On days when I did not work, I walked around the city. I listened careful-ly, trying to learn the Russian now being spoken on nearly every street. I watched Russian soldiers and officers, with their thick wool uniforms, their Slavic faces, and their motorcycles that roared down the roads, belching clouds of dark smoke. It was a strange, exotic world.

At home, my world was wonderful and warm. As the months wore on, the family continued to embrace me with a special kindness. The woman and her husband also had a twenty-three-year-old son and a seventeen-year-old daugh-ter, both tall and striking. Like my mother, this woman wanted very much to marry off her daughter. It was wartime. I was young. She knew my family and knew that I had a good name. The longer I stayed, the more certain it became that the daughter and I would marry. So no one encouraged me to leave. And the longer I stayed, the more I also came to love the family as my own.

Daily life in the house had a comforting routine. We woke before dawn and ate thick black bread smeared with cooked fat and onions. Then the father and son would go off to deliver water. They owned a wagon with a big bar-rel, which they filled with water each day. The two would go house to house in the community, selling the water. It was steadier work than peddling. People can do without chickens, but not without water. In the winter, they also logged wood. A number of times, I offered to help them, but they insisted that I did not have to do their work. Ironically, even though the father and son were able to make a respectable living, because they worked as *beligoulas,* or haulers, they were considered part of the lower working class.

Every Friday night, we shared a Shabbat meal. Come evening, candles were lit. We ate Challah bread and often fish or chicken soup with matzo balls. For this family, not having a Sabbath meal was like not having a front door.

I spent relatively little time with the father and son, but the mother doted on me. She mended my clothes and slipped an extra spoonful of sugar into my tea. We reminisced for hours about Radzyń, laughing and joking. She had a wonderful laugh, which seemed to rise from deep in her chest and light the skin around her eyes. Her daughter, however, was shy and quiet. She wanted to be a teacher, and each morning she diligently went off to school. In the afternoon, she cleaned house and worked on her studies. During the days, we rarely spoke, exchanging only slight glances and nervous blushes. When she handed me a plate at dinner, she bowed her head to avoid looking straight into my eyes.

It was not considered proper for us to be together unsupervised, but sometimes, in the late afternoon, when I was certain her back was turned, I would stand in a doorway and watch as she bent over her books, the light from a lamp picking up the flecks in her hair. After months had passed, at night, after the rest of her family had gone to sleep, I would occasionally sneak softly into her room, and we would talk in whispers and tell stories. The moment, however, that I heard even the slightest noise, I would bolt from her room, rush to my bed, and cover myself with a blanket, pretending to be fast asleep. Once, as I sat in her room listening to her soft voice, I reached out my hand to touch her cheek. She quickly turned away. Even just the simple touch of a hand was not considered proper. A kiss was unthinkable. Only once did my lips touch hers, my hand hold hers.

As the months wore on, I got to know the closest neighbors in the courtyard. To the right lived a woman, about thirty-five, the wife, and perhaps by then the widow, of a Polish army general. To the left lived a family who had had a beautiful teenage daughter. Her story was a tragic one. She had fallen in love with a Catholic Pole named Vladec, and defying their families, the two ran off to marry. But, away from Brest, the girl fell ill with typhus and died.

Vladec returned to Brest, devastated. He grieved over the loss of his love as if he were mourning the loss of the entire world. His devotion moved me, and we became friends. He was a Pole who loved a Jew, and in our friendship,

I felt a new hope. I decided to invite him to come with me to visit my brothers and sisters in the south, a journey I also felt would be safer with a Pole. Our first stop was the town of Rozyszcze, a bustling town in Polish Volhynia, which was now under Soviet occupation. My brother Ytzel lived there, and I imagined I would find a quiet place, a little larger than Radzyń. What we found was a city under occupation, patrolled by armed brigades.

Ytzel told me that right after the Soviets entered Rozyszcze, a Communist youth organization, previously banned and forced underground in Poland, seized control of the town. But their reign in Rozyszcze was very different from my brother Luza's vision of a communist utopia in which everything was equitable. Instead, these young Communists marched on the streets of the town with guns. They wore red armbands to identify themselves and arrested people thought to be fascists or enemies of the communist cause. I was afraid just to walk from the train station to Ytzel's house. I was afraid even though some of the young men with arm bands were Jews.

Vladec and I did not stay long. Within a day, we were heading southeast, to see my sister Esther and my brother Srulke some forty miles away in Olyka. Olyka was a town perhaps the size of Radzyń, also in the Volhynia region. Although small, Olyka's Jewish community was one of the oldest in the area, dating back to the mid-1600s. Nearly half of Olyka's population was Jewish, so, surrounded by the lush green and heavy mud of the Ukrainian countryside, Olyka seemed like a safe haven from the Germans.

While Rozyszcze had scared us, Olyka soothed us. The houses were clean and small. Flowers bloomed in almost every yard. There was a sumptuous farmers' market filled with fresh produce and a neatly trimmed town square for leisurely strolls. My sister Esther welcomed us into her home.

One warm afternoon, Vladec and I wandered out to a lake nearby. As he dove into the water, a ring that his love had given to him as she lay dying slipped from his finger. When he felt it slip off, he emerged from the water with a horrible cry. Madly, he dove down again and again looking for the ring. He scoured the lake's muddy bottom for the band, filling his lungs with air and then disappearing into the darkness. I watched, terrified, on the bank. Finally, panting and exhausted, he crawled to shore. I tried to console him, I tried to explain that the ring was not the girl. But Vladec would not be consoled. It was as if she had died again. Overcome with despair, Vladec could not bear another moment in Olyka, so we returned to Brest. But when he returned to his home, things were no better.

In the ominous year of 1940, not long after 330,000 British and French troops fled the European continent from the beaches of Dunkirk, Vladec, his world shattered at the loss of his love, killed himself. For so many others, the shattering of their worlds had just begun.

As 1940 drew to a close, Russian soldiers still swarmed on the streets of Brest. Sometimes, after they passed, groups of residents would quietly taunt under their breath, "Yes, the Russians freed us. They freed us from sugar and meat and bread and clothing."

Whatever the Russians could transport out of Brest, they did. Whatever remained was rationed. A black market appeared almost overnight. Shops that had been stocked in the early days were now barren. Soviet officers sold available supplies on the side, and residents eagerly bought and traded. Increasingly, we spent most of our time trying to find food and staples, following up on rumors that lard or potatoes or cheese could be found in one particular store or market. Despite the shortages, most residents believed that the conflict had been resolved, that Russia and Germany had made a lasting peace. The grim images of September 1939, the looted shops, the kidnappings, the wanton destruction had been replaced by very different ones. For over a year and a half, we saw pictures of smiling blonde German families standing in front of snow-capped mountains. The Soviet press presented Germany as an engine of peace and progress. Nazi campaigns against Jews went unmentioned. On the streets of Brest, the future seemed secure. Overhead, the skies did not darken.

As I worked on the Bug, I had no idea that by early 1941, across the river on the German-controlled side, Jews from the Polish and Austrian ghettos were arriving at labor camps by the trainload, that across the river from me, other Jews with picks and shovels were being forced to build fortifications for the encroaching Nazi war machine.

5

Running East Alone

On June 22, 1941, I was riding on a train, heading south and west away from Brest to the loamy fields of the Ukraine. I was on my way to Olyka to tell my brothers and sisters that I was going to marry and to invite them to the wedding. In the late spring of 1941, I had become officially engaged to the water carrier's daughter. For months, her parents had openly suggested marriage, and now they had decided that the time had come. Arrangements began. Even with the Soviet occupation and the shortages, the wedding was going to be a celebration. Whatever food we had would seem like a feast. If the only music was the clapping of hands and the sounds of a hand-hollowed pipe, it would be as good as a complete band.

Long before Poland had been overrun and occupied, only the wealthy had elaborate weddings with festivities lasting for a full week, a week of lavish meals, gift-giving, and a ceremony outside under a *huppah*, or wedding canopy, to be followed by still more food and dancing. For poorer people, a wedding was quite different.

Sometimes, the bride's family could not even afford a new dress for her. There would always be a huppah and a ring, but the cakes and sweets eaten after the ceremony were baked by neighbors—ten or fifteen families might arrive, each bearing a single cake for the celebration. Music for dancing might be made by the groom himself, by rubbing a stick against a washboard. A wedding could be made for the cost of about five U.S. dollars. At my own sister Serke's wedding, I did not even have a pair of shoes to wear.

For our wedding, my bride was going to have a remade dress and a simple veil. Her mother had already worked on both. I had watched her bend over the material for hours, taking tiny stitches with the thinnest possible needle. I had already selected the ring for my bride, a rather plain one, because there was not much to be had in these times and it was all I could afford. Still, everything about the wedding promised to be joyful, and I wanted my brothers and sisters to share in that moment. Unfortunately, I could not send word about the wedding to my parents, trapped in Radzyń, inside the German zone.

As the train headed east, I thought about all that had happened since I had traveled this route with Vladec nearly a year earlier. I felt excitement, optimism. It was warm, by the calendar, the very beginning of summer. Grass waved in the fields. Flowers dotted the landscape. Animals were grazing, and farmers were working in plowed patches and long, furrowed fields.

The train reached Olyka in the afternoon. By then the news had already spread through the train cars. The German army had attacked the Soviet Union.

Olyka was the same small place, with wooden houses and a market square that I had visited earlier. Within minutes, I was at my sister Esther's door, and soon after, we left in search of a home with a radio for news. As we huddled around the speaker, I heard the announcement that the Germans had crossed the Bug River, and I knew I could not go back to Brest.

Inside, I felt as if something had been ripped away. My chest tightened, my limbs felt heavy. It was as if a dulling numbness had overtaken me. Watching my fiancée's delicate hands, hearing her soft voice, seeing a pink blush overtake her cheeks, I had grown to love her, and I considered her parents my second family. They had given me a home, and I loved them. Many times during the war years, I would wonder what had happened to them, would hope for them.

After the war, I learned that almost no Jews from Brest survived. My second family vanished, like so many others, without a trace. There were no bones to honor, no cemetery plot to visit, nothing that remained, nothing for me to bury, except their names.

To this day, I have pushed them down in a place so deep that though I can still picture their faces, I cannot say their names.

During those late June days in Olyka in 1941, once again I was with my brothers and sisters, fearing the advance of the German army. Although all the towns in the region were plunged into confusion, Ytzel, Esther, Srulke, Genia and I managed to unite in Olyka. When the German bombing started, Genia, along with many others, had fled from Lvov into the countryside. Ytzel and his wife had already moved to Olyka from Rozyszcze several months earlier. But even in Olyka, things were hardly calm. In Olyka, we had no way of knowing if the Russians had been able to stop the Germans. Radio news was unreliable, and things were happening far too quickly for any word from refugees heading east to reach us.

Esther, Ytzel, Srulke, Genia, and I began to discuss what we should do. This time, I had not run off at the first sounds of war, but I also had not lost any of my fear of the Germans. My brothers and sisters felt differently. Having fled once as refugees, they were not eager to set out on unknown roads again. And they, like so many others, including me, had almost no idea what German occupation meant, especially what it meant for Jews.

Ytzel and Esther especially wanted to stay. "It is far more unsafe out on the roads," they argued. They had visions of hunger and hostile peasants. I listened to them, but inside myself all I could hear were German planes opening fire, all I could feel were troops coming toward me. Once again, something inside me was screaming, "Run Yankel, run." Fear consumed me. I tried to figure out how I could know when the Germans were coming. I had no way to find out, but the more I thought, I began to wonder if perhaps the Soviet forces would warn the local NKVD, the Soviet secret police, later known as the KGB, before the Germans arrived.

Olyka, like nearly all Soviet towns, had an NKVD office, and a number of residents knew its location. Listening to my brothers and sisters, I began forming a plan. I decided I would go and wait by the NKVD office. When the NKVD started packing to leave, then, I told them, it would be time for us to run. I hoped my logic would sway them, but my brothers and sisters did not agree. They believed it was I who would be running back to them. Only Srulke wanted to come with me, but the rest of the family was opposed.

"You're going to kill yourself," Ytzel said to me, upset, frustrated. "I don't want you to kill your brother too. I don't want you to go at all, but, if you go, go alone."

The words stung. But something, an instinct, was driving me. I shoved my hands in my pockets, went to the NKVD office, and hid nearby. I sat all day. I slept on the ground at night. I only left briefly, to get food and to report back to my brothers and sisters, to try to convince them to leave with me. But I could not persuade them, and they could not stir me from my vigil. Two days went by. Then I saw the office erupt with activity. The NKVD men were packing, furiously shoving things into trunks and cases. I barely said good-bye to my brothers and sisters. In my mind, there was time for nothing but running. Within an hour, I was gone.

Once again, I was heading east, running for my life from the Germans. Once again, too, I had left behind family, family whom I would never see again.

When you run, you try not to think about these things. You try not to think about who will or will not survive. You try to have hope. I held onto my hope for over three years. I held onto my hope and nurtured it until I returned. Then I had to bury it, to bury it in place of bones.

Leaving Olyka, I began to walk deeper into the Ukraine. I tried to avoid the main roads, for fear of the army, either army. I just kept walking, asking the way east and walking. I knew the names of certain towns and villages to the east, and I looked anxiously for them on road signs. My greatest fear was that somehow I would become turned around—and thus actually be walking backwards, toward the Germans. Even after I had been walking for more than a day, each time I came upon a signpost, I would start to shake, afraid that perhaps for hours I had been going the wrong way.

At first, the roads were filled with other people running away, Poles, and Czechs, and Jews. Mostly Jews. Soon, though, I discovered even smaller back roads, where I could wander for hours without seeing a soul. I always walked with my hands loose, so that in an instant I would be able to use them. Walking alone, I had to be on my guard constantly. I never knew when someone might appear and I might have to fight. Hardly any carts traveled these back roads, which were really more like paths, barely wide enough for one cart, certainly not for two. When I did see a horse and wagon, the feeling was terrible. My body would stiffen, my mind and my heart would start to race, like someone caught in a hard, sudden fall. I sensed every second of danger, and yet I had so little control. I quickly learned that many Ukrainians hated Jews even more than we were hated by Poles. I was spat on and chased. I found no one willing to offer me food. To eat enough just to survive, I had to watch for empty houses and try to steal scraps. Unlike my escape from Branica to Brest, this time I was careful always to choose isolated houses near wooded areas. When you're running away through a field, it's easy for someone to catch you. When you can flee into the woods, it's much more difficult.

Sometimes I would watch a house for hours, only at the last second to see an occupant moving inside or nearby. Even the sound of an animal, of a horse or a pig, would drive me away. I would have to sneak off and find another secluded farmhouse, hide myself, and wait all over again.

I remember finding one small wooden house, watching it, and then entering to search for bread. I quickly found two loaves and glanced about as I ran out through the doorway. Then, coming over the rise, I saw them. People, running toward the house, running toward me.

Maybe there were three. Maybe there were four. I did not stop to count. I just ran, squeezing the bread in my fists. The people from the farm were swinging hatchets and screaming. They were close enough that I could hear them swear at me, hear them curse me and scream over and over, "*Yivrey,*" Russian for Jew, and, more often, "*Ghid,*" a slur word for Jew.

I looked back at them once as I neared some woods. I could see the glint of the hatchet blades and the heavy wooden handles in their hands. Not knowing where I was or where I was heading, I fled into the dark safety of the thick, green woods. If I had been older or weaker and they had caught me, I would have been killed. Many escapees were. On those back roads and paths, I came to fear everyone, Ukrainians as well as Germans. I made my loaves of bread last a very long time.

Gradually, I worked my way back to the road, and, then, I began to walk again. For several days, I followed that road. I kept going until I could not walk any farther. In the fading light, I saw a farm, and I took a chance. I walked up to the door and knocked.

The farmer and his family came out, and I told them everything, except that I was a Jew. I told them that I was running away from the Germans, that I was too exhausted to keep walking. I knew as I spoke those words that, if the farmer did not take pity on me, this could be the end.

The farmer looked at me for a minute and then said, "Come with me." He led me to a barn, a fair distance from the house.

The barn had straw for sleeping, and the farmer brought me a large basin of warm water and towel, so that I could wash. He left and came back with food. It was like a dream. Never before had I been so grateful for straw, a barn, and sleep.

He woke me before dawn the next morning. He spoke quickly. "I'm not Polish, I'm Czech," he said.

"I wish I could help you, but you must leave right away because there are rumors that the Germans are close by. You must leave before the Germans have surrounded this place." He gave me a package of food and gripped my hand. I wondered if he suspected that I was Jewish or if he simply did not want any strangers in his barn when the army came. But then as he looked at me, his eyes grew watery. He blinked back tears. I felt my throat tighten, but there was nothing that could be said or done. I started walking again.

I tried to make the food from the Czech farmer last, breaking off small bits of bread and slivers of cheese. I would chew first on one side of my mouth, then on the other. And after each time, I would tightly tie the bundle back up.

I lost count of how many days I walked alone. Fear, hunger, and exhaustion were constant. During the nights, I was afraid of animals, during the days, I was afraid of men. The steady clop-clop of a horse and roll of a wagon were terrifying sounds. Sometimes I would hear a step, the crack of a branch, or the squeak of a wheel, and my heart would pound. I would think for a second that this was it, that this was the end.

Time passed, and only the weather changed. When it rained, my feet sank in the thick mud as I walked. When it didn't rain, the slightest breeze would stir clouds of gritty brown dust. I remember the fields being as beautiful as fields around Radzyń. They were lush and green, thick with crops and flowers. At night, they offered cover while I slept, sometimes hidden under a layer of straw. During the day, these fields sometimes made me ache for home.

By July 1, only days after I fled Olyka, the German army had in some areas swept more than a hundred miles into Soviet-held territory. By July 16, some German forces had already moved close to Kiev, the capital of the Ukraine.

At the time, I knew none of this. I only knew what I could see, what stretched from the horizon behind me to the one beyond. But from the speed with which German tanks and troops rolled over the Ukrainian landscape and from the fervor with which some Ukrainians welcomed the Nazi invasion, I can only imagine that, had I been walking a few miles to the north or south, I might well have died early that summer, shot or axed in some nameless green field.

It was well into July when I came upon another young man at a crossroad. My hands were loose, ready for anything, but every other muscle in my body was tense and waiting to react. Crossroads were dangerous. Because there were two separate roads, there was twice the risk that someone might approach. Instinctively, as I walked, I would prepare to fight, not knowing what would happen.

This time, too, I was ready. But, as I drew closer, I could see that this fellow was also running away. His clothes were worn and splattered with mud. He was tired, and the skin under his cheekbones was already sinking into hollows.

We started to talk, and for the first time since I had started running on that late June day, I heard Yiddish spoken, just as I had heard it around Radzyń since I was a little child. We were Jews, both from Radzyń, Jews now once again fleeing the Germans. And this man had known my brother Luza.

It was odd to meet someone from my town, but war creates strange coincidences. For all the lives and limbs war severs, it also brings people together, families hiding in the woods, soldiers separated from their units, even refugees from the same small town. Then, too, war makes people hunger to find those connections. When you are alone, you start to become desperate to be with somebody. I do not know whether he was waiting for someone or walking. I do not know whether it was an accidental meeting or whether he met me and I fit into his plan. I only knew that I was so glad not to be alone. And only when I knew I could be killed because of him, only then did I truly want to be alone.

We started to walk together, day and night. The roads twisted and curved, and often we did not know if we were walking in the right direction. We wanted to go east. But many times we began to fear that we were lost, and so we would take a chance, asking lone farmers or other wanderers to point the way, and then we would worry that they were wrong.

To eat, we would sometimes grab a chicken in the field, wring its neck, and run with the carcass into the woods, where we would pluck the feathers and pierce the bird with sticks to roast it over a small fire. We ripped the charred meat from the bones with our hands.

We preferred to sleep in the fields, under straw, away from the animals who roamed in the woods, but sometimes we did rest under the cool tree branches, on the damp ground. Grass and mud and rotting leaves stuck to our clothes when we slept, usually in the motionless hours before the first light of dawn.

When we could, we walked at night, searching for ruts in the road by threads of starlight or, as the evening hours deepened, by the round, warm glow of the moon. In the beginning, we talked almost constantly, each telling his story of what had happened since leaving Radzyń. Repeatedly, we asked each other, "Are we doing the right thing, running away?" And each time, one would reassure the other. But, in truth, we did not know. We had both heard comments like my landlord's "I'm going to kill all the Jews." But, while we did not know what was to become of the world we were leaving, we knew even less about the world we were entering. As the days dragged on, we talked less and less, traveling instead in a kind of shared silence, broken only by an occasional wind or the scurrying of some nocturnal animal. I did not mind the quiet, as long as I had a companion, as long as I did not have the constant fear of being alone.

One evening, shortly after dusk, we heard the whir of an engine and saw a plane swoop down very low over a thick field next to the road. Bodies tensed, we prepared to jump into a ditch the second we heard the crack of gunfire or the whistle of a bomb. But we heard no explosions, no sound except the gradual fading of the engine's whir as the plane flew out of sight. I was still wondering about the plane when several minutes later, a man emerged from the wheat stalks and made his way onto the road.

The man wore a long coat, which made it difficult to see if he was a large man or a small one. He greeted us in Polish and said that he was also running away, naming a city in Poland where he said his family had lived.

He was a talkative man, full of questions: where were we going, how long had we been on the road, where were we now? He asked and described many things, speaking in Polish, but I did not listen. Every chance I could, I glanced at him in the dark. Even if he was running away, it was summer, a strange time of year for a long coat, and I knew if I were hiding in a wheat field, I would not come out if I heard strange voices. Most of all, he was clearly not a Jew. No Jew would speak to other Jews in Polish, and since I had left Olyka, I had not met any Poles who had fled this far into the Soviet Union. Something was not right. I looked over at my friend, and he looked back at me, but we had no signal, no plan, no idea what to do.

We walked with this man for several hours, but every moment I was thinking, wondering what to do. I had already decided that I did not like this strange, Polish-speaking man. I kept swinging my arms as we walked and watched for him to move, ready to attack him the first instant I suspected he was reaching for a knife or a gun.

It was a dark night. Our only light came from a thin slice of moon. I could barely make out the trees and the large, cleared fields and the low, straggly bushes sprouting beside the road.

I did not see the Soviet checkpoint until we were almost upon it, and then, at first, it was only an indistinct mass of shapes, but I hoped it would be our release.

The Soviet guards stopped us, and my companion and I explained that we were "Yivrey," Jewish refugees. The usually very talkative man in the long coat now stood silently beside us, simply nodding in agreement. I wished the guards would ask us for papers, but they did not ask to see anything, they seemed completely uninterested in searching us. For the first time in my life, they treated us perfunctorily and let us go. We had no choice but to continue walking, this man in the long coat, my friend, and I.

The checkpoint had just receded behind us when I decided on what to do. Saying I needed to relieve myself, I ducked into the woods alongside the road. I slipped from tree to tree and ran back to the Russians. Every twig that cracked, every heavy step I made, sent a shot of fear through my body. I wondered if the sounds could be heard from the road, if the noise would somehow give me away.

Breathless, I reached the Russian guards. I spoke fast, reaching for the right words, my hands making quick gestures. I told them about the plane and about how this man had emerged from the field. I held my arms out straight like metal wings, and spread my fingers to part imaginary grain. The guards did not wait for me to finish. They grabbed their guns and ran up the road. I followed behind.

By the time I caught up to them, the Soviets had already stopped both my friend and the man in the long coat. The guards stood firm, pressing their bayonets into each man's side and stomach. I pointed to the strange man, and the guards opened his coat.

Inside he had grenades, a gun, and bullets. The lining of his coat was a series of bulges, presumably each bulge marked a spot where still more things had been stuffed and sewn into the lining. He was almost certainly a spy or a saboteur, perhaps German, perhaps a Polish collaborator. Blending in with refugees was a perfect cover. There were so many unknown stragglers wandering across the region.

The guards dragged the man off, leaving the two of us to continue walking alone in the darkness, along this nameless Ukrainian road, terrified, yet relieved. We tried to piece together all that had happened, from the sudden appearance of the plane and the man emerging from the wheat field to what else he might have carried in his coat, but our excitement soon wore off, replaced by exhaustion. The tension that had collected now felt like lead in our limbs, and, finding an open field, we crawled in among the grasses to sleep. At dawn that morning, we awoke, a damp dew clinging to our skin. We searched for a stream for water to drink, and then we began walking again.

During the day, we said very little, but by now both of us were quite glad not to walk alone. With a companion, we both could survive much better. We could keep watch for each other when we had to steal food from farms, and on the roads, the people were less threatening when we were two rather than one.

Except for a brief time on a train, we walked for over a month to reach the Ukrainian capital of Kiev. Some stretches had thick, loamy fields, others were paler and covered with a scrubby brush. We had to cross small brooks and larger, faster streams and then walk for hours with soaking shoes and heavy, wet pants plastered against our legs. Bugs crawled over us and bit us as we slept, and sometimes in the low, swampy places bands of mosquitoes swarmed around us. We would cover our faces with our jackets to drown out the constant buzzing, but our bodies were still vulnerable. The mosquitoes entered through the smallest opening between cloth and skin and left us covered with itchy red welts.

We preferred to walk at night, under the protective cover of shadows, but some nights were too black to walk. Some mornings, a soupy fog clung so thickly to the ground that we had to feel for the road with each step. Stray branches and holes were hidden under the fog's whiteness, and it was easy to stumble or fall. We were hungry all the time. We chewed on green wheat kernels and ate wild berries, but they only left our jaws tired and our stomachs raw.

When we came upon Kiev, enveloping the high banks along the rushing Dnepr River, when we saw the sheen of the gold leaf on the distant onion domes, we felt like animals emerging from the forest. In filthy, burr-covered clothes, our hair tangled and dirty, we were willing to do anything for a loaf of bread, for any bit of food.

6

Fleeing Kiev

When we reached the city limits, we began to search for a flea market. We wanted to sell something, anything we had for food. We found a sprawling place, with stall after stall of vendors. They stood with their wares in baskets or spread in front of them on the ground. Sometimes they would show only three potatoes, or a woven market basket, or a hand-carved pipe. There were heavy, thick-knuckled peasant women with bright kerchiefs covering their hair and ample, fleshy faces. There were thin women too, hunched, bony, toothless women, and lean men whose clothes hung on their bodies. Some had hard, reddish noses and spat a yellow, pasty phlegm. All had come to sell and trade.

Farmers brought food to exchange for clothing, soap, flint, pans, nails, whatever items they needed. In every corner, voices rose as the bargaining grew heated, and carts and wagons clattered in and out. Not everyone was willing to barter, some vendors wanted rubles, but countless others just wanted anything.

Scattered among the seasoned traders were refugees, hawking their jewelry, books, and any remaining possessions for a bit of food or money for shelter. Some desperately approached customers, holding out whatever they had to sell. Others, their goods in their hands or spread out around their feet, stood passively on their little spots of ground, their heads bent, thin and waiting.

I walked up to one vendor who had a stall and sold clothes. He was a tall, handsome man, maybe six feet, and about forty years old. I took off my black jacket. I asked the man if he would buy it, and he countered, asking me why I wanted to sell it.

"What's the difference to you? I want to sell it." The jacket was heavy in my hands.

"I'm not going to buy it," he said. "Why do you want to sell it, it's your jacket?"

"I need the money for food."

The man looked at me and at my friend. He told us to sit down, and he sent another man to his house to bring back some food. The vendor started to talk to us. He ignored the crowds, his business, and any chance for sales. He wanted to hear our stories, to hear any news we might have. He wanted to hear everything. He was a Jew.

Around five o'clock, the man folded up his stall and took us to his home, nearby, on the outskirts of Kiev. "You will stay here with us, with my wife and me," he said.

By Russian standards, his house was luxurious. He had four rooms, three bedrooms, plus a living and eating area and a place for cooking. He and his wife also had a little garden behind the house where they grew vegetables. His wife was lovely, very warm and welcoming. They had two children, a boy, eighteen, and a girl, seventeen.

The man prepared water for us to wash. The bath water turned dark almost as soon as I submerged myself in the barrel. I clawed the dirt off of myself, scraping my skin again and again with my fingernails to remove the layers of grime. When we were clean, the merchant gave us fresh underwear and new clothes to wear. He threw our old clothes in the garbage heap to be burned. We had not washed them in six weeks.

For the first time in as many weeks, we also slept in a bed, not on the ground. We ate a meal that was not stolen from a field but was fixed in pots and served in bowls. We had to remember not to scoop the food into our mouths with our hands.

The next morning and every morning after that, every morning until that final day, we went to the market to help the clothing merchant. We searched for customers and traders and also for news. The German army was approaching Kiev.

Several units had reached the area around the city as early as July. We did not know if the Russians would hold the Germans. We did not know how many Germans had advanced how far. I wanted to believe that Kiev would hold, that the forward march would stop. But when I thought of the plane and the spy, and the ease with which he moved unchecked along that country road, I felt more and more afraid.

I also began to feel increasingly uneasy about my companion. He had a lewd, foul mouth, which I had largely ignored while we were on the road but which was now unavoidable. He swore, he spoke about sex. He embarrassed me in the marketplace until I no longer wanted to be within earshot of him. In the marketplace, he hustled, often trying to do people out of what little they had. Now, instead of a companion, I saw him as a conniver. He was often at his worst in the merchant's home.

He had started to play up to the merchant's wife, speaking to her in a casual, flirtatious style, as though she were a loose girlfriend. When mopping or sweeping needed to be done in the house, he would never offer to help. He never carried a flour sack, never did a thing. I was embarrassed to be associated with him, and I longed to tell him to shut his foul, obnoxious mouth, but he made me nervous, even afraid. He would linger about the house in the morning, catching up to us after the merchant and I had left for the market. He concealed things, made up stories that could not be true. He made me feel that I always needed to be on my guard. But soon I had an even greater fear.

Before dawn on September 2, exactly two years after the Germans had overrun Poland, the merchant woke us. There were tears in his eyes. His voice was thick. "I have to ask you to leave," he said.

I knew he did not want to say those words. He held his voice steady as he spoke, but his hands trembled. "The German army is on the outskirts of Kiev. We Russians cannot run away. You, you are considered refugees. You can go, we cannot. I do not want to see you go, but you must. You must save your lives."

He went on, trying to banish any hint of uncertainty. "I am a citizen of Kiev. I must shoulder a gun and defend my city. We will face the Germans. We will fight to defend Kiev."

What he did not say, but what we knew, was that refugees were not wanted for the defense of Kiev. The Soviet army did not want to take and arm refugees, whose loyalty to Stalin could not be counted on, who could be plants or spies. Stalin and the NKVD had other plans for the refugees. Many would later be sent to labor in frigid Siberian camps, where they would die, not in the lightening heat of battle but in the slow, debilitating misery of dysentery, hunger, and cold.

But on that morning, we could not contemplate such prospects. We could only think of running. The merchant packed a traveling case with food. He gave us money and told us we should head east, toward the city of Saratov. He would see us off. We left within minutes. I looked back once at the house. His wife stood in the doorway, twisting a rag tighter and tighter in her hands.

I later learned that for the next two weeks, German army divisions encircled Kiev, tightening like a noose. On September 19, the battle was over. A Nazi flag flew over the Dnepr. Jews who survived the failed defense of Kiev were liquidated by the Germans. Some were deported, some were shot, house to house. Many were lined up and sprayed with machine-gun bullets, their naked, riddled bodies, alive and dead, toppling into a pit called Baba Yar.

But on that early September morning, there was still time to flee. The merchant went with us through Kiev, along the city streets, past crumbling czarist architecture, to the docks along the Dnepr River. There, everything was in chaos. People were pushing, screaming, shouting, stampeding to board boats to cross the river, to reach the eastern bank.

We could hear the distant thunder of guns. Children clung to their mothers. Men scrambled to hold onto belongings, to keep sight of their families. Stronger ones pushed aside weaker ones. Faces were grim, eyes were filled with fear. An elbow was thrust into my ribs, and I was almost knocked down as hundreds of other refugees surged forward to board a waiting ferry.

The merchant handed us the suitcase filled with food. He put one hand on my hand and the other on my arm. He hugged me and kissed me on each cheek. He did the same to my companion. Then he said good-bye and stood at the dock as we joined the crush of bodies toward the ferry.

We made it onto the boat, but each of us was standing on a different section of the crowded deck as the ferry pulled away from the dock. Within moments, I heard an unmistakable sound, a sound I had not heard for two years. Overhead was the whir of an engine and the crackle of gunfire. A harsh, metallic hum droned in my ears. Then came the explosions.

Worse than the horrible loudness was the shaking that followed each bomb, the tremors in the air, the violent pitch and roll under my feet. People screamed, smoke rose into the sky, but the engine hum above was relentless, the hum followed by thunder, as if the whole world were breaking.

One bomb either hit the ferry or exploded nearby. The boat shuddered and seemed to buckle. Frenzied, panicked, people ran to side rails and began to jump into the swift waters below. People were screaming, but I didn't hear them. At that moment, I felt certain that I would die.

My hands were like ice as I reached the rail and gripped it. The boat was already heaving to one side as people rushed to the railings to jump. I looked down at the choppy water below. The boat leaned harder. I could not swim, but the boat was sinking. I had no choice. I let go.

My muscles stiffened as I hit the water. Water was in my eyes, my mouth. My clothes stuck to me like weights. Arms were flailing around me. I could not keep fighting the water that surrounded me and was now pulling me down.

Then I felt a single arm. Something was turning me, pulling me onto my back. I felt as if I were suffocating. I gasped for air. Each breath seemed like a knife, puncturing my lungs. For what seemed like an eternity, I struggled to breathe again. My head throbbed. Then, I looked around for the owner of the arm, the arm that had kept me from going under. Floating next to me was my companion from Radzyń.

He told me I was all right, and he began to maneuver us toward a small boat, one of many that had sailed out to rescue the ferry passengers. I felt stunned, my body heavy and swollen with the filthy, cold water. My companion guided me onto a boat, and I sat, dazed, dripping, gradually becoming aware again of the unrelenting gunfire, the crackle and thunder that persisted above the screams and cries.

The small boats returned to shore, and we scrambled away from the river. We had lost almost everything. The food and the clothes were gone. We still had some money stuffed in our pockets, but much of it was now in the Dnepr. And then we saw him. The merchant had waited at the dock, he had watched the boat pull away, and then he had heard the planes. He saw us go in the water, and he would not leave the shore until he had found us again.

Exhausted, the three of us began to make our way back through the chaotic streets, up the hills, to the merchant's home. His wife was there. She cried when she saw us at the door. She dried our clothes and prepared some soup for us. The merchant left for a while and returned with another traveling case, more clothes, more money, and more food, even more than he had given us that morning. We slept in his house one final night, a fitful sleep, listening for the sounds of gunfire.

At dawn the next morning, the merchant left with us for the train station. I was still numb from my near drowning the morning before. We knew now that we could not just walk east and hope to survive. We barely spoke as we made our way through Kiev once again.

When we arrived, hundreds of people had already jammed the train station. The station was dark and cavernous, with imposing arches and thick columns. Only a single electric light dangled high overhead, and it had been shut off. Inside, some of the people fought and shoved their way to the ticket line, which stretched up to the tiny slits in the ticket windows. Others would not wait. Massing together, they forced their way through the station doors, a great human wave, overwhelming the guards who remained, rushing toward the tracks.

We had tickets. I don't remember how we got the tickets, but we had them. The merchant must have paid for them. On the platform, there was pandemonium. People were thrusting themselves through train widows, hauling their families in after them. Some clung to the outside of the train, straddling open windows or even the connecting rods between cars.

Inside, there was nowhere to sit down at first, but the chaos finally began to subside. The air was filled not with screams or gunfire but with the sounds of every possible language, Polish, Czech, Russian, Ukrainian, Hungarian, and other unfamiliar tongues, even a rolling speech, which I imagined to be Italian. People were positioning bundles on the wooden boards overhead and piling into the wooden seats. There were no cushions, but the wood was slightly curved to fit the curve of a back.

We walked from car to car, searching for an empty place, and at last we found one in the far end. Then suddenly, the car lurched. The train whistle sounded, the wheels began to turn, and clouds of steam rose as we left the station for Saratov, deep in the heart of Russia.

7

A Chance
on a Collective

Kiev vanished behind us. The landscape turned rural, and the train stops became just small towns. We did not get off, we stayed on the train. I could not sit for very long on the wooden seats. The hard boards made my back ache, and I often had to stand, my body swaying as the train shuddered along.

The train was a collection of about twenty cars lashed together. None of the cars had nicely paneled walls and rows of comfortably upholstered seats. Rather, all had wooden seats and racks above, where at night many of the passengers lay down to sleep. Families would set up camp on the seats and even on the floors and in the corners of the cars. Bodies rested on top of each other, a different weight pressing in on either side. This, however, was infinitely preferable to the long open flatbed cars in which some desperate refugees rode for days, literally piled on top of each other, constantly exposed to harsh sun, rain, and cold darkness.

The train plodded eastward as men and matériel rushed west to the faltering front. It was an agonizing journey. The wheels crept along the worn rails, and often there was a sudden lurch as we were forced into a sidebed to wait for a military train with carloads of soldiers and ammunition to pass, whistle blaring, metal wheels throwing sparks and heat off the metal rails. Babies cried and people waited. But, as long as the military trains continued westward, it was a good sign.

I listened to the people around me. They had fled on trains, in carts, on foot. Sometimes entire families had left together, sometimes only a few members or just one. "Surely, Kiev will hold," they repeated. "Surely."

But we were all fleeing Kiev.

Although we were not being shelled or shot at, everyone on the train shared a feeling of fear, and even on a train, you had to think about survival. Anything could happen.

At first, my companion and I tried to make our food last. We ate it quietly, in small quantities. But others knew when you had food. They would watch you eat, watch each bite and swallow with wide, open eyes until you tore off some bread or somehow shared. We tried to be discreet. We would put a piece of bread in a pocket and tear off small bites and ease them into our mouths.

Except for mealtimes, my companion was often gone, wandering through the train cars. I was glad for the familiar face, glad not to be totally alone, yet even so things around me took on a blurry cast, like the landscape bobbing outside the window, new, unreal, one scene indistinguishable from the next. Once again, I was on the run. Watchfulness was extracting its own toll.

I had many empty hours on that train, hours when my mind wandered back to Radzyń, to Olyka, to Brest-Litovsk. I thought about my family, about my fiancée. I saw their faces, my father's long dark coat and graying beard, my sister rocking her new baby, my fiancée holding a bowl of soup in her pale, industrious hands, and I felt myself draining away with each new mile of countryside.

When I slept, I dreamt, large chaotic dreams. I would wake anxious, tired, as if even in sleep vigilance were inescapable. And yet I was relatively safe, inside a sealed, moving train.

One night, about halfway between Kiev and Saratov, I awoke and at first saw only blackness around me, but gradually I could make out the shapes of other sleepers. I don't know why, but I stuck my hands in my jacket pockets. I felt watches, rings, the stiff paper of passports, all filling the pockets. Suddenly, I was wide awake. My hands froze. Slowly, I pulled my fingers out of my pockets, afraid that anything inside would fall out, afraid that something inside would make noise, afraid that someone else might be awake. I lay there very quietly, taking shallow, short breaths, stunned. Was I loosing my mind? Slowly, I reached back in a finger. I touched the cool metal case of a watch, the round curve of a ring, the crisp paper of official documents. They were all very real.

I had to start thinking. My companion, as he wandered through the cars, must have stolen these things. He wandered and watched and must have gone back in the dead of night. I listened for him, somewhere around me, but heard nothing. My mind was moving. All the mistrust that I had felt before this man had saved my life returned. I had traveled with him for two months, and yet I did not know him. Only my instincts had been right. Yes, he had saved my life, but now I feared that he would ruin it.

I also knew that I could not confront him. The stuff was in my pockets. There was no proof. If I said one word, I would certainly be hauled away by the NKVD or at least be thrown off of the train and left for the advancing Germans.

I had to get away from this man. I had to get rid of the stuff in my pockets. My old fear was gone, a new, immediate fear had replaced it. Eyes open, body almost completely still, I waited for the dawn. Once again, everything seemed to be at the end.

He found me soon after the other passengers began to stretch and rouse themselves for another cramped, repetitive day, and he gave me a knowing glance and a smile. I looked back and then quickly looked away. My hands felt like ice. I hunched my shoulders lest anyone notice the fresh bulges in my pockets. Each moment as we rolled along the tracks was agony. I tried to move as close to the other passengers as I dared so that he could not say anything to me. Then all I could do was wait. I did not even know if the train would stop at a station that day. I did not know anything except for what was in my pockets.

The train slowed down several times but never stopped, until finally we reached a station. I do not even remember its name. I tried to stand, casually, and move toward the door. Always, a few men would jump down onto the platform to walk, breathe air, search for hot water in the station, just to be off of the train. I waited for quite a while until a crowd had gathered on the platform, then I eased myself down onto the hard surface and glanced up at the car windows. He was watching. He smiled, showing his teeth. I smiled back, motioning something about wanting a drink. His smile faded. He moved toward the exit.

I walked quickly into the station and looked around for someplace to run, to hide, to dump the stuff. Behind me, I heard the door open, and in a loud voice I asked for water. A heavy, red-faced woman in a corner looked up and then looked down again. There were men in uniforms standing off to the side, and suddenly I became very conscious of my pockets. I wanted very much to leave.

When I stepped back out onto the platform, he was waiting for me, a bit apart from some men milling around. I forced a smile and nodded my head toward the car where we sat. I tried to moderate my pace, to move but not too fast, as I made my way to an opening between the cars and eased myself into another cluster of men. Then I saw it, down the platform, at the edge of the station, an outhouse. Moving along the side of the train I headed for it. Someone was inside. I waited, and when the door opened, I pushed it in and then shut it tight behind me.

I was sweating. From my pockets I pulled the gold, the papers, the stones, and the chains. I did not even stop to look, I threw everything down the hole. I hunted around for a long stick and finally pulled something off the wall. Then I pushed the stuff deep into the hole, smashing it, burying it in the waste. My hands shook, my shirt stuck to my sides. I checked my pockets again. Empty. The stuff was gone.

I leaned against the wall, trying to calm my breathing. I was worried that someone had heard the noise of the stick or that they would simply come to check why I had taken so long. I knew I had to get far away from that out-house, but I also did not want to be back on that train. It seemed, though, that I did not have a choice. I tried to walk casually back down the platform and reboard the train. I saw my companion watching me from a window as I climbed up the steps. Then his face disappeared. Instantly, the thought flashed through my mind: he must be walking through the cars, toward me. I had deliberately gotten on far away from our seats. My heart pounding, I waited, expecting him to appear in the crowd at any moment. I waited, and I listened. I listened for the high, wailing whistle of the train.

When I heard the first whistle, I did not move. I kept watching the crowd in the car. I saw the crowd by the door part to allow someone through as people were jostled into their seats. In my mind, I thought it could only be him. I had to fight the urge to run. Then I heard the release of steam and felt the lurch as the train brake was loosened. I stepped back until I was standing at a door that opened to the outside. As the train began to move, I jumped down onto the platform, hitting the concrete with heavy, hard thud. The train was gathering speed, and it was then that I saw him, in the very spot on the train where I had just been standing, only farther down the tracks, holding on to the door handles, yelling, cursing, his face tight with rage. But with every second the train was moving faster, carrying him farther away.

I had fallen onto the ground, and only then did I pick myself up, wipe the dust off my jacket, and watch the train grow smaller as it receded. I felt like a man who has been condemned to death and at the last moment is given a reprieve. I felt free, even as the Soviet police ran down the platform, grabbed my arms, and arrested me. I was still afraid of the NKVD, but not nearly as afraid of them as I would have been if I had been caught with all the documents, rings, and watches in my pockets.

The NKVD men were holding my arms, asking me why I had gotten off the train. I had to think fast and to say something that would keep them away from the outhouse. And then it came to me. I told them that I had dropped my identity papers when I climbed on, that they had fallen from my pocket, and that when I realized they were missing, I jumped down to look for them but had not found them. The words were coming out in a jumble, but once I had spoken them, they became my story, a story I would tell again and again. I hoped none of them had seen me visit the outhouse or would remember it. The Soviets held me and searched every inch of me. Then they questioned me once more. I repeated that I had jumped off to look for my documents, thinking only about losing those precious papers and not about the moving train. They did not react. I was panicking. I took a chance and looked at them, saying, "I am a Jew, a refugee, do you expect me as a Jew to be a German spy?"

They did not answer. Instead, the circle of police opened, and two of the men led me away from the station. We headed to a building in the city. I was praying they would not look in the hole in the outhouse. I don't remember anything about the city or the place, only that I was taken into a room where there were still more men, and each asked me questions around a table, trying to get me to contradict myself. I told my story over and over. I told them I had worked in Brest-Litovsk before the Germans had attacked. They kept asking questions. Then they brought me food and left me alone in that room for what seemed like several hours. But a short while later, everything began again. Two new men came in and started to question me. I don't know how long I was there, but eventually the NKVD gave up and let me go. They sent me back to the station and gave me a little food. I ate silently, chewing big mouthfuls. Around me were women weeping as their husbands boarded trains to take them to the army and the front. So many grim-faced men setting off to stop the enemy. I watched families being wrenched apart right before my eyes. The NKVD men said nothing. A few hours passed, and then they let me get on another train, heading east.

My relief at leaving was soon tempered by new worries. What if my old companion was waiting for me when I got off the train in Saratov? The thought of seeing him again made me fear for my life. I knew I would have to disappear almost from the moment I arrived.

This new train did not have just refugees. There were some Soviets on board as well. I listened carefully as they talked about collective farms scattered through the region and especially about one called Iminia Krupskaya, which was located right along the train line. When we reached that stop, a little ways before Saratov, I got off the train.

Officials of some sort were waiting inside the station. They came over to question me, and I said I was looking for work. After more questioning, they took me to the collective, Iminia Krupskaya, named after Lenin's female companion, Krupskaya. There were about twenty-five other refugees on the collective farm, other Poles, Hungarians, Czechs, even a couple of German Jews. Most of them had come from Saratov. They had been the lucky ones. Many of the refugees who had asked for work in Saratov had been turned away by the Soviets and forced to get back on trains and head still farther east, into Siberia.

At the collective, we were each assigned to live with a Soviet family. I had my own room in a tiny wooden house. It was really like a closet with straw on the floor and a quilt filled with feathers, but the material was rough and the quilt was old, so the feathers had matted into a ball in one end. I did not care.

I could sleep on a floor, not in a field. I had hot food to eat. I had stopped running.

I loved life on the collective. I watched cows and horses give birth, watched the mothers lick the new calves and foals as they struggled to stand on shaky legs. I rode some of the horses, and I learned about bees, because the collective produced a lot of honey. I learned that if I walked unafraid, without running or making sudden gestures around the hives, I would not be stung. People who worked with the bees wore little masks over their faces, and after they had drained the honeycomb, we enjoyed the sweet smell of fresh honey as the nights turned cool and we began to think about the impending frost.

The house where I lived had rough wooden walls and a slanted straw roof, or at least a thick straw covering over the roof. The outside looked very old, as if it had never been painted. Most of the other houses on the collective looked the same. Inside, there was often a picture of Lenin or Stalin on the wall. The furnishings were simple, a few wooden chairs and maybe a table. Some people used little barrels for tables. Everyone cooked in their homes using wooden stoves, although there was not much variety in what they cooked.

Our diet was black bread, eggs, and milk. But the people made more out of what they had. They left the milk in a cold area so the cream would rise, and then they would skim the cream off the top, sometimes churning it to make butter. When the milk had turned sour, it was poured into a tight burlap bag and covered top and bottom with wood with a heavy rock on top. The weight would push the liquid through the burlap and curds of cheese, "farmers' cheese," would be left inside, clinging to the sack.

I ate what the family in the house ate. Sometimes they even gave me a bigger portion of food or the last scrapings from the pan. They were very nice people. They did not look down on me because I was a refugee. Instead they treated me warmly and shared the very little they had. The man was about forty, his wife maybe thirty-five, and they had two children, a boy and girl, ten and twelve years old. They felt bad for me because I was alone, without a family. They even tried to set me up with a young woman on the collective farm, so I could settle down. But although they were kind, I did not want to get too close. I had already left three homes and two families.

In the evenings, after work, they took me to dances on the collective, where some of the residents would form circles and a few farmers would play the balalaika, a stringed instrument that made vibrant, melodious sounds. I learned some Russian folk dances and some Russian songs, and for a few hours in the dusk and darkness of a fall evening, we would forget the stiffness in our muscles, the numbing exhaustion, and lose ourselves in the sounds and steps of what now was another time and another place. But all too soon the music would cease, and we would wander home, to sleep and wait for the first hint of dawn.

Before the sun rose in the morning, the head of the collective, known as a *nayalnik* in Russian, would go around to each house and bang on the windows, hollering for everyone to get up. During the harvest, we would assemble in groups, and then five to seven people would be given scythes and sent off to a field to cut grain. The work was backbreaking. We stood far apart and swung the crescent shaped blade from one side to another to cut the stalks of pale yellow wheat. My arms ached, until even turning over at night was excruciating. We cut wheat, we cut rye, we cut hay, we cut a little flowered grass that made cows' milk sweet, we cut everything. But that fall, we cut mostly wheat and rye and stacked hay.

We used a wooden fork to pitch the hay onto a pile, which grew higher and higher, until other men made it into a stack. The rye was stored in barns or silos, and the wheat was also stacked, waiting for a threshing machine. But much of the wheat was lost because it was not taken in on time. The residents of the collective didn't rush to gather the wheat. Rain clouds appeared, and no one hurried. Rains came, and the wheat stood out in the fields, soaked and ruined.

At first, I didn't understand why the residents did not hurry to bring in the wheat. I thought of the Graboevitzs, in Radzyń, who feared allowing one potato to rot in their "rented" field. On the collective that fall, all the refugees worked very hard. We were afraid not to. But we soon learned how the Russians felt. "Everything goes to the government." That was all they said.

The refugees soon discovered that the Soviet government set quotas for the harvest, and regardless of how bad a harvest, the collective had to meet its quota of wheat, milk, rye, and hay. The collective had to give a set amount of what it grew to the government, and there were no adjustments, no compromises. The people on the farms were given only a minimal amount of the harvest, whatever was left over after the government quotas were filled. Some years, they could be left with barely anything at all. Small, private plots sprang up for vegetables and foods, but the farm harvests yielded less and less. There was no desire to work because they did not get anything in return. And the refugees soon came to realize that, aside from not keeping much of the harvest, no one got any more food or better shoes or clothes for a good day's work. We were thankful, however, just to be able to eat and sleep.

Gradually, though, by the end of the harvest, we had begun to learn more about the land in which we were living.

One day in November, after it had already turned cold, the Soviet police and some members of the Soviet military selected twenty to thirty people from the collective. I was one of them. We did not know where we were going. I had heard whispers of men being rounded up, being removed from their homes in the middle of night, and never being seen again. We said nothing as the Soviets led us away. But we soon discovered that the Soviets had taken some men from every collective and had put them, in groups of fifteen, on trucks. Everything had been done in secret. We were driven away from the farms over a bumpy, rutted road to a region we did not know, to a colony of fields and clean, sturdy wooden houses. The walks were swept, there was smoke rising from the chimneys. We were given guns, and each one of us was assigned to stand guard over a house while Soviet police and military cleared out the inside. "Do not let anyone inside run away," we were told.

We watched as the people came out, men in trousers, strong, solid looking women, and children. They were speaking strange sounds, not Russian, with its rolling *o* and *e* sounds and its curt *k* sounds, but something deeper, throatier. Then I heard one of the Soviets say it, "German."

Several hundred of them were lined up in the cold. Some didn't even have coats. They took nothing. No suitcases, no bundles. Instead, they were led to the waiting trucks and loaded on board, and then, with us following, they were taken to a train stop, loaded into windowless cattle cars, and sent east, into Siberia, the Soviet graveyard for millions of its own citizens.

But these people were different. They were ethnic Germans, or *Volksdeutsche*, one of many independent German communities inside the Soviet Union, Poland, Czechoslovakia, and indeed all across eastern Europe. The people in the colony had lived there for generations. Especially up and down the Volga, there were small German communities started by Catherine the Great, the eighteenth-century czarina who induced the Germans to settle there, in the midst of rich, dark farmland. The descendants of these original German settlers still farmed, not as a collective, I was told, but privately. They did not have to turn over a portion of their harvest to the government, though they were forced to pay taxes to the state.

Recently, however, the NKVD had discovered that German planes were dropping off guns and ammunition to this colony so that it could help start a second front in the rear as the German army moved closer. Or at least this is what we were told. A roundup had been planned, and extra workers had been recruited from surrounding collectives.

As they came out of their neat, little houses, some of the women were crying, and the men were quite pale. Children tugged at their mothers' skirts. I watched. I knew they were Germans, but I had never seen people taken from their homes and rounded up before. Only later, when I had seen many more things, did this seem quite minor, this loading of people with nothing onto trains.

The winter was cold, cold that I had never felt or known. On Iminia Krupskaya, the happiest person in the world was someone with good shoes. If you had a pair of boots, you were rich. To have holes in the bottoms of your shoes was torture. People wrapped string around their shoes to hold the soles, and they wrapped newspaper around their feet to keep warm. The boots we had from the collective were made of felt, all one piece, with no hard soles, just material. If it was close to freezing, water would soak through the material, ruining the newspaper and making our feet throb with cold. The collective also provided clothing, either two sizes too big or too small. The material was rough, shirts felt like burlap, and there were not enough jackets to go around. A group of women in the collective washed the clothes once a week, but of course that was much more difficult and irregular in the winter, when everything froze.

Inside the houses, we could not get warm. Wood stoves could not keep out the winds. We had to move to keep warm, and yet moving around was torture because it seemed to use up the strength needed to stay warm. Night came early, and the days seemed more like breaks between long stretches of darkness.

Even during the bitterest cold, the people on the collective were caring and kind, but they were afraid. Everyone knew there were NKVD informers on the collective, but no one knew who they were. It was dangerous to mention the Soviet leader Stalin or the government. As refugees, we quickly learned that we could talk about politics only among ourselves, not with the Russians. Over time, we heard stories of people who were taken from their homes in the middle of the night for saying something against the government, of children who turned in their parents to the state for a simple remark or a quick outburst of frustration. Everyone suffered under Stalin. The only people who might be considered happy were either Communist party members or part of the NKVD. Ordinary people lived with a constant fear that they would become a target of the state, that their lives would be ruined. The hardship united all of us, but the fear drove a wedge between husbands and wives, between even the best of friends. Trust evaporated, and the word *Siberia* hung like a cloud over our heads and like ice around our hearts.

While Hitler tried to eliminate the Jews, Stalin and his supporters would eliminate anyone about whom they had doubts. They would jail them, send them to labor camps, or shoot them. But if you were a small man, like me, a laborer, who kept your head down and tried to follow the rules of the communist system, you had a chance to survive. With Hitler, I did not even have that chance.

At Iminia Krupskaya, we heard almost no news from the outside world. Only people passing through the collective could tell us how the war was going, and many times they did not know or would not say. We did know that

Germany had tried to capture Moscow and had failed, but we also knew that Germany was still entrenched in the Soviet Union and was waiting for spring.

As the winter months dragged on, we were thinking about the war, but we were also thinking about staying warm and about cigarettes. They weren't actually cigarettes, made from real tobacco rolled up in fine paper. Rather, they were made from something called *mahorka*, a leaf similar to tobacco, which was wrapped in strips of newspaper and then smoked. *Mahorka* was like poison. It had a bitter, burning taste that scorched your tongue and throat. But to us, even the harshest, strongest tobacco seemed sweet. We savored the aroma, the filling of the lungs. Cigarettes were a sought-after luxury, and they were in very short supply. People on the collective catered to anyone with cigarettes. Sometimes, we wanted a cigarette so badly we would even give away our bread for one.

A number of the refugees who came to the collective arrived with cigarettes and quickly found people lining up to trade. Not even the remains of tobacco were wasted. Kids hung around smoking areas, gathering up crushed cigarette stubs. They would carefully remove the last shreds of tobacco, mix them together, and reroll them into another cigarette to trade. It was not even shameful for a man to pick up a used butt from the ground, try to relight the last frail leaves, and inhale a few more puffs. We took joy in cigarettes, a very fleeting joy.

After many months, spring came. The newly thawed air smelled fresh and sweet and did not burn in my lungs. The hard ground became soft and then quickly turned to mud. Everywhere I stepped, something wet soaked through my shoes. Wagons, people, shovels, everything stuck in the mud. The rain created deep puddles, and the earth itself seemed to become a liquid, sliding mass. The mud covered everyone, and no matter how hard the women scrubbed, they could not wash it all off. Many days, I slogged through this mud to take the cows to pasture. It caked my pants and boots and then dried hard and crusty. When I rode a horse to herd the cows to a more distant pasture, the mud would fly up and splatter me, clinging to my legs in small drops, as if God had invented a thick brown rain.

Riding the horse made me feel free. I loved the sudden rush of speed and the feel of wind on my face. There was a sense of complete abandon to be moving over the earth with such power, to feel the heat of the animal and the rhythm of its breath, to race without running.

One afternoon however, as I was leading the cows from atop the horse, my horse reared up, throwing its weight onto its hind legs and nearly flinging me from its back. I wrapped my legs around its belly and gripped its mane in my hands. It rose up again, squealing, and then galloped off. I was shouting, and a few people nearby looked up, but the horse was unstoppable. I tugged on the mane, hoping to slow the horse, as my legs slid along its sides and I felt myself rising up off of its back.

I held on as it ran, striking the ground like thunder, kicking up clumps of grassy earth. Finally, exhausted, its sides caked with foamy sweat, it slowed. My legs ached, my arms were nearly frozen, each beat of my heart rang in my ears. I guided the horse around, and we headed back toward the cows.

When we returned, a Russian from the collective was waiting. He told me the horse had smelled a wolf lurking not far away. "Wolves go after the throats of horses," he explained, showing with his hands how the wolf's jaws rip into the vulnerable flesh. "But," he said, "maybe the wolf did not attack because a human was there. Perhaps because a human was there, you saved the horse."

8

Taškent

There were dances in the spring, happy evenings filled with music and sing-ing as the days held out longer against the night. But by summer, things had begun to change. People from Saratov were coming to the collective for food, for a place to sleep, for protection from the advancing Germans. The German army was closing in on Stalingrad, which lay below Saratov on the winding Volga River. By August, the assault had begun.

By October, the German forces were near the heart of Stalingrad and barely half a mile from the Volga, but I was already gone. When the first chill nights settled over the region, marking the coming of fall, I knew I did not have enough clothes to survive another winter on the collective. And there were no clothes to be found. Everything was going to the troops as the Germans closed in. I had not been assigned to the collective by the Soviet government, which meant I was not bound to the collective, no governmen-tal authority or fear was holding me there, and I could leave. The Soviet gov-ernment, desperate for laborers as the war dragged on, would round up ref-ugees and send them to work camps far east in Siberia, but it did not restrict their movement throughout the rest of the country as efficiently as it con-trolled Soviet citizens.

I had spent months listening to people talk about the warmth of the south, the perfect climate, the beautiful land. Sometimes they were only people re-telling others' stories, people who had never actually been, never actually seen. But as the air grew cooler and the Germans drew closer, I decided that my time had come.

I informed the head of the collective that I wanted to leave. I was noth-ing to him, so he released me. I hitched a ride to Saratov, where I boarded a train. Until then, everything had seemed easy. Until then, it had all seemed possible.

I spent over two weeks on that train, over two weeks traveling the fifteen hundred miles from Saratov to Taškent. Almost as soon as it had left the station, the train was forced to pull over to a sidebed and wait while high-speed military trains rushed past. Inside, the passengers would feel the cars shudder as the train switched onto another track, then the jolt as the train stopped. After that, we would wait, listening for a whistle, feeling the vibrations as yet another train sped by, rocking our own motionless cars. Eventually, our train would begin to move again, the engine chugging and steam filling the air. But as soon as we had covered one hundred or two hundred miles, the train would grind to halt, and the waiting would begin all over again.

Sometimes, we would sit in a sidebed for days, watching the blurred images of tanks and machines as they passed. At several points, the trains were coming every hour, a brief, violent rush before we were plunged back into stillness, with no movement around us other than our own restless limbs. Inside, the train had grown filthy, and there was little, if any, food. Those who had money could buy bread and other simple items in the train stations, and, as we drew south, we sometimes found melons for sale. What other remaining food there was had been rationed.

Most of what we did eat came from old men and women who swarmed the train when it came to a halt in an open space or alongside a station. They would arrive with thick loaves of bread, eggs, and chunks of lard, eager to barter them for salt or soap or whatever the refugees had. I watched women rummage through clothes and hold up blouses for eggs. Some removed their rings, twisting and tearing the bands off their fingers in return for bread for their children. Always, there was the confusion of arms reaching up and down, the bare white arms of those inside the train and the thick tanned arms of those outside. I heard the plaintive cries of those who waited until the final moments, reaching out as the train was moving away.

When we stopped at the stations, we drank *kipjatok,* the Russian word for boiled water, which was kept, ready to be tapped, in kettles along the wall. People lined up by the kettles, using and reusing chipped cups, cans, even narrow-necked bottles, although those using a bottle ran the risk having their hands scalded by the steaming liquid. There was nothing else to drink but *kipjatok.* Anyone who drank unboiled water usually contracted dysentery.

All the passengers on the train suffered together, and many of them shared what little they had. I remember people opening suitcases, taking out carefully packed foods, and sharing, even people with children. Mostly, the passengers were refugees. By now, we were used to running and waiting.

We had almost no news, only the fragments we picked up in stations, and they were hardly reliable, so we speculated. We could not have known everything, and yet, if we had known, what would we have said then, what would we have thought, hour after hour and day after day in those sidebeds?

People asked how Hitler could have become so strong, how could he have taken over Poland and Czechoslovakia, how was he able to attack the Soviet Union? Some believed that England could have stopped Hitler, and they blamed England for what had happened. Others wondered about the United States, and why it had not joined in the war. But most people had no answers, only a sense of exhaustion. The war was on everyone's mind, but so too were their own lives. We held onto Taškent as we would a dream, envisioning it as a place where we might begin to make our lives better.

When the train finally ground to a halt in this dry, Moslem city, east of two deserts and at the foot of a mountain range, I said to myself, "I should never have left Saratov."

The gray concrete train station was packed, but it was nothing compared with the streets outside. There, stretching before me, in the hot sun was an enormous human camp. Hundreds, perhaps thousands of people lay on the sidewalk and street in front of the train station. Some rested against little bundles, but, for many, their only pillow was their fist. I caught sight of open sores oozing on swollen legs. Lice crawled over their bodies and clung to their hair. I had never seen such filth. The stench from sweat and waste was sickening. I listened to the sporadic outburst of hacking coughs and to the deeper, rattling sounds made by the very ill, who lay, almost prostrate, on the ground. Here were men, women, and children weak, exhausted, some all but unable to move, living worse than wild animals.

The local police and NKVD would conduct sweeps, trying to disperse the human mass, but even those who left were quickly replaced by another fresh trainload of refugees. The trains kept coming, one after another, only increasing the misery. Many of the people who arrived were simply put on other trains and sent to Siberia to work in labor camps.

I had nowhere else to go, so I stayed with this wretched mass. The expressions in their eyes frightened me, the way some rolled their faces up when a new person passed, the way many others never stirred, but only stared off into the same direction. I did not know what to do. I dreamed that someone, maybe even my father, would appear, point to me, and say, "You are my son."

I waited, but no one came. I wandered around the nearby streets, afraid to venture too far from the train station. Mostly, I counted each new day among the filth and stench and waited for something to change. Then, late one morning, a Soviet military officer appeared. Several times, I had watched Soviet soldiers drive up to the station in flatbed trucks. Rifles cocked, they would line up groups of refugees, sometimes by occupation, calling out for tailors or shoemakers or whatever profession they chose. Then the Soviets would motion to those who looked strong and healthy, and often also to those who did not, telling them to board the trucks, that they would be cared for and that they were going to work for the motherland. With nearly every young man in the army, the Soviets were desperate for laborers.

This morning, however, there were no trucks, just this one man, asking in Russian if any of the refugees knew how to finish furniture. I quickly raised my hand.

In Radzyń, a little less than a year before the war began, I had worked for a casket maker, and I had learned how to mix a furniture lacquer. But I had never actually finished a piece of furniture by myself.

The man in uniform looked at me, nodded, and told me to come with him. He took me to a military canteen and gave me lunch. The food was simply army rations, but to me it was a feast. I tried not to eat like a ravenous animal, I tried not to let my hunger overtake me. But I was constantly shoving in a new mouthful of food before I had swallowed the old one. When I had eaten everything before me, I ran my spoon up and down the edges of the container, collecting any remaining drops. As I licked the last bit of food from the utensil, the officer asked how I would go about finishing the furniture, wooden covers for sewing machines.

I went over each step in my mind, slowly and methodically, trying to collect my thoughts before I spoke. First, I would wipe the wood with a damp rag to force out the air and any fine shavings still trapped in the grain. Then I would rub sandpaper across the surface and wipe it again. Next, I would mix bismark and alcohol to make a lacquer finish and pour some of the finish on a rag. Finally, using pumice stone and a drop of oil, I would rub the finish into the wood, filling in the grains, making the color even and smooth.

The officer listened. He asked how much of each ingredient I would need to finish five hundred sewing machine covers. I made some quick calculations using some very vague figures and gave him some numbers. He seemed satisfied. He stood up, and I quickly got up after him. "Let's go," he said, motioning toward a parked jeep.

Once or twice in my life, I had ridden in a truck and also in a few busses, but I had never ridden in a jeep before. He got in with ease, and I followed, gripping the seat with both hands, my knuckles turning white at the first bounce as we began to move. I did not know how I would stop myself from falling or flying out, how I would stay in my seat. But I held on, and slowly a new feeling overtook me, a feeling of exhilaration. It was both frightening and exciting to feel my body rise up and fall back into the seat, to feel the breeze in my face and hair.

Our destination was a factory, a rather small place in a single-story building. I soon discovered that the factory belonged to the military and that it made uniforms and clothes for the soldiers. There was one room with thick bolts of material and another section where the workers, mostly local women and some men, who were either older or unfit for the army, hunched over sewing machines, stitching yards of fabric. The officer, however, led me into yet another room, empty except for five hundred sewing machines with unfinished wooden tops. He pointed to a bucket and some sandpaper and told me I should begin work.

I filled the bucket and grasped the sandpaper, but my heart was pounding. With every splash of water, every stroke of the paper, I feared I was making some deadly mistake. Slowly, I began to mix the ingredients for the lacquer and build up some color on the wood, but I knew I was no good as a furniture finisher. Something would have to be done.

Early in the evening, I returned to the train station, and I began asking the refugees, in Yiddish, if anyone there was a furniture finisher. A man who looked to be about fifty, gaunt, with wrinkles that cut into his skin like scars, laughed at me as if I was making some cruel joke. "That was my life," he said. "What, do you want me to teach you?"

The next morning, I took this man and one other from the crowd to the factory to work. "With three, instead of one, we should be able to finish three times as fast," I explained.

The two men began washing, sanding, and coloring. Everything was going very well, but still I was watching the door. When I saw the officer enter, I quickly grabbed a rag out of the old man's hands and began to rub it across the wood myself, pretending that I was teaching the old man, who looked at me for an instant, but said nothing. The officer nodded approvingly, ran his finger along the edge of one of the sewing machine tops, and left, satisfied that the job was being done.

From then on, for several weeks, it was as if we had entered an easy dream. Immediately, we were able to leave the squalor of the train station. The Soviets sent each of us to live with a local family and even gave us ration papers so we could buy food. Each morning, the military man picked us up in his jeep to take us to the factory, and when the day was over, he was back, waiting to take us home.

My "home" was with a ruddy, round-faced older man and his wife on the outskirts of Taškent. They were Tadzhiks, not ethnic Russians, and their son had been sent off to the front to fight. After the weeks of living either on a train or in a train station, I was grateful for a bed and a bit of peace. But I had never before seen such a house. Its walls were cement, and its roof was made of clay. In the very middle of the house was a big pit, dug right into the floor. They cooked in that pit, and if it grew chilly, they kept a fire going in the pit for warmth. Smoke escaped through a chimney in the roof.

Sometimes, I would come home and find people gathered in a circle around the pit, drinking tea from a single cup, which they would pass from person to person. Sometimes, they would pass a pipe in the same way around the circle, with each person pausing to smoke it.

The man and his wife treated me very well, and they were glad to have me in their home because my extra money allowed them to have a little extra food. My life seemed almost normal, except there was nothing normal about how I had come to this dry place with its old, tiled buildings and round, colored domes. Each day as Germans and Russians slaughtered one another at Stalingrad, as entire communities were marched off to their own destruction, I woke up, ate, and rode in a special jeep to a factory, where, along with two other men whom I did not know at all, I methodically sanded and stained the wooden tops of sewing machines.

We worked to the rhythmic whir of the sewing machines and the sounds of hundreds of needles piercing the thick green and brown cloth in nearby rooms. Our hands and clothes, even our hair, smelled of furniture lacquer, and our fingertips had a kind of permanent brown stain. We said very little. Circumstance had pulled us together, soon enough it would pull us apart.

I spent a lot of time watching for officers or officials, and in the course of all my watching, I also began to notice what was going on around me in the factory. One day, as I peered into the room next to my work area, the room with the bolts of material, I saw a man and a woman huddled in a corner, taking off their shirts, and wrapping yards of the fabric around their bodies. Then they put their shirts back on and waited for their shift to end. I could not believe they would take such a chance. To be caught smuggling material surely meant jail or Siberia. But at the end of the day, the guards at the gate just watched the two of them pass, along with all the others who poured out of the gate. As I watched, I learned that, while any bag or a bundle carried by a worker would be searched, people could easily come and go with yards of material wound around their middles.

Five or six times, I found some extra material and, when I was sure no one was looking, I tied it around myself. I brought the extra yards home and gave them to the Tadzhik and his wife. They were thrilled because fabric of any kind was almost impossible to find, and, for them, this material was like gold. But I was afraid of being caught. So after those few times, I stopped my smuggling.

With three of us working on the sewing machine tops, it did not take many weeks to finish the job. Once the tops were ready, the officer handed me a packet filled with money, a certain number of rubles for each top, and then we were all cut loose from the factory. I did not think about whether it was common to be paid under communism, I simply shared the money with the two other men, who quickly receded back into the anonymity of the refugee crowd. The rest of the rubles I shared with the Tadzhik man and his wife.

For two weeks, I wandered around the city. In the best spots, it smelled of oils and spices, but mostly the scents were of heat, decay, and dust. The streets were lined with a mixture of newer buildings, flat, square, and decidedly solemn in the austere Soviet style, built with cinder blocks, and older, far more ornate structures with curving lines and oriental domes.

The city seemed to sprawl over the land, its streets cluttered with horses and wagons and obstinate donkeys hauling carts or bundles strapped to their backs. Many were heading for the market square, where vendors set up hundreds of little stalls winding across the square like the corridors of some unfathomable maze. There, I also saw refugees, part of the endless stream of new arrivals who came to the market hoping to be able to buy food or find a day's work in exchange for something to eat. If they found neither, some, in desperation, would resort to stealing. I could see from the remnants of their clothes, from their faces and hands, that many of the men had been professional men, that they had standing in their communities at home. Now, hungry and destitute, they were trying to learn the art of stealing a simple loaf of bread.

Most of the refugees were gaunt and thin and pale, easy to spot, wandering amidst the market stalls and the rising din of bargaining and the clattering of carts drawing up and driving away. They shuffled past stalls selling fruits and vegetables grown in the farmers' own backyards, stalls selling extra eggs and tubs of freshly churned butter. Some stalls had only piles of melons, plump, round, and achingly ripe. Chickens squawked in cages on a long table of a long maze.

Other stalls sold pottery, metal work, rugs, baskets of spices, and countless odds and ends. The sellers were mostly old men and women, with gnarled hands and faces darkened like leather. Some of the men would squat in a corner, sucking on long pipes and then exhaling clouds of sweet smoke, while the women watched them with their dark, almond-shaped eyes.

To me though, the people in Taškent seemed to live better than people in other parts of the Soviet Union. Some still dressed in traditional embroidered blouses and wide, flowing pants. They had more things, more food, and, of course, the climate was warmer. But there was still fear.

Some of the young men from the area, almost as soon as they were conscripted into the Soviet army, shot themselves in their trigger fingers, so that they could be discharged or at least avoid going to the front lines. The Soviet military quickly discovered the pattern of these self-inflicted wounds and promptly lined up a large group of men and shot them dead. There was no mercy. But, for many people, there never had been.

One afternoon, on what had so far been an average day, I returned to the house to find the Tadzhik woman waiting. "Pack your things immediately," she said, grabbing my arm and pulling me towards my room. "You've got to get out of here. Two men were here just a little while ago, looking for you. I think they were NKVD men." She tried to whisper, her words were practically falling over themselves in a kind of hysterical motion of their own. "They were asking questions. I think they want you for capitalist activities."

"I don't want to lose you," she said, "but the safest thing right now is for you to disappear."

She told me to leave Taškent and go up into the mountains to some of the local collectives. There, she said, I could hide and work unnoticed, there the NKVD would not find me.

Any sense of security or ease I had was suddenly drained away. I felt as if a cord were being pulled tight around my throat. My hands grew cold, my whole body shivered. All I could see was the packet those men in green uniforms had given me for finishing the cabinet tops, that packet full of money. I had heard stories of men being arrested as capitalist conspirators for taking money in return for their work, but I had never before connected those stories to myself. I had been too trusting, too carefree. I thought that I had outsmarted them, getting a room, a salary, as well as a bit extra for food, because I could talk them into believing that I could finish furniture. They were the ones outsmarting me. They had needed easy help, so they had paid me. Now, they no longer needed me, so they could arrest me, send me to Siberia, and take back the money. As I shoved my things into a satchel, I vowed never again to let myself wander so recklessly into such a trap. Within fifteen minutes, I was gone.

There were collective farms throughout the region, and many of them had refugees working as laborers. Local trains wound their way up to these places in the mountains above Taškent, where wagons or even trucks waited to meet the refugee laborers, who sometimes had to go miles to reach the farms. With so many young men in the army, the Soviets needed more people to work on the farms, which were vital in supplying food to soldiers at the front. As I had seen at the train station, the local authorities would randomly round up refugees and transport them to the countryside to work, so if a refugee appeared at a collective, the authorities did not ask too many questions. I boarded the first available local train.

The train groaned along the tracks, and when we finally disembarked, the local residents waiting in the station stared at us as though we had come from another planet, their eyes were riveted, their mouths hung open. The refugees were dressed differently, and we were generally sallow or red-faced, not from health, but from the sun and wind and constant exposure outside the train station. In the marketplace, the people had become used to us, but here in the hills, disheveled bands of Europeans were still an inexplicable phenomenon.

The region was pretty. Uzbek houses, called *kishlaks*, had been built up and down the hillsides. Above them grew leafy fruit trees. Old men with long thin beards and round caps sat in the doorways of the houses or shuffled down the streets to the village tea house, where they drank tea and smoked pipes at long, low tables covered with rugs and surrounded by pillows. For the refugee laborers, however, life was quite different.

I ended up in an Uzbek collective that stretched across a valley ringed by hills. The work was typical farm work, caring for animals and working in the fields to bring in the harvest. But everything was done on an enormous scale. The collectives seemed to swallow the land, every corner of it seemed to belong to them and their activities. Barns held hundreds of animals. There were a hundred cans just to collect milk from cows.

Almost as soon as I started working, a representative from another collective came looking for additional laborers. Since I was new, it was easy for the collective to send me. But at this new collective, I was the only refugee. Everyone else was a Moslem. They wore little round caps on their heads, and they spoke their own language, which I could not understand.

The Moslem farmers reminded me a bit of Orthodox Jews. They rinsed their hands before they ate, they would not touch pork, and even their greeting in the morning somehow sounded like the Yiddish greeting of shalom aleichem. But in every other way, they were different.

They cooked their food, mostly lamb and rice, in a single big pot, which they placed in a hole in the ground, over a fire made from cow dung. First they heated the oil inside the pot, and then they added fistfuls of onions, which sizzled and darkened, sending up curly wisps of smoke. Next they added the meat, and I heard the soft hiss of rice pouring out of a sack into the pot, and the plop of raisins. The mixture bubbled and steamed for hours on end.

Once the fire had died down, the men ate right out of the warm cooking pot, plunging their arms in up to their elbows, and scooping their food out with their hands. After each mouthful, they licked their fingers, and then plunged their arms back into the pot, as the remains from the last mouthful continued to run down their skin.

These people used cow dung not just as fuel for their fires but also as mortar for their houses. Dogs ran in and out of the homes, they ran all over. After the first night, I could not take it. I could not take the filth and the constant smell of burning cow piles. I could not understand what the people were saying. I watched them cluster around their pots, laugh and speak their language, and I grew afraid.

The next afternoon, toward sunset, I ran away. I spent the night sleeping in a field, inside a big mound of straw, and then I made my way back to the first collective. From there I was sent on a train along with some other laborers to cities throughout the region, and from each city out to still more collectives to help with the harvest. The names reeled off the tongue like an ancient, rhythmic chant: Samarkand, Namangan, Astrakan. They were names called out in train stations and along train tracks. They were places that melted into each other as the frenzied pace of harvest labor accelerated. Then, almost without warning, we were sent back to the very first collective, in the now familiar valley, surrounded by the now familiar hills.

But soon I did not feel safe in this collective. One of the local Uzbek women kept inviting me in for tea, and it became clear that she wanted to have an affair with me. That could only lead to trouble. Since the afternoon when the NKVD had come looking for me, I could not shake that feeling that there was always a shadow behind me, that at any minute someone would tap me hard on the back and say, "Come with me." I decided that I could not stay in the collective. At that moment, it seemed my only alternative was to return to Taškent.

9

To Siberia

I went back to the train station where it all began, and I waited. I sat in a corner, my back hunched, my collar up. I stared at the floor. I wanted no one to see me, and I wanted to see no one. All around me were cries and coughs, shouting and the sounds of comings and goings. But I did not move until the announcement that a train was arriving, a train heading east to Alma-Ata.

Alma-Ata, I was told, literally means "fruit town," because throughout the region people grow large, sweet melons, like cantaloupes and honeydews. There were so many melons, more than could be eaten or shipped fresh, that, as in Taškent, often they would be cut up and left to dry in the sun, shriveling and crystallizing into long, sweet strips that were chewed like candy. But I wanted to go this city in the lush, hilly lands of central Asia because it was farther away from the Germans, because it was warm, and because, while not as big as Taškent, it was still a big place, which is far easier to get lost in than a small one. So, still looking over my shoulder, afraid of any shadow that drew too close to my path, I headed toward Alma-Ata.

For refugees, a train station was like a headquarters. It was a meeting point, a place for news, a place to live, a place where anything could happen. And it was at the train station in Alma-Ata where I found Shlomo Shumlek, the brother of one of my closest friends in Radzyń. He was there with his father and mother and younger brothers and sisters, who were huddled together in one corner of the station. My friend David was not among them. He had become separated from them farther back along the train lines. I did not ask them why they were in the station. I was simply overcome by stumbling upon people from Radzyń after so many months of loneliness, after journeying so far from home.

Despite my surprise, the coincidence was not as unlikely as it may seem.

There were a limited number of major train lines heading eastward into the Soviet Union, away from the German front. Refugees followed these lines and each other, as if traveling in the same direction would somehow give meaning to our confused wanderings.

Inside the station, I do not remember whether I saw Shlomo Shumlek first or he saw me. I hardly remember anything, except the embrace, some tears, and the news that the Shumleks had seen Moshe, my eldest brother.

I knew Moshe had registered to return to Poland. I knew that he and his wife and their daughter, Bella, had boarded a train. I had heard the rumors that the trains had been sent east, not west, that the people on board had been taken to Siberia. I had heard, but I had never known for sure. And even if Moshe had made the journey east, that itself was no guarantee that he was here. Many other refugees had not survived. Now, however, Shlomo Shumlek was standing before me, telling me that Moshe was working at a collective outside of Alma-Ata.

My knees began to shake. One moment it seemed as if my muscles were surging with energy, the very next moment, I felt on the verge of collapse. For close to two years, I had not known whether anyone in my family had survived. For close to two years, I had hoped yet not dared to hope. And then I had heard the words, "Moshe is alive."

Those words brought me such joy, and then, without warning, that joy was destroyed. I walked away from the Shumleks for an instant. It was an instant that became an eternity, for in those moments a deadly roundup began.

I did not see the guards until they were inside the station. Then, among the dusty, dirty, weary refugees, it seemed as if they were everywhere, an ever-expanding mass of green uniforms with bright red Soviet stars. They clutched their guns. Their thick-soled boots echoed like thunder on the floor. They took those of us who could stand and marched us onto the platform, herding us into boxcars, attached one by one to the train engine. And one by one we boarded, leaving behind the dry heat for the foul stench of each other and our waste.

At first, I did not want to believe what had happened, but as the thick air closed in, like a weight being lowered onto my chest, I knew. With each minute, my brother was receding, and miles of frigid steppes and dark forests were overtaking each one of us, fresh conscripts into the *trudovoye*, or working army. Not trusted or wanted as soldiers, we had been rounded up to labor for the Soviet war effort. We were an army of muscle, each one expendable.

As Soviet soldiers doggedly repelled German troops from the frigid land around Stalingrad, we were being sent to cut the trees that would fuel Soviet ammunition factories. And as the chill air outside began to penetrate our collective heat, the first of our "army" began to fall.

I lay back as the air cooled. My limbs were numb. I looked at my hands, which might at this moment have been holding my brother. His name and his face ran through my mind, but my mouth could make no sound.

From Alma-Ata, we headed north over a series of rivers and then east around mountains. The journey seemed endless. Time lost all meaning, and soon I forgot how many days I had been riding on the train. It did not seem real to be shut inside this car and unable to see outside except through the cracks. Sometimes, for an instant, I caught sight of women working along the railbeds, and for a moment I remembered the feeling of freedom and the smell of clean air. But then those glimpses would fade, and once again I would be overtaken by the slow monotony of the train.

Sometimes during the day, we would stop at small stations, where the waste pail would be emptied and the doors would be opened to allow in some new air. Some days, we simply stayed in our car, with only the strengthening and weakening of daylight through the cracks to tell us how many hours had passed.

Gradually, through cracks in the car slats, we glimpsed snow covering the land. Inside, the cold all but extinguished any feeling in our fingers and toes. The car had a small, wood-burning oven, with a pipe for the smoke that extended up through the roof, and that was all we had to keep warm. Without it, we might easily have frozen to death. We had a pot to make *kipjatok*, the ubiquitous boiled water, on the stove. And to make the water boil faster, some of the men, including me, began to push the lid tight, down onto the pot. The water would heat silently into a bubbling, raging force.

One afternoon, the pot was left on the stove. Usually, we heard a slight whistle as the steam pushed through any available space between the lid and the pot. This time we heard nothing, until the explosion, which sent the lid flying through the car and sprayed scalding water on anyone close by. A few men in the car were rather badly burned, their skin bubbling and crackling with heat in the midst of such immense cold.

But the cold in the car was nothing compared with the bracing, bitter chill when the doors were at last flung open in Irkutsk, a city in eastern Siberia, lodged amidst the sprawling Siberian lowlands and uplands that housed the gulags, first controlled by Russian czars and now by Soviet Communists. It was colder and bleaker than anywhere I had ever been.

We were taken on trucks to camps outside of the city. Each place housed between two hundred and three hundred people, and, like links on a chain, these little compounds stretched across the frigid land.

When we arrived, camp officials lined us up for questioning. "Who is a shoemaker? Who is a tailor?" the officials asked, and each time, up went a few scattered hands. Then they asked, "Who is sick?" Many people raised their hands. I kept mine down. The question seemed too easy. Illness never meant better treatment. The officials said nothing, and we were sent to our barracks.

We were mostly anonymous men (some women, usually wives, also lived and worked in the camp), a disjointed bundle of nationalities and ethnicities—Jews, Czechs, Poles, Hungarians—all thrust into this primitive camp and horrible cold. Many here had fled east as the Germans advanced to avoid being fingered as leftists by Nazi collaborators in their own villages. Others had simply fled from the violence. We were all people who had run away.

Our only place of refuge now was a long, dark barracks, with a hallway running down the middle and small rooms along either side. Ten people were crowded into each room. We slept in the same ratty, straw-covered space, sometimes on the floor, sometimes in a box with a piece of cloth laid over top, and we defecated and retched into the same holes. We began and ended our days staring at the same thick walls. We encouraged each other not to die, offering a word or an arm to the frail and sometimes a bit of soup or a bite of bread to those closest to us. But many mornings, I felt there was little difference between living and dying.

We were awakened by screaming, one of the camp officers yelling at us to get up. Yelling was common practice. An officer who was unwilling to yell could easily be replaced by one who was. Once up, we were given a cup of watery soup and a cube of bread, and then our labor began.

The work was punishing. It was mostly cutting and splitting wood. There were groups assigned to cutting and others assigned to splitting. There were groups who collected the wood and still others who loaded the wood on trains, which carried it to factories in the region and beyond. The trees supplied fuel for ammunition factories molding bullets to fight the Germans. Our trees fired their furnaces, and with the German army still inside the Soviet Union, the factories were desperate for wood.

From the first, I was assigned to a crew and sent out into the woods to cut down trees. It was winter, and the snows kept coming, piling layer upon layer until the light flakes had been compressed into sheets of ice. We did not have enough warm clothes, and, for shoes, we wrapped our feet in rags and then tied strings around the rags. We did not even dream of owning boots. A few lucky men had felt boots, into which they stuffed old newspapers to keep their feet warm. Most days, we tried to pour some water on the outer rags or even on the felt just before we walked outside. The water would immediately freeze into a tough layer of ice, providing a bit of extra insulation for our feet.

Outside, the cold was unbearable. We wore layers upon layers of old clothes provided by the camp, not caring if they fit, only that they offered a bit of protection from the wind and the soft, constantly falling snow. If you complained about the cold, the Soviet officer would tell you to keep working, that working would make you warm. But sometimes crews had to walk for over fifteen minutes through several feet of snow just to reach the work site, just to begin cutting trees.

One Soviet guard refused to allow us to cut the trees above the line of ice. Instead, he ordered us first to use an ax to chip away the band of ice that encased the tree trunks, and only when the ice had been removed and the dark, damp bark exposed could we cut down the frigid, quivering pines, slicing through them inch by inch with a sharp-toothed cross-saw. Fortunately for our brigade, however, this guard was given a new assignment, and we were given a new guard. But little else about the work changed. When we grew thirsty, we ate handfuls of fresh snow, letting it melt on our tongues and moisten our dry, burning lips, raw from the wind and cold. We also took handfuls of snow to rub on our hands when they lost all feeling from the cold. The snow shocked our hands back into feeling again. We wore gloves and sometimes wrapped cloth around our heads, but the cold was unrelenting. Many days, temperatures dipped to thirty or forty degrees below zero as the brigades marched out into the woods to chop.

We had quotas to meet for cutting the trees and quotas to meet for splitting the tree trunks. Soviet managers picked crews to work in the woods and crews to work at the wood-splitting machines. Those who did not meet their quotas for either cutting or splitting were given smaller rations of food.

Splitting was tough work. The wood splitters ran for twenty-four hours, and three different crews worked day and night, using about fifteen machines. The machines were set up in a work area in the camp. They stood on the hard, frozen ground, and whether the snow fell as soft flakes or as icy pellets, it vanished as soon as it came close to the splitters' heat.

To split the wood, two men would stand beside a machine with a constantly sliding metal blade. Together, they would pick up the tree trunk, lift it onto the machine, hold it as the blade sliced through once, and then turn each of the halves so they could be split again. Sometimes the trunk slipped out of the men's hands, and we would hear the thud as it fell. Sometimes the trunk would splinter, and we would hear the crack of the wood. Sometimes the only sound we heard would be a piercing human scream.

The days became indistinguishable from one another. They existed only through a frigid, monotonous haze. We could only ask ourselves a question without an answer: when would this all end?

We woke, we worked, we returned to collapse from our exhaustion around a stove, our only real source of warmth, and to feel the full force of our weakness and our hunger. People thought of little else other than where and how to get more food. In the summer and fall, some of the people in the camp had scoured the forest for wild mushrooms. Not everyone knew which mushrooms were poisonous and which were not. A number of those who harvested, boiled, and ate the mushrooms died from the poison. But even after those incidents, other people in the camp continued foraging because hunger itself was a kind of slow death, in many ways far more certain than the mushrooms.

Newer arrivals heard these stories from older survivors. Those who had arrived together had a certain bond, something linking us. Among my train-load were a husband and wife from Czechoslovakia. They were around forty, and we were an unlikely set of companions, but something drew us and held us together. The wife stayed with the other women, who cleaned and washed and in the warmer months took care of cows. The husband stayed near me.

They had brought some extra food with them, and while it lasted they shared it with me. When their supply was exhausted, I shared mine. Because I was able to fill my quota, I usually received a larger portion of food. I also helped the Czech fill his quota for chopping trees in the woods. He was a gentle man, even gentle in the way he took an ax to a tree. Every day, he prayed in secret, so the Soviets would not notice, and he hid himself in the mornings to wrap the leather *Tefillin* straps around his arms and another strip around his head. Wearing *Tefillin* is an old Jewish ritual that literally binds the book of prayer to your body. Each leather strap is attached to a container that holds lines from the Torah. When the straps are tied to the body, so too are the words of faith. The Czech maintained such faith even in this place. It brought back images of my father, and I wondered if he was still binding his arms and covering his head with a prayer shawl.

In the camp, we had almost no news, only the word from some newcomers that the Soviet army was still fighting at Stalingrad and that the men from Siberia had been sent to the front lines, where, twice a day, they were given vodka to fortify them against the Germans. Hearing so little, we speculated, wondering who would survive if Hitler took over Russia. What we did not know was how many people, how many Jews, how many of our own families had already died at the hands of Hitler and the Nazis.

I kept working, cutting and splitting, and the Soviets who ran the camp seemed pleased. Some of the officers were the second generation to live in this frigid wasteland. Their parents had come here to build communism and had stayed through Stalin's purges and the bloodshed of the 1930s, into this war. They rewarded my work. They let me help with dividing the food for the camp. Once, they even let me travel on the train to Moscow to collect some supplies, cans of fat, sugar, and salt and packages of tobacco and tea. This excursion also allowed me to acquire some extras for myself, which I shared with the Czech and his wife. These bits and pieces, culled from any source, were essential for survival. Without any extras, many quickly fell sick and often perished.

In addition to cutting and splitting, I was assigned to guard duty. Several refugees were selected to stand guard over a large number of boxes, housed in a little square building, which stood alone, away from the camp and the town. I assumed it was an ammunition stockpile because it was in such a relatively remote place, visited only by large trucks, which regularly came to collect the boxes and carry them away. The dangers of ammunition, especially its volatility, were already abundantly clear. We were always hearing stories of explosions at the ammunition factories. Once in a while people out on work crews even felt the jarring aftershocks of a blast.

By now, however, I had learned not to ask too many questions. I simply reported for guard duty and hoped that nothing happened during my shift. If you made a mistake, the guards would not think twice about taking your life.

To keep warm, I paced the floor, back and forth, across each board. I came to know their subtle warping, to know which ones squeaked, which rocked, which made no noise at all. One evening, I looked down at a crack in the floor. A single light illuminated the darkness beneath. I could not believe what I saw. I got down on my knees to look, and sure enough, there, beneath the floorboards, was a cigarette butt.

Cigarettes, even the remnants of cigarettes, were valuable, especially in a desolate place like this. They could be traded for food. As I stared at the crumpled bit of newspaper, which was used to wrap the tobacco, I could only think: perhaps there were more. Working at a feverish pace, I began to rip off the plank. Underneath were maybe a dozen or more butts, with one end gnawed down into a fine thin line and the other brown and singed. I picked up a butt and gently unrolled it with my fingers. Inside was a little wad of the dark *mahorka* leaves. Most of the *mahorka* had been smoked, but a few untouched spots remained.

I gathered up the butts and replaced the plank. Then, worrying every second that I would be discovered, I pried up a second plank, right next to the first. Again, the space was filled with discarded cigarette butts. It soon became clear that this place had not always been an ammunition storehouse. The more I saw of the floor, the more I thought that it had to have been some sort of a bar or club, a place where people smoked and where the remains of their cigarettes were swept under the floor.

For several days, during each of my shifts, I systematically ripped up the floor, plank by plank, scooped up the butts, and then replaced the boards. Then, I cut up the butts, scraped out the remnants of the *mahorka*, and rolled new cigarettes, which I traded for food with some of the local people who worked in the camp. The cigarettes bought me some additional sustenance and time, but not nearly enough.

When I had first arrived at the camp, I was relatively healthy and strong. Not only was I able to meet my quota, but also I managed to arrive on time for the work crew. Being late, even as little as five minutes, carried severe penalties. Three late arrivals resulted in a one-week incarceration in a jail about five miles from the compound. Jail did not release you from labor, however. Each day, the detainees were sent out to work, but after their shifts were over, they were confined to their cells, unable to go outside or walk around. Once I was given the job of taking an offender at gun point to the jail. Within a few weeks, someone else from the barracks was taking me.

I had tried to maintain the stamina and strength I had in the early days, but the cold and the conditions were draining both away. Even when we met our quotas, we received only meager rations of food. Our meals were mushy cubes of black bread and watery soups. Short of diving into the pot itself, we could barely hope to find a whole potato or scrap of meat. Soon, my pelvis and ribs jutted out. My stomach had shrunk until I could easily feel my intestines. It was as if my body were consuming itself day by day. The work, however, did not lessen.

I struggled simply to lift myself from the bed each morning. Once up, I moved slowly and, consequently, was late. After the third time of arriving late to line up for the crew, I was ordered to spend one week in the dark confines of the hated jail.

The jail was a dank, concrete building, used mainly for political prisoners, and it reminded me of the camp barracks, except that each person was placed in a tiny, individual cell. It was cold, cramped, and agonizingly lonely. At night, I would awake, my heart pounding from nightmares, and hear nothing—no restless sleeper, no rumbling snores, only a desperate silence closing in on me from every cramped corner of the room.

Each evening as I waited for sleep, I tried to recall the warm lands to the south. Soon, my thoughts would drift to returning home, to escape. I fantasized about fleeing the camp, slipping unnoticed through the woods and onto a truck or a train. In my thoughts, for a few brief moments, I was warm and free. But as soon as I lapsed into sleep, I would see women, men, and children, all dead, rise up in their crisp, white burial shrouds and follow me down endless winding roads.

I longed somehow to stop imagining. The dreams were unbearable. My fantasies about escape only made reality all the more miserable.

After that long week of loneliness and confinement, my punctuality improved, but not my health. The weakness set into my arms and legs first. My hands shook when I had to use the wood splitter. Then one day, as the metal blade methodically pushed its way through a trunk and the room buzzed with the sounds of machinery and the constant drumming of falling wood chips, I felt everything fade before me, and I passed out.

Somehow, a few men dragged me into a warm room in a nearby building and poured hot soup down my throat. I rested for an hour or so, and then I was sent back to the wood splitter. This was not unusual. Men were continually passing out. You simply hoped it happened to you in the camp and not in the forest.

In the forest, cutting down trees, there was no warm room, no cup of hot soup. Crews of a hundred men would leave in the morning, walk a mile or more to cut wood, and return by evening as a crew of seventy. Men in their forties or fifties were the first to fall. But the young ones collapsed too, and were it not for the fresh trainloads of refugee recruits for "the working army," the compounds would have quickly become ghost towns.

At the end of each crew, the officers sent a wagon through the forest to collect the dead. They piled the bodies on the back and carried them to an area away from the camp. I don't know whether they buried them or how they disposed of these corpses in the freezing cold. All I saw were the wheel ruts from the wagon in the new snow, light marks for coming and heavy for going, and I feared being carried away from the woods in that wagon.

Even among those of us who managed to stay alive day after day, only luck seemed to keep us from death. Some refugees had stores of money or gold and could buy morsels of food or a piece of clothing from the Soviets. But most of us had nothing. A few men resorted to removing rags from the dead to wrap around their feet. Even surviving could be grisly, and we all knew we would not likely survive for long.

I was often selected to work at the wood splitter, partly because I could still lift the heavy trunks, although several more times I passed out next to the machine. That, however, was less of a problem than the toothaches. What had begun as a dull throbbing in a single tooth soon progressed into a blinding pain. We had a doctor in the camp, but there was no dentist, and aside from numbing my gums with handfuls of snow, there was nothing to ease the pain. It woke me at night, and my body pulsed with the horrible combination of exhaustion and agony. Finally, I could not take it anymore. A Pole in the barracks offered a solution, and I took it.

At night, we unraveled a section of string, breaking it down into individual heavy threads. The Pole wrapped one end of the string around my tooth and tied the other to the door. He paused and then swung the door open, throwing his full strength into the wood. For an instant, I felt the string grow taut, followed by a sharp tug and a long pull as the tooth was ripped from the gum. Blood began to pour from my mouth. I bent my head over a bucket, spitting, but the blood kept coming. There were other teeth that needed to be pulled, that even now were throbbing in my gums. But nothing seemed able to stop the blood from this single tooth. Blood filled my mouth, until I was almost choking.

The blood continued to pour from my gum. Methodically, I tore up a cotton undershirt, already soiled and well worn but not encrusted with filth like some of the other rags. I bit down on the material, trying to stop the bleeding. As each piece of rag became soaked, I replaced it, but the bleeding would not stop. I grew more and more scared, wondering if I might bleed to death in my pile of straw. I spent the entire night biting on rags, my mouth throbbing, tasting my own blood in my throat. By dawn, the bleeding had slowed, but it was still several more hours before it finally ceased altogether. When the bleeding stopped, the awful toothaches returned. I tried to wait, but I could not stand the pain. More teeth would have to come out. Two nights later, the Pole wrapped another string around a second tooth and ripped it from my feeble gums. Once again, the bleeding did not cease until the following morning. I spent a third horrific night like this until finally the most painful teeth had been removed. It had taken almost a week.

I don't know whether it was a lingering weakness from the loss of my teeth or whether I was just weak in general, but after a few days back on the work crew, my body succumbed to a fever of such intensity that I was only semiconscious, and even the guards' screams and kicks could not induce me to move. I lay on my bed, shivering convulsively and uncontrollably. Sharp flashes of pain struck my muscles, growing more intense each hour, until I lapsed into violent, soaking sweats. Afterward, the pain would abate for a bit, only to return and build until once again my muscles were wracked with pain. I was weak and helpless. Why they did not leave me in a room to die I will never know.

But instead of a quick grave in Siberia, the camp doctor had me loaded onto an open train car, a flatbed used for transporting goods and animals, and sent me to a hospital in the neighboring city of Irkutsk. I don't remember whether there was anyone else from the camp on the train. I only remember how I lay in that car, with a blanket and coat covering me, my face exposed, my body on fire, as snow fell. The frozen white flakes spiraled down and vanished on my face. Even in my delirium, I still remember their feathery sensation, that endless, weightless dropping.

In Irkutsk, no one was there to meet me and take me off the train. Instead,

I continued on to the next station down the line, and I had to be moved to another flatcar on another train heading back to Irkutsk. From there, I was taken to the hospital, where nurses with large hands and stained white smocks moved in and out of the room and among the row of beds. My fever and delirium accelerated. I had full-blown typhus.

I do not know how long I lay in the bed, almost burning myself alive. I just remember the sharpness when the fever finally broke and my mind and body began to cool. I was lucky. Many of the others lying in the ward died. You could smell death everywhere, in the soaked linens and urine staining the floor. It was on the hands of the nurses. Unlike the frigid, odorless deaths of the men on the work crews, here the scent of dying clung to every corner. I looked around me. I knew I had recovered only to go back to the "working army," which now seemed to mean almost certain death amid the Siberian snows.

And if I died in the forest, in this frozen land, if they buried me here, no one would ever know where I was, no one in my family would ever find me. I would always be completely alone. I thought of this, and I began to cry.

As I boarded the train for the ride back, I eyed the station at Irkutsk. I noted where the Soviet guards were standing and what people looked like as they boarded the trains. The way I was returning was my only possible way out of this frozen wasteland alive.

10

An Almost Certain Death

It was still cold when I returned from the train station to the camp. Snow continued to fall, and the wind howled in violent shrieking gusts. It sprayed sharp pellets of icy snow into our faces and was like a crushing wave bearing down upon us with every step. In the woods, the trees bent and swayed above us as we chopped, and they fell unpredictably. We struggled to clear away the soft outer layers of snow that banked up against the tree trunks. Beneath us, the weight of each new snow hardened and solidified the old flakes into sheets of ice, but we barely noticed as we sawed through tree trunk after tree trunk. Sometimes, however, the ice from layers of snow had risen so high on the tree trunk that we had to cut very high on tree, leaving us with far less wood for all our effort.

There was little to say on these crews, which each day seemed to fan out farther into the woods. Sometimes we were even loaded on trucks and taken to other villages, where we were housed with families at night and by day sent to new stretches of forest to cut. And each day, usually some men did not return alive. Weakened by hunger, cold, and disease, old and young together were dying in the snows. We were told to wait for the thaw, that after the thaw things would improve, but for many, their bodies could not wait.

We did, however, have a glimmer of hope before the thaw, when news came that the Soviets had defeated the Germans at Stalingrad and were driving them westward, back to their borders. Suddenly, we could really dream of the war ending, of returning home. All we needed was more time so that we could go back to our homes, to the places we knew, to things as they were. But all around us, each day, we saw men who were never going back.

I became more and more consumed with escaping. I could not truly believe it would ever happen, but neither could I stop believing, because then it seemed that any chance to survive would be gone.

I told no one of my thoughts and plans, except for Kalman Schweitzer and his wife, a couple who had arrived on another train. The Schweitzers were a few years older than I and came from Chełm in Poland. Kalman and I were housed in the same barracks. In the biting cold of the camp, we talked about life, about our hopes to survive. Kalman was small, slight, and often sickly, but his eyes burned with an unusual intensity. He loved to think and look into the world around him.

For an hour or two, Kalman could take my mind away from the desolate camp, from the hopelessness. We talked of Poland, of Central Asia, of dreams and ideas. We imagined all the things we would do once we were free. We had passionate discussions, using energy we could not afford to expend on emotions and ideas, Kalman least of all.

Even the first signs of the thaw were not enough for him to hold onto. One morning, he left with his crew for the forest. As dusk fell, Kalman's wife watched, as she did each day, for the men to return. She saw them dragging themselves back, and she saw that Kalman was not among them. He had died without warning in the snow that afternoon.

Kalman's wife was devastated. She herself seemed to go from living to simply existing. There was nothing to be said or done. We recited the *kaddish,* the prayer for the dead, and we felt the ache of once again being more alone.

About ten days after Kalman died, his wife gave me a document, a document with Kalman's name, residence, everything that gave him his identity. Documents were precious, like gold in wartime. They gave you an identity, a freedom, an ability to move about. I had nothing to prove who I was, nothing official that might offer me a bit of protection outside of the camp, nothing until now.

I looked at Kalman Schweitzer's widow and thanked her. I should have said more, but I did not know what to say, I could not find any words. She wished me luck and told me to use it well. She said Kalman wanted me to have it. Then she left to return to her barracks, with nothing. I have always regretted that I did not find a way to do more, that I did not try to take her with me or find her after the war. Logic tells me that it would have been too dangerous, that we never could have survived together. But logic can never erase regret.

For several days, I planned my escape. I had saved some cigarette butts, and I traded them with a Soviet man for a pair of very worn shoes. I knew I could not run far in rags tied with string. I decided that I would leave after the work crew returned, before people ate and settled in. I would walk to the train station, which was less than a mile away, and I would find my way onto a train leaving that night, so when they realized my absence, I would already be gone. I tucked the document, with its official seal but without any identifying photo, inside my shirt and buttoned it closed.

All day, as I worked, I could barely concentrate. I was constantly going over the plan in my mind. I could feel my stomach tense and tighten as each hour drained away. By the end of the crew, I was existing on nervous exhilaration.

It was a little before dusk when I set out. I walked quietly through the snow, constantly glancing over my shoulder to see if anyone was behind me. It did not take long to reach the train station. In the fading light, I saw the building, wide and imposing, made of rough logs, round and uncut, piled on each other and cemented in between. Lanterns hung along the side, and two or three tracks ran next to the platform. There were mounds of snow from where the tracks had been cleared, and everything had a quality of isolation and bleakness.

I eyed the entrances, with their solid benches for passengers, but I knew I could not risk going near them, let alone using them. In the semidarkness, I stole around to the side of the building, near the tracks, to watch and wait. Very soon a train passed, ten or fifteen flatcars piled with logs, no doubt cut by some other work crew at some other camp.

Half an hour passed. My feet were growing numb with cold, but I dared not stamp to try to make them warm. I dared not move at all. Night had arrived, bathing everything in blackness, except for the faint glow from the lanterns. A passenger train was sitting on the tracks, facing the direction of Irkutsk and far-off Novosibirsk. I did not take my eyes off that train. Only the front cars had pulled inside the station. The rear ones were well away from the platform and actually protruding out from the building. The whole time I watched, no one wandered back to the rear cars. I knew I had to make my move.

Hunched over, I dashed to the far side of the train, the one facing away from the station and the platform. I pulled myself up onto a tiny lip above the train's wheels, and I began to try the rear doors. The metal was bitterly cold to the touch. I pulled the latch on the first door. It was heavy and unyielding. I pulled on it with all my weight. It was locked. Even in the chill air, as every breath turned to ice in front of me, I started to sweat. I could feel my heart throbbing in my chest. Trying not to make a sound, I eased my way along the metal lip down to a second door. I pulled, and the latch stayed frozen in my hand. It too was locked. Panic was rising inside me. There was one more door in the rear car. Resting all my weight on it, I pulled the latch. I heard a click. The latch gave, and the door swung open.

I barely looked around before hauling myself up from the lip and inside, so great was my fear that someone would see me sneak in. Now I had a few minutes. The Soviets would check the passengers' papers in the station and then right as the train began to move. But until that moment, inside the car, no one would bother me.

I had no document to allow me to travel, nothing except my paper identifying me as Kalman Schweitzer from Chelm, Poland. Until this moment, I had concentrated on getting on the train, giving little thought to what I would do once on board, whether I would try to pass myself off as a passenger or whether and where I would hide. Inside the car, I knew I could never be a passenger. I was pale and gaunt, my clothes were soiled and did not fit. I looked like a refugee, a refugee on the run. Shaking, I began to search around.

I knew I wanted to stay to the rear because it would be easier to exit once the train came to a stop. The middle, I felt, was too restrictive, too many people, too many chances to be caught. Behind me was a maintenance area with supplies and, secured at the top, was a little compartment, a tool chest, with a small sliding door. I pushed the door to one side and climbed into the chest, curling up my body and squeezing my limbs into the box. Then, I pulled the door closed, leaving just a tiny crack for air. My knees were pressed against my chest. My feet and hands began to sting from the sudden warmth. It felt as if my flesh was being struck with a thousand small needles, but I knew could not move, could not make a sound.

I stayed in that chest, unable to see, unable to stretch, unable to relieve myself, and only barely able to hear and breathe. There were muffled sounds of passengers boarding, then a whistle, and finally the chugging vibrations of the engine being fired and the wheels beginning to turn. I felt the jolt as we pulled out of the station and switched to another track, then the faster, rocking motion as we began to pick up speed. I prayed there would be no need for anyone to open that tool chest.

The minutes passed slowly. I did not move, and it was not long before I felt the shooting pains as my muscles stiffened. My back was so contorted that it began to have spasms. Then, twisted, drained of blood, my muscles began to lose all sensation. I longed to stretch, but dared not. The lack of fresh air was making me dizzy, and I could feel everything sinking away.

How long I stayed like that in the tool chest, I do not know. It seemed like hours, but it was probably only a single hour, maybe slightly more or slightly less, when the train creaked and groaned to a halt at its final destination, the sprawling concrete station of Irkutsk. I could feel the train slow down to enter the station, and only then did I slide the door open ever so slightly, listening until I was sure the room was empty and I could safely extract my cramped body from the chest. Once freed, I could barely straighten up and walk, my legs wobbled beneath me. I tried to regain a bit of steadiness, but as each moment passed, I grew more frightened. Now that I was here, I did not know what to do.

Looking out a tiny window I could already see local Soviet police, the

NKVD, and military personnel patrolling the platform, checking identification papers and travel cards. In the vast expanse of concrete, they were everywhere. I knew the moment I stepped onto that platform any one of them could walk up and start to interrogate me, asking me who I was, where I was going, what I was doing, and I would have nothing to show them, except a certificate stating that I was Kalman Schweitzer. But I also knew that I could not stay on the train.

Once again, I opened that third door, and as the latch released I glanced around, to check for anyone close by. I saw no one close and decided if anyone was looking and saw me, I would simply have to take the chance that I could lose myself in the station before they would be able to find me. With one final look, I jumped down onto the track bed, as the door shut hard behind me. I walked quickly along the rocky bed and around the train to the far end of the platform. Raising myself up with little metal handles used by maintenance workers, I headed toward a pile of crates to hide myself and gain a little extra time. The station seemed far more enormous than I had remembered it being after my release from the hospital. Then, however, someone had accompanied me to the train, then I was enjoying the first blush of good health, and then my mind was darkened only by thoughts of returning to the camp. Now, everything had changed. To my ears, the tiniest squeak from a train car echoed into a thunderous noise filling all that vast space. The heavy tread of a few feet sounded like the marching of an entire army.

Irkutsk was a military junction and a key transport point for prisoners and now refugees being sent to camps in Siberia. It was not a place for passengers. As I peered around the crates, I became aware of the full enormity of what I had done. Leaving Irkutsk would be all but impossible. Train personnel were everywhere. Even if I could find a train heading west, I could not open one of the doors and enter unnoticed to hide in another tool chest. There were people all along the platform, at both ends of the train. Even just inside the station, cowering, hidden among the crates in my ratty, shabby clothes with my very worn shoes, I obviously did not belong.

I knew I could not stay among the crates for long. I had to keep moving to make it harder for someone to notice me and come over to check. I tried to stay close to the walls and away from any crowds in uniform. I barely noticed anything, except how modern and how vast everything was around me. This was not an ornate, detailed station found in Europe or a rough, small country stop. It was sleek and massive, like a mechanized concrete monument, a gateway to a land from which few returned.

I found a side door and slipped outside. The drive in front of the station was paved with smooth stone. I knew that I could not linger too long in the front, that somehow I would have to move back into the building. If I walked in alone, without a purpose, I would almost certainly be stopped. My mind began to work. Perhaps I could carry something. Or move with a crowd. Then standing at the entrance I saw a man. He was tall, with dark eyes and hair but a fair complexion, not the swarthy coloring of the south. He looked regal in his long army coat that swept down to his ankles, just brushing his boots. On his head, he wore an officer's hat. The red stars gleamed, every piece of metal shone. I could tell from the bars and epaulets on his shoulders that he was a general. He looked majestic, even with one apparently useless arm, tied against his chest in a rough, white sling.

I do not know what possessed me to approach him or to ask, in my still awkward Russian, if he wanted help loading his suitcases on the train. I knew from watching him that he did need help, and without papers or a ticket, this was about the only way I could ever hope to board the train. I had reached the point where I felt there was nothing left for me to do. I had to gamble, otherwise I would certainly lose.

As I spoke, the general looked down at me. I froze. He said nothing. Any second now someone would come up to him, and also to me. I felt I had made a horrible mistake. I was convinced that I had. Then, slowly, he nodded his head up and down and said, "Da," the Russian word for "yes."

I gathered up his bags and followed him onto the platform, to the track for his train, a train heading west. I set the bags down, and he turned and in a low voice asked me who I was. My mind raced through the possibilities. He had already agreed to let me help him. He had offered to trust me. I had no choice. I had to trust him. In a whisper, in Russian, I told him that I was a Jewish refugee from Poland, that I had almost died in a camp near Irkutsk, that I wanted to find my family. He asked me how I had left the camp, and I told him, on a train, in a tool chest. He stood there in silence, his left arm motionless in its sling. "Stay right here," he told me. I did, and he did not move from my side.

We said nothing, even once the train came, releasing clouds of white steam and little traces of soot, chugging to a slow, screeching stop. He motioned to the bags with his good arm, and I gathered them up and followed him on board, into a private compartment, with a door that closed. I stowed the suitcases underneath the seats. The compartment had a row of seats below and a bed above, as well as a little built-in table for eating. Just as I finished with the last bag, he told me to lie down in the bunk and not to move, not to say anything. He spoke to me in a whisper, in Yiddish.

I scrambled into the bunk. My heart was swelling inside of me. The words were like music, like the first sounds of home.

As soon as I was on the bunk, the general lifted his long coat with his good arm and spread it over me. The coat was warm from the heat of his body. "Do not move," he repeated. I did not make a sound. I lay motionless under the weight of the wool, completely hidden, and waited.

Minutes passed. Then I could hear the muffled sounds of compartment doors opening down the corridor, the sounds of papers being handed over and scrutinized. I heard voices rise. As I strained to understand what was being said, I heard the sharp click of the NKVD opening the door to the compartment. Blood was surging through my veins, my fingertips and head pulsed and throbbed. The heavy coat felt like a vice, compressing my lungs. I struggled for breath. The agents were curt, they wanted papers, identity cards, passports, travel documents. The general produced his. One agent immediately asked about me. Suddenly, I felt a hand grasping my foot and shaking my leg, yelling at me to get up.

Then, as quickly as it had started, the shaking stopped, the hand left my foot. In a firm voice, I heard the general tell the agents not to touch me. "*Kontuzeja,*" I heard him say. A head wound. He told them that I had a head wound and was traveling under his orders to receive special medical care and that we were not to be disturbed. His papers were in order. He was a general. The NKVD agents assented and left.

For several minutes, I lay motionless, expecting that at any minute the agents would return and drag me from the bunk. But instead all I felt was the jolt as the train brake was released and the momentary pitch as we began to roll forward and build speed. As a whistle sounded, the general reached up and pulled off the coat. I felt a bit wobbly as I sat up, but as I looked at the general and he at me, we each started to laugh.

I thanked him. I was not sure if it was too little or too much, I knew I could do nothing in return. The general took out some food, which we shared while we talked. I learned what I already knew, that he was Jewish, but beyond that, he revealed little else. He wanted to know about me, where I was from, what I had done, my stories of running away. He asked questions, and I talked, grateful at last to have a sympathetic ear, someone who was concerned. We spent hours in the private luxury of the compartment. It felt like freedom.

He asked me where I wanted to go, and I said Alma-Ata, to wait for the day when I could at last return home. He stared out the window at the landscape, watching the snow and trees rise and fall from the motion of the train, and asked me if I wanted to travel to his home and live with him. It was a kind, generous offer, but I did not take it. I felt freer on my own, and I still nurtured the hope of finding Moshe and the rest of my family, wherever they were. He repeated the offer once more and then, with a shrug, let it drop.

We rode on the train for a while longer, until his stop approached. I wanted to stay on the train as it curved around and crossed the grassy Central Asian plains. I helped him gather up his luggage. The general told me to wander into a crowded passenger car and try to blend in among the people. He handed me a part of his ticket to use for proof if I were asked. Then, with his good arm, he gripped my hand and wished me luck. I took one backward glance as

I headed out of the car, and I saw him at the edge of the compartment, standing so straight that his long coat formed a clean line from his shoulders to the floor. He was holding his hat, waiting to don it, giving me full view of his neat hair and the lines that cut across his face.

That was my last look at the man who saved me. I never even knew his name.

11

We Embraced,
Then Cried

No one stopped me in the passenger car. No one asked to see my papers. Still, in my mind, I rehearsed my answers and practiced my name, Schweitzer, Kalman Schweitzer.

The car was filled with thick blue *mahorka* smoke, curling up from the disintegrating edges of newspaper cigarettes. Gradually, however, as the miles passed and the acres of upland pine were replaced by more fragile, flowering trees, we were able to open the windows more than a thin crack, bringing a bit of relief from the choking, stale odor. The hours lengthened into days, and the days themselves seemed to grow long. But as the time passed, I could see from the window that every tree was covered in new, light green leaves, and in brief gusts I savored the sweet, warm scent of the outside air. It felt like months since I had fled from the icy Siberian uplands. But in truth it had only been a little more than one week.

Time on the train moved in fits and starts. I wanted the journey to be over, and yet I did not know how it would end. There was the lingering fear that all my hopes would vanish in Alma-Ata. There was the fear that Soviet authorities would swoop down upon me, like a wide-winged bird upon its prey, as soon as I entered the station. As the train rolled over the landscape, past the distant outlines of sheep herds and carts making their way along dirt roads, my mind was numb, my thoughts haphazard. I was exhausted. I could not even plan for a second escape.

It was night when we pulled into the station. After a long day of cramped sitting, my legs felt weak as I stepped onto the hard, concrete platform. Even at the late hour, the station was busy, crowded with refugees and Soviet personnel. There were mounds of goods for transport. It was the wrong season for melons, so their sugary, ripe scent did not fill the air, but in their place I heard the now familiar, throaty tones of the Turkic language, which fanned out to the east and west. I paused for a minute on the platform to get my bearings, knowing I could not stay long. This time, I was not even carrying a bundle, and my tattered layers of clothes would easily betray that I had come from somewhere else.

It was mostly dark. Only a few lights hung overhead, spraying their beams out in a wide circle, which grew weaker and weaker at the edges, until it finally plunged into shadows and darkness. I followed some of the passengers from the train into a waiting area, which smelled of unwashed human flesh. There, crammed on benches and sprawled on the floor were bodies, some awake, some asleep. Discreetly, I headed toward one edge. I could hear the sounds of coughing, the stir of restless children, and the wails of hungry babies, but I had heard them before, and bending my arm underneath my head, I lulled myself into sleep.

I woke a little before dawn, just as the station began to swell with activity, with loading and unloading and people preparing to move. I was incredibly hungry. I had no money, but I was desperate to find some food. Already outside of the station, farmers were arriving in the city and heading toward some market square, with their carts of vegetables to sell, late season roots and greens, things stored from last fall's harvest. And along the streets were stalls with thin, steaming breads. I asked at one stall if I could do some labor in return for bread. The women answered in broken Russian, telling me to go somewhere else. I tried several stalls until finally I refused to move on and the woman relented. I hauled some flour sacks, and she handed me a long flat bread. I tore at the fresh dough with my teeth as I walked back to the station, to begin my search for Moshe and my family.

The Shumleks had given me the name of a collective, and I planned to see if a train stopped near the place and then to volunteer to work on the farm. Perhaps I should have asked in the market or even tried to ride out to it on an empty farmer's cart, but I assumed that, like those in Taškent, this collective farm was far enough away that it was reached most easily by train. Also, I had met the Shumleks at the train station, and so I assumed that Moshe had also been at the station and had been taken away. I was going over the questions in my mind when I returned to the station, about midmorning. I walked inside and saw hundreds of weary people, their clothes stained and torn, their eyes and cheeks scooped out like hollows between bones. They were standing, milling about. Immediately, my muscles tensed. I could see Soviet men in uniform. A shrill train whistle sounded, and I jumped. I turned my head and saw that one of the Soviet men was staring straight at me. He walked over and asked me for my documents. Trying to steady my hand, I pulled out the paper saying that I was Kalman Schweitzer. He pulled it from my hand. Suddenly, my whole body grew cold. What if he never handed the document back?

What if he confiscated it? My whole identity would vanish, my thread of protection would be gone.

He looked at the document, at the unfamiliar Polish. He turned it over. He asked me if I had anything else. I shook my head. He told me that I was a refugee and that I was going to be sent to Siberia to work for the cause of the great war, and then he motioned for me to move over to the group of refugees. I froze. It seemed impossible, after everything, now to be returned to Siberia. The Soviet man's eyes narrowed, he thrust out his arm and pointed. Slowly, I shuffled over to the wide-eyed band, lining up for selection. Moving toward the back of the group, I began to search for an escape. I could not bolt and run. I had to make it appear as if I were complying. As long as I simply avoided this roundup, I believed I would be free to slip away, to find Moshe.

Could I simply hide behind a crate and emerge with the next trainload of refugees? I saw no isolated crates. Craning my head around, searching each corner, I caught sight of the bathroom. I waited as the officials began to move the group, readying them to board a waiting train, poised like a horse behind the starting gate. Clouds of steam filtered out across the platform. I walked out with the others, and then moving casually, my hands in my pockets, I drifted over toward the bathroom and walked straight inside. It was a row of stalls without doors and wooden seats. The entire room was filled with a foul odor. I loosened my pants and balanced on my toes, leaning slightly toward the wall, listening.

I was waiting for the rapid pumping of the engine, for the shrill whistle signaling departure. I could feel the warmth of my thighs pressing against my elbows as I stayed crouched down. I heard the first whistle but did not move. Only when I heard the massive hiss of steam escaping and the clacking of the wheels turning did I raise myself up and move toward the door. As the train began to move, I ran out onto the platform, clutching the waist of my unbuttoned pants, waving my one free arm, moving awkwardly and too slowly to catch even the last of the cars, now gathering speed along the tracks.

Panting, still holding the waistband of my pants, I turned back to see two Soviet guards moving quickly in my direction. They grabbed me by the arms, and my pants dropped to my knees, making it impossible for me to walk. Angry, the guards stopped and ordered me to refasten my pants. They were yelling, cursing me for not getting on the train. One guard's face reddened, and he sputtered as he spoke. I held my ground, repeating that I had tried to make the train but that I was forced to answer a call of nature. One continued to hold me while the other scoured each line of my document. Then they shook me and said, "We will be looking for you specifically when it is time for the next transport."

They could look, I thought, but by then I would be gone. That afternoon,

I returned to the market area and asked the way to the collective. An old man with a rickety, empty cart offered to take me in that direction.

It was not far from the city, I remember. I watched as the urban limits quickly dissolved into fields, freshly plowed, the dark underlayers of the earth turned over. I wanted to find my brother, to see his face, but I dared not hope too much.

When I arrived at the collective, I avoided any of the main buildings. I did not want to have to go to an official office and present my papers, because my only papers identified me as Kalman Schweitzer, not as Yankel Pomeranice, Moshe's younger brother. Instead, I stayed at the edge of the collective's vast fields, even sitting down so that no one would notice me off in the distance and come over to inquire. The sun was already high overhead, giving off a powerful heat and a blinding light. I felt it burn into me, making my skin grow hot to the touch. I waited in the fields until late in the day, when laborers would be leaving from their work. As the sun dropped lower in the sky, I saw a young boy approach, and I asked him to point the way to the *berzentse*, to the refugees. He turned and extended his arm, and I followed his finger back toward the horizon.

It was then that I spotted them coming in from way out in the fields. I did not know whether to walk toward them or stand still. I decided to walk. About twenty-five men, their skin dried and cracked from the wind, looked at me as I drew near them. In their faces was more exhaustion than emotion. Their eyes all had the dull, receding look of men who endure hunger, except for one who had carefully concealed a flash of recognition. In the camel-trodden pathways of Central Asia, I had found my brother, whom I had not seen since a few weeks after the shiny German planes unleashed their bombs and bullets on Radzyń.

My feelings can hardly be described. For nearly two years, I had been alone, running. At nights, I would dream of my family. Sometimes they would be so close I felt that I was touching them, but when I awoke, no one was there, their faces and voices had faded from my mind. Already, it was growing harder to recall exactly how my mother sounded when she spoke, the rhythms of her voice. No matter how tightly I tried to hold onto the sounds I remembered, they slipped from me, each day growing a bit fainter, a bit more unclear. I frightened myself by wondering what if a day came when I could no longer remember.

Pursued by those thoughts, I constantly teetered between moments of hope and hours of despair. In the hopelessness of Siberia, I almost lost myself to them. Now, to find Moshe was like a new beginning, a chance to fill in the hole that had been chipped away in my heart. It was like a promise against forgetting. A warmth of emotion that I had never before known flooded me. And safe among the other refugees, we embraced, and then we cried.

Moshe was already a man in his thirties, a man who had had a family and a business in Poland, a young man who over the last four years had begun to grow gaunt and old. He had lost everything. Sent east into Siberia by the Soviets when he believed he was returning to his home in Poland, Moshe had labored in fields and barns. And he had gone alone. He had been separated from his small family, sent off while his wife and daughter watched from a train station. He had tried to keep sight of their eyes as he had been dragged away. Now he did not know where they were or if they were still alive. Many nights he lay awake, staring off into the darkness, imagining the details of their faces.

As Moshe told me these things, his voice grew thicker and throatier. I listened, and then I told him about my life in Brest and later on the run, about Siberia, about my escape, about how I had at last arrived here. We talked all through dinner and into the night. Even when it was already quite late, we stayed awake, adding fragments to our incredible tales. It was as if we were racing against time to release all that had been buried, to tell everything before we were torn away.

After months of being alone, I was suddenly surrounded by familiar faces at the collective. In addition to Moshe, the Shumleks, my neighbors across the street in Radzyń, the ones who had first told me about Moshe so many months ago in the Alma-Ata train station, were now sleeping in the nearby bunks.

I was grateful to see the Shumleks, but here in this place they were also a reminder of all that now seemed lost. I looked at them, and I recalled the Saturdays when I had walked down the main street of Radzyń with David, each of us dressed in our best clothes, his always better because his father was a tailor. I looked at his father's weathered face, and I thought of my own father, of my own family. But if the Shumleks were reminded of anything by me, they did not show it. Instead, we talked cheerfully about the old days, about how things had been. We made light of any differences, or perhaps it was that the differences seemed so much smaller so many miles from home.

I was a young survivor, but the Shumleks were old survivors, determined to beat death and return home.

The next morning, Moshe and Mr. Shumlek accompanied me to the office of the collective farm's manager. The manager was a squat, dark Tartar man.

Moshe introduced me as his brother and explained that I had lost my papers. The manager said nothing. He looked at me and then at Moshe, squinting, trying to make out the resemblance. It was irregular, he said. "How does someone find a brother so far away?"

"My brother is a good worker. He will help your farm," Moshe replied. I turned and looked at my brother. It had never occurred to me that he had learned to speak Russian.

Moshe's words just hung there, unanswered. So I spoke. I told the manager that I had spent a year working on the Iminia Krupskaya collective and was released because the German army was approaching. I recounted the types of field and farm labor I was able to do. The entire time I spoke, the manager said nothing. I paused, and he shrugged his shoulders. That was all. He had accepted me with a fierce glance followed by a shrug, and it was settled. He needed more laborers, but he would never take the risk of actually saying "Da," or yes, to anything. He motioned us away.

Life on this collective was far from easy. It was a massive, sprawling place, thousands of acres of pastures and fields. We did have somewhere to sleep and even showers for washing once or twice a week, real showers, complete with a steady stream of water and a room for changing. I was also given shoes and a few clothes. But the collective was months away from the harvest, and the food stocks were low. What remained was routinely shipped off to soldiers at the front, and we, as refugees, received the very least of the rations.

So in the midst of what should have been abundance, we lived on watery soup, sometimes a borscht, sometimes a cabbage soup with a few bones and small cubes of bread. When the new potatoes were ready, we ate them, washed down with a watery yogurt. Whatever there was, there was never enough. We were fed in our own canteen, with long tables and hard benches, almost like a military mess hall, and the portions were slopped into bowls by women recruited to work in the kitchen. We always left the table hungry, some days even hungrier than when we came.

The work was demanding. We were constantly moving dirt, plowing, and planting. We harnessed bulls to plow in the fields. My arms throbbed as I tried to guide the reins and the plodding animals across the long acres. I did not know how to plow and could not make the animal or the blade obey me and move evenly across the earth. Sometimes, I would have to go across the same section again and again, trying to churn up the soil. Other days, we squatted in the freshly plowed fields, planting until our backs throbbed and we dreaded the very act of straightening. Dirt seeped into the cracks in our fingers and under our nails, and our hands never seemed to come clean. When we were not shoveling or turning dirt, we were taking the cows and sheep out into the fields to graze, milking the cows, feeding chickens, and gathering chicken eggs. To take the cows out to pasture, we had to get up before the first hint of the sunrise, about four in the morning, and, fighting sleep, lead and prod the animals out into the grassy fields to eat.

The only relief was the weather. Spring was in its full warmth and glory. Trees and flowers blossomed, thin green shoots began to thicken and rise from the ground. We walked around in light clothing, and at night my body was no longer wracked with chills and shivers. The air did not stab at my lungs but flowed in, gentle and warm. But even the warmth did nothing for our hunger, which followed us through the day and invaded our dreams at night.

The constant hunger made our stomachs churn and our heads ache. We felt our muscles grow weak by midday. And we had no stored strength to draw upon. As I struggled with my hunger, I did not know that the Shumleks had a plan. I did not know until the middle of one night when I felt an arm shake me and a hand cover my mouth so I would not make a sound. Since the refugees lived in a separate barracks near the animal barns, removed from the residents of the farm, we had unexpected freedom in the dark of night, as long as we were quiet and careful. I opened my eyes and saw Shlomo Shumlek standing over me, dressed. He motioned, and, rubbing my eyes, I rolled out of bed and began to put on my clothes. As I looked around, I discovered that more men were up. Silently, the band of men left the barracks. Moshe, Shlomo, and I were among them.

We stole through the darkness to the chicken coop, only a building away. The now familiar thick, heavy odor of chickens grew stronger with each step. Suddenly, the plan became clear to me. One man undid the bolt on the coop door. Slowly, it swung open. Two men stepped inside. The chickens were asleep, bundles of feathers in the foul-smelling air. They were packed in tight and thick on the muck-covered ground. Having managed to enter without disturbing the flock, the men then moved aside slightly so that two more could enter. They paused and stood perfectly still.

Then, with two quick motions, each man grabbed a chicken. There was a brief squawk, a beating of wings, but with lightening efficiency the men snapped the birds' necks. Even those sounds, however, had disturbed the remaining live birds, which began to rustle and wake, squawking. Two more chickens were grabbed and their necks snapped before our group, clutching the carcasses, closed the door, replaced the bolt, and began a dead run away from the coop.

We headed out into the fields that surrounded our barracks. It was only then that I realized why this night had been chosen. The ground was dry, too dry to reveal our footprints, and the grass, wet with dew, would spring back, giving away nothing. Once we were near a newly plowed and planted field, we began to walk carefully, single file, around the edge. By that time, the rest of the refugees had joined us in the darkness. Then, silently, at the far end, we squatted down and began to pluck the feathers from the lifeless chickens. We formed a pile of feathers to be scooped up later and buried in a distant field. Two men in the group made a quick fire, while the rest of us stood around the burning embers, trying to shield the light and the sparks, to hide the flames. We roasted the chickens, watching the skin char as the birds turned on a makeshift spit. Once the first three were cooked, we ate them, like animals, attacking the flesh, ignoring the heat and clouds of steam that rose as we tore off the skin and stripped the meat from the bones. I had to chew slowly. My remaining teeth were weak, and I had gaping holes in my gums. But nothing could prevent me from consuming the wonderful, tough, charred chicken.

Squatting in that field, we ate every last ounce of the chicken. The left-over bones and feathers were carefully gathered in a single piece of newspaper and carried several fields away to be buried deep down in the freshly plowed soil. The rest of us plowed under the ashy remnants of the fire and swept the ground clean. Not a single shred of evidence remained.

It was still dark. Only a few stars hung in the sky, and they were often covered by clouds moving silently through the night. None of us said a word as we moved cautiously back toward the barracks. We stayed at the outer edges of the field, and our eyes kept scanning the darkness for the slightest movement while our ears listened anxiously for any sound. The crack of a twig or the rustle of grass made my heart race, but the Shumleks did not bother to stop for such sounds, except once, and then we quickly began to walk again. We all knew that once inside the barracks, we could say nothing, and nothing the whole next day. Noiselessly, we stepped inside the barracks and returned to our beds. Our stomachs full, we collapsed into a deep, easy sleep.

The next morning, as we were getting dressed, the door burst open and officials from the collective descended upon us. They scoured the barracks. They checked our beds, pulling off blankets, rooting through straw. They sniffed our clothes. They looked everywhere, but they could find nothing. "Six chickens are missing," they told us.

We played dumb. No one spoke, no one flinched, there was not even a glimmer of recognition. The officials were angry they couldn't find anything, but they just shunted us off to the fields. All day, we pitched dirt and did not let a word escape. On the collective, the officials had about as much regard for us as they did gypsies. We were foreign drifters, not trusted, not wanted except for our ability to work in the fields. No one understood this better than the Shumleks and my brother. They knew the dangers facing us, and they knew the risks that had to be taken if we were to survive.

We waited over a week, and then we returned in the dark to the chicken coop and stole three more chickens. But stealing chickens was too dangerous. We heard from the Kazaks who lived on the collective and worked alongside us in the fields that the officials had ordered residents to take shifts standing guard over the coop at night. The local people on the collective were all very friendly to us, perhaps even secretly rooting for us in our struggle to outsmart the officials, whom they hated as much as we did.

It was clear, however, that we needed to devise some other way of obtaining food. And it was also clear that whatever we did, the officials would be watching. During the days when I worked in the fields, my pulse quickened every time I saw a new figure approach in the distance. Our nighttime forages were keeping us alive, but they also filled us with fear.

One afternoon, in the pasture, the Shumleks proposed another scheme. We would slaughter a cow at night and bury the meat in the ground, so that we would have a steady supply of food and not be forced to steal just enough for only one brief meal. At first it sounded impossible, but the more we discussed it, the more logical it became. The ground was soft, it would be easy to bury the animal, and it would provide us with food for quite some time. We began to plan.

We managed to steal a bag of salt from the collective's warehouse and some wooden slats to line the hole for the carcass. Someone also stole a sheet of plastic. During the day, the Shumleks searched for a site where we could bury the cow. At last we were ready. The nights were growing warm, and the cows often stayed out in the pens. We waited for a cloudy night, and then slowly and quietly we led a cow out into the fields. We must have walked over a mile out into those fields with the cow. We wanted to be far enough away from the other people on the farm.

Someone in Mr. Shumlek's family had been a butcher, and he knew how to slaughter a cow. He slit the animal's throat while the rest of us held it and muffled its mouth. When the animal was dead and the blood was carefully drained away, some of us cut up the cow, while others prepared the hole, about six feet long and two feet deep and lined with the wood. We skinned the flesh and rubbed salt into the meat to preserve it, then we rolled the skin over the meat to protect it from the dirt. Next, we laid the pieces one by one into the lined hole. We worked quickly, worrying about the mess and about our blood-stained hands. Once the pieces of meat were stacked against the wood, we stretched the remaining skin over top, then a layer of wood, then plastic, and finally dirt to cover everything. We had to scoop up the bloody earth and bury it in another part of the field. Lastly, we had to scrub our hands and clothes. It had taken us several hours, and it was nearly time to rise when we returned to the barracks, exhausted.

By the next morning, someone realized that the cow was missing. People were sent to check the fields. No cow. More officials came to inspect our barracks, but they found nothing. Still more people were sent to interrogate us. For days, we did not even dare to walk in the direction of the hole. We said nothing and did nothing. The search for the missing cow continued, but still nothing was found. Nearly a week had passed when I felt Moshe touch my arm. I did not need more than a touch because I was already awake, waiting. Tonight, I knew, we were going out into the fields. We were going to build a small fire and eat meat.

Silently, we trudged across the dirt to the covered hole. We checked carefully all around the area. Nothing. No one appeared to have been there. The ground was undisturbed. We bent down and scraped off the dirt until we reached the plastic. We removed that and then the wood and the skin, pulling out some of the meat. The salt and the cool earth had kept it well preserved. We built a low fire some ways away and cooked the darkening meat. That night, we did not eat the food, we sucked it in. We tore at the tough flesh with our teeth, savoring every bite, quickly filling our shrunken stomachs. Even in the darkness, even though we were exhausted, we were jubilant. The plan had worked. We could almost feel our strength returning, our hunger at last being assuaged.

We waited two days and then stole back in the dark of night to eat again. Sometimes as we sat around eating, or after we had finished, we would wonder out loud about what was happening to everyone we had left behind.

I looked forward to these forays in the night and thought about them as I worked picking the first fruits of the season from the collective's heavily laden trees. Before, I would have crammed piece after piece of fruit, green or only partly ripe, into my mouth just to fill my stomach. But, now in the mornings as I reached up under the branches to twist and snap the stems, my stomach felt full, and I could still taste the chewy, salty beef, tough and stringy, and more welcome than anything I had ever known.

Our success with the beef prompted us to become more daring. We decided that we needed some sugar, for what reason I am not quite sure. We knew that the collective kept its sugar supply in a warehouse located at the foot of a high hill. On top of the hill was a cemetery, and that location became the site for our latest plan.

The warehouse was filled with bags of sugar, and we thought that a few bags would certainly not be missed. So once again, under the cover of night, we silently left the barracks. We unlatched the warehouse door and removed a few bags of sugar. We carried the bags on our backs up the hill, and then we wrapped them in a heavy covering to protect the sugar from the dampness. When the bags were ready, we walked into the cemetery. In the darkness, I could feel the dead everywhere, almost as if they were next to my shoulder. Even though I was not alone, the place still had an eerie stillness. We walked among the stones, until one of the men stopped and extended his arm, the signal to begin digging. We turned the earth slowly, knowing that bodies lay buried close by. When we had finished the hole, we filled it with sugar, carefully making a soft mound above.

The missing sugar was quickly discovered, and the officials on the collective wasted no time in coming to search the refugees. They came and turned over everything. Then they waited two days and returned. It seemed as if they were constantly searching for the sugar, but once again they found nothing. We waited a week and then returned to dig up the sugar. We walked through the rows of graves looking for the mound. The moon hung above us, but we could not see very far in the darkness. We paused to dig at a few spots. The dirt came away easily, but underneath we found nothing. Every night for a week we returned. We retraced our steps from the warehouse, up the hill, and into the cemetery. We covered each row of graves. We retraced our steps again, and still we could not find the sugar. If no one has been buried in that spot, the sugar is probably still there. And if a body has been buried close by, there is enough sugar for its entire afterlife.

12

A Second Siberia

The sugar incident seemed to have soured the collective. Summer, with its high scorching suns, was close at hand. Planting had ceased, and the fruit trees were ready for harvest. Peaches were turning the color of flame amidst the green leafy tree branches, and melons were growing soft and sugary on the vines. It was then that the head of the collective released us and returned us to Alma-Ata.

On the road into the city, we passed donkeys laden down with woven baskets full of produce for sale in the peasant market. We passed brightly dressed women who wore round high hats and black veils and had bands of decorative coins swaying across their breasts. We saw old, weather-beaten men and young boys. And then, after we entered the city limits, we began to see the refugees. They were most often in clumps and clusters, aimless, hapless, drifting along the streets. Their skin had yellowed and cracked, and it flapped like excess cloth over their bones. There was nothing full or fleshy or whole about these men and women and children in dirt-encrusted clothes. Some were barefoot, some wore sandals made out of strips of tire rubber tied over rags. They were what we were, and, at that moment, I was glad I could not see myself, because in my face, I might also have seen them.

The NKVD police were out in force on the streets. They were requiring all refugees to register. Technically, whenever foreigners arrived in a new city or town, they were required to register with the local authorities. They needed papers and would likely be interrogated, sometimes even if everything was in order. But in the big cities, registration was difficult simply because of the size of the refugee population and its fluidity, its constant movement from spot to spot. Many refugees spent their days on the move, from one part of the city to another to avoid the NKVD. But Moshe and I wanted no trouble, so we decided to register together, as Yankel and Moshe Pomeranice. Whatever happened, we were determined to stay together. We had become very close on the collective, constantly looking out for each other, sharing, caring for each other. For survival, each of us could depend absolutely on the other. And for the first time in years, I did not feel the emptiness and fear of being completely, totally alone.

It turned out to be very simple: we registered, along with the Shumleks, and we were sent to Siberia. We were packed onto one train, the Shumleks were packed on to another, and with a whistle and a lurch we were off. Once again I was heading north. It was summer, and at least that meant some kind of hope, even the hope that by some miracle the war would end and Moshe and I would return home, together. I prayed we were not headed to Irkutsk. The train wound its way back along a now familiar route, to Novosibirsk, but there we boarded another train, which took us north and east to the small town of Berozofka, where we were released along with twenty other refugees.

The area, we soon learned, was filled with tiny towns and fields, a few miles apart, separated by heavy thick woods, a jumble of pines and birches, so thick and full that even by day the forest was plunged into a kind of semidarkness. Dirt roads crisscrossed the land, roads that widened in the towns and grew narrow as they trailed off into the woods, becoming barely wide enough for a horse and buggy. The houses that lined the roads were old wooden houses with massive stoves, which was all we needed to see to know about the winters.

Berozofka was little more than a collection of such houses lining either side of a road that abruptly led into the woods. A community of collective farmers, Berozofka was now home to the very old, the very young, and women. The men had all gone off to fight. Those few who had returned were little more than shadows of themselves, men without arms, legs, hands, feet. They sunk their shoulders into crutches. Their stunted limbs swung carelessly as they moved. Such men were everywhere, in the big cities, in the Siberian uplands, and even in these small villages. Yet for every one of them, there were many more who would never be returning home.

As in the south, here refugees were sorely needed as laborers, and we were easily housed in the village's homes. I lived with an older couple whose son was fighting on the front. They were warm and welcoming to me, and they doted on me the way the old often dote on the young.

Our band of refugees had arrived weak and exhausted from the journey. Days of cramped inactivity, of pure listlessness, of waiting for time to pass while not knowing what awaits, had drained us. It was not the brutal physical exhaustion we knew after long hours on the collective with only meager food, but it was exhaustion nonetheless, the kind that cannot be erased by the simple acts of eating and sleeping. And even if it could have been, we soon discovered that there was no food. All around us, people were hungry. There was not enough bread, and meat could rarely be found. And now there were more than twenty new mouths to feed.

In addition to a lack of food, we had to cope with illness. One of the men had been sick since we boarded the train, and we had not been there long when he grew worse. The refugees had formed their own committee to make decisions, and somehow it was decided that I should be the one to walk through the thick woods to another village, where a doctor lived. I remember setting out and making my way there, only to discover that the doctor was a young woman, perhaps a little older than I.

Her name, or her last name, as much as I have remembered, was Vrublefska. She was blonde and thin. Young Russian women were usually thin, until children and years of eating starchy food thickened their waists and limbs. The war and hunger, however, had taken a toll on many of these women, newly hollowing their cheeks, making their ribs protrude.

Vrublefska, while still young, did not look young. Her hands and skin were rough, and lines already cut across her brow. She was pretty, but it was in a round-faced way. She rarely parted her lips when she smiled, perhaps because her teeth had started to go bad and decay. As we were leaving, she said very little. She merely grabbed a few things, and we set out for Berozofka. It was late afternoon when we returned, and Vrublefska was able to examine the sick man. She emerged saying that he should be all right but would need some medicine, medicine that she had in her home. It was already too late to walk back to her village, though. Dusk was descending, and the woods were filled with bears. The local people were afraid of bears, a fear that I shared after hearing only a few stories of these bears mauling folks under the dark cover of the forest.

Stories abounded of bears scalping people, ripping the skin from their skulls and pulling it over their faces. Already this year, two men had been killed by bears, and many people refused to travel between towns, except in groups. Vrublefska would have to spend the night.

What a night. She was staying with another woman in the village. When everyone else had gone to sleep, the three of us stayed awake, talking. We didn't close our eyes the entire night. Vrublefska and the local woman wanted to know everything, where I had come from, what life was like in Poland, about Central Asia, everything. And I wanted to know about their lives in small Russian villages. I had always been shy whenever I talked with girls, sometimes so nervous that I could barely utter a single word. Never before had I just simply enjoyed the easy, frivolous flow of conversation. But for some reason, talking was now easier. Or perhaps it was simply that it had been years since I had shared what seemed like light conversation and banter among new friends. We traded questions and answers until deep in the night, almost until the first threads of pink light of the dawn.

The next morning, the refugee committee met again to decide who would accompany Vrublefska back for the medicine. No one in the village looked askance at my spending the entire night with the two women. It was something that was accepted. In fact, the only ones who said anything about it were the other refugees. They could not be convinced that nothing had happened. With my brother standing right there, the committee declared, "You slept with her, you have to go with her for the medicine."

I had very little choice. Vrublefska and I started the trek back through the woods to her home. I could see that Vrublefska was happy. She walked with a light step, and, when we were under the dense cover of the trees, she reached out and took hold of my hand. When we reached her house, she took off my shoes and washed my feet with soap. Then she insisted that I sit down. "You cannot leave without having a meal," she insisted. "You will be too tired to walk."

I was hungry and tired. I knew I should be starting back, that all too soon darkness would begin to fall, but still I stayed. Vrublefska busied herself in the kitchen. She lived well. In addition to a small kitchen area, her house had three rooms, a large living room with a fancy tile stove, a bedroom, and a little sitting room. Like all of the homes in the town, this one had no bathroom, only an outhouse. Inside, everything was clean, and there were lovely old pieces of furniture, delicately carved, much finer than anything I had seen in any other Russian homes. I was amazed that she had this house and the garden out back all to herself.

While I looked around the rooms, I heard the sizzle of fat in a pan as Vrublefska began frying cheese pirogi, a kind of pancake, which she served with a homemade drink that tasted rather like bad beer. The food was thick and rich, and she piled my plate high, until I could not swallow another mouthful. Outside, the sun was slowly sinking, and a thick darkness seemed to be rising up from the trees. It was too late to walk back.

The fullness in my stomach was slowly being replaced by a sinking feeling. I had no choice but to spend the night. Vrublefska began to clear away the dishes and then quickly produced two glasses and a bottle of liquor. "I am only going to give you a little bit," she said, as she carefully measured the clear, strong liquid into the glass. "Otherwise, you won't be good." There was a mischievous tone in her voice.

I was confused. I had little experience with Russian men and their drinking sprees. In fact, I rarely drank any form of liquor. But it soon became clear just what Vrublefska intended. After we had raised our glasses and pounded them back on the table, Vrublefska leaned over and kissed me. It was not a gentle kiss on the cheek or lips, but a fiery kiss, laced with passion. Tonight, it was clear that Vrublefska was not interested in talking. She wanted me.

For two years, almost every young male who could hold a rifle had been plucked from the region. The towns were decimated. And when some of those called up returned, it was without arms or legs or even both. They moved on crutches, hauling about listless stumps, often wearing the remnants of their uniforms, as if that was all they still owned.

I was young, intact, and male, and anyone would have to be naive to think that I would not provoke at least a passing interest. But I was naive, and I did not see where this interest would lead. In some ways, at a time when it mattered most, I did not think. I reacted. That night, we were alone, and I made love with Vrublefska. It was not out of any deep feelings of affection or even deep attraction. I certainly did not love her. But we were young. It was wartime, and we shared desires. And, too, this house, this woman, this place, all of it seemed so unreal, so new that it was unbelievable. I wondered if I would simply wake up and discover I had dreamed the whole thing. Only afterward, as I lay there in the dark, half expecting a fist to pound against the door at any minute, did I regret what I had done. All I wanted to do was to return home.

I lay awake most of the night and was up before dawn. I knew I had to be back at work. Already, I was worried about being punished. When the first rays of light crept across the sky, I woke Vrublefska and told her that I needed the medicine, that I would be in serious trouble and had to go. She looked at me, her eyes still somewhat swollen with sleep, and she giggled. I found nothing funny about the situation and was growing more irritated by the minute. "Don't worry," Vrublefska told me, "I will give you a letter, a medical excuse."

In the Soviet Union, medical excuses were a sought-after prize. They were, like identity documents, a kind of gold, something accepted by the state, something that permitted you to move outside of very set rules. I did not know, however, what Vrublefska could write that would excuse me. I was in a relatively good health. I continued to insist that I had to leave.

Sighing, she dragged her naked body from the bed, and, pulling on a skirt and throwing a blouse over her shoulders, she walked to a desk, where she began to write. When she had finished, she sealed the note and returned it to me. Then, she went into the kitchen, saying she had to prepare the medicine. She emerged carrying two bundles, a small one and a large one. On the table she had already placed an entire loaf of bread, some cheese, and some sour milk for breakfast.

I looked at the bundles and at the food spread out before me. It was mystifying. With shortages everywhere, how could a doctor in a small rural village afford such food? I soon discovered how.

Stacked in the corner of her kitchen were empty cans that she used to collect the sweepings from the stove. The cans were stamped with strange letters, letters I had never seen. I picked up a can and asked her where it came from. She answered that her uncle supervised a warehouse that stored food being sent from the United States to help the Soviet war effort and that he was able to give her a little extra. I quickly realized, that, like the factory workers who walked out with bolts of material strapped to their middles, he was able to benefit from his position, even more so, because he was the top authority and no one, it seemed, would question him.

I was ready to leave, but Vrublefska insisted that she walk with me part way through the woods. I could not convince her otherwise. I insisted on carrying both bundles, one in each hand.

Last season's dry brown pine needles snapped softly under our feet as we trod along the path. The air was cool under the trees, and everything had a dark cast, pierced only by shafts of bright sunlight, which sliced like a blade through the weighty, thick trees. As we walked, smelling the pine and hearing the occasional rustle of branches above, she told me how she wanted me to visit again and how she would invite me. I said almost nothing.

When we were nearly three-quarters of the way to Berozofka, Vrublefska said she must go back. She reached for my hand and, clutching it, kissed me, a kiss of passion and parting. Then she brushed my cheeks lightly with her lips and squeezed my fingers. "The second, larger bundle is for you."

At that moment, I felt like a man descending into water, with each second I had sunk deeper, and the vast surface above had receded still farther away.

As I walked on alone, the consequences of the previous evening rippled through my mind. I did not want to become involved with Vrublefska. I certainly did not want to fall in love. I had visions of myself trapped in Siberia with Vrublefska, unable to return to Europe, unable to return home to Radzyń. The farther I walked, the more afraid I became that if I became involved with Vrublefska I could never go back, that this dense forest and these dark trees would be my future and my fate. I decided I did not want to see Vrublefska again.

When I returned to Berozofka, I immediately delivered the medicine and then went in search of my brother. I told Moshe everything that had happened. I was still clutching the second package in my hand. Moshe told me to open the package. Inside was some smoked meat and a can of lard. Moshe looked carefully at the food. I was in shock and simply stood there, saying nothing. At last Moshe spoke. I don't know what I expected him to say, but I was not prepared for how he put both hands on my shoulders and, looking straight at me, said, "Do you want to be buried in Siberia or do you want to live to go home?" It was not meant as a question.

He paused. "You have found an opportunity, a chance for us to survive. This girl likes you, maybe she will help you. Maybe she will help us all."

I did not want to listen to Moshe. He was right, but I did not want to listen to him. I did not want to think about what was happening. I did not want to think about consequences, and I did not. You are reckless when you are young.

Mail came to Berozofka on horseback, carried by a man who rode from village to village in a kind of wide circle. You didn't need stamps to send a letter, but if the man missed your village, you waited until he returned. It was slow and, if the hushed talk was true, screened by the state, but eventually the mail came. I had barely left when a letter from Vrublefska arrived, inviting me back to visit. And right after the letter, packages began arriving, packages with bread and canned goods, in one even some salami and a bag of sugar. After the second package, my brother told me to go to visit. I went on a Sunday, my day off, but I told her almost as soon as I arrived that I had to return, because I had to be at work the next day. The old rule still applied. Three times late to work, and I or anyone else would be sent to solitary confinement in a nearby jail. But Vrublefska had an answer.

"It doesn't matter," she told me. "I will give you a signed, sealed doctor's note saying you were ill and could not work. That will take care of everything."

I stayed. I stayed for two days. We took walks around her garden and around the little town. She introduced me to her neighbors and to her best friend, Natasha, a beautiful young woman with long dark hair and laughing brown eyes. Vrublefska cooked for me and fussed over me. Throughout those two days, she wanted me by her side day and night. Gradually, I began to enjoy the attention, the company, the desire. But in my mind, an uneasy feeling kept nagging at me. I couldn't express it in words, yet it was most certainly there.

When I returned on Tuesday, the authorities in Berozofka accepted the note. They examined the paper and said very little. Then, they let me go. I was relieved, and as I walked back to my home, I carefully ran my hands along the knapsack Vrublefska had packed for me. It was practically bulging. I could feel the edge of cans and thick parcels. It was a weighty package, and I tried again to recall all that she had stuffed inside. There were cans of oil and fat, bundles of sugar, tea, coffee, dried meats, things we could never hope to find in Berozofka, things that were to us the finest luxuries. Once again, I went in search of Moshe, and when I found him with some of the other refugees, we immediately began to open the bundle, to pull out canned treasures with labels none of us could read, from a country none of us could truly imagine, but a country that must, no doubt, have an endless supply of oils and fats, so many that they could send these away. I thought of my American shoes and the five dollar bills my mother saved, all from a place with extra fats and oils and sugar.

With each item that came forth, up went another cry of delight. My brother turned to me and, grabbing me in his arms, whispered in my ear, barely able to conceal his joy. "Yankel," he said, "We're going to live. We are going to survive." And I looked at the fats with the strange foreign labels and for a moment, I too believed.

I went back again. I stayed, and Vrublefska gave me another doctor's certificate. After the third time, the local authorities grew suspicious. It did not take much for them to put everything together. I would leave and then return with a doctor's note. I was called in and warned that my first duty was to the war effort and the Soviet Union. But they hesitated. Vrublefska's uncle was a powerful man, and no one wanted to offend him or to incur his wrath in any way. So while they warned me, sternly, no one wanted to be too stern with Vrublefska. It was a game of boundaries and degrees. And until they resolved to move beyond warnings to actions, I was not wholly deterred, for each time I returned from Vrublefska's, I returned with a package, and even in summer, even as the crops ripened in the fields, these packages meant everything to us. They provided the food that made the difference for our survival.

And it wasn't just the packages I carried back through the woods. In between my visits, Vrublefska sent others, sometimes full of canned foods, sometimes even foods she had prepared. Some of the packages she brought to me herself. A few times she tried to stay over, other times she came and left on the same day. And when she did not come herself, she sent the bundles with others. It seemed that every time anyone was traveling to Berozofka, Vrublefska sent me a package. She would press them into the hands of the mail carrier or random travelers. She might even have bribed people to carry them safely. I do not know. All I knew was the packages kept coming, and the entire village of Berozofka was talking.

The old women in the village told me that Vrublefska had put a special ingredient in the *bobka*, the plain Russian cakes she baked and sent, an ingredient women used to make men fall in love with them. They giggled and smiled when they told me, smiles that crinkled their skin and showed their nearly toothless mouths. I was horrified. From then on, I refused to touch the cakes. The other refugees were happy to eat them. One said to me, "I don't give a damn if I fall in love with her." He was hungry, and before him stood a cake.

My visits to Vrublefska continued, and so did the warnings. In the Soviet Union, people quickly learned that you do not do what you want, you do what the government wants. After my fifth or sixth visit, the authorities on the collective farm told me that in their judgment I was not sick. The head of the collective instructed me not to visit Vrublefska anymore. Vrublefska received an equally strong warning, and she cursed the officials who gave it. The situation was becoming dangerous. Afraid of what might happen, I resolved not to visit her anymore, except on my day off. In addition to the warnings, I was still receiving the packages. My brother and the other refugees were at a loss to know what to do. My involvement with Vrublefska could cause trouble for all of them, but none of us wanted to forgo the packages. My brother mentioned that I had to be careful, that maybe I wanted a different kind of attachment to Vrublefska. But no one talked about a wedding.

One Sunday morning, my brother and two other refugees appeared with four horses. They told me we were going to a party and proceeded to load me onto the empty horse, and we rode off into the woods. It was a beautiful day. The leaves on the trees were lush and green, the air was bursting with the smell of flowers. It was as if the land had been doused in a warm, rich honey, which made even the musty forest seem sweet. My brother and the two men appeared to know exactly where they were going. I watched the branches dip and rise as we passed, and I felt the gentle motion of the horse beneath me. A million questions rushed through my mind, but nothing prepared me for the final destination.

We dismounted in front of a long hall. Inside was a table that seemed never to end, covered with steaming plates of food, fresh meats, cheeses, vegetables, and, of course, bottles of clear vodka. Benches ran along the table on both sides. There were already people waiting. The head of the collective was there, and so was the family I lived with in Berozofka. Everyone was dressed in their finest clothes. Men wore flowing white embroidered shirts, tucked into slim dark pants. The women wore dresses, and many had put up their hair. Moshe took my arm and led me to the head of the table. A seat was waiting. Next to me was the town magistrate, a balding man with a firm grip and a vast, protruding belly. I was told he was seventy-five years old, but he was not wizened, like so many of the men I had known. His cheeks were full and red, with streaks of broken capillaries tracing unusual patterns just under the surface of the flesh. He grabbed my hand and offered me some vodka, and we raised the glasses. And as I felt the liquor heating my lips, rushing like a fire down my esophagus and into my stomach, he proclaimed it "the toast before the ceremony."

It was then that I saw Vrublefska come toward me, wearing a simple dress with embroidery at the edges. I took a step back as Moshe quickly grabbed my arm. "A woman will take much better care of a husband than she will of a boyfriend," he said in low, strong voice, his lips almost touching my ear. "You'll worry later about what's going to happen."

I said nothing. I could find nothing to say. I felt shaky, my head seemed to be revolving, spinning, until I felt dizzy. "He is the man who will marry you," Moshe explained, his voice laden with authority, gesturing to the sweaty balding man who had so tightly gripped my hand only moments ago. "You and Vrublefska."

The vodka was already working its way through me, warming and numbing me, making everything around me feel easy and far away. My mind wandered back to Radzyń. I remembered a time when I had been so shy and scared to speak to a girl on the street that I had taken a sip of liquor just to give me the courage. Now Radzyń seemed very far away.

The mayor asked me very perfunctorily if I wanted to marry Vrublefska. In my mind, I knew there was only one answer that I could give. "What am I going to say now," I thought to myself. "No? If I say 'no,' who knows what terrible things could happen."

Somehow my lips formed "Da," and Vrublefska said the same. The mayor announced that we were officially married. Vrublefska gave me a long, passionate kiss. My brother and the two other refugees who had ridden the horses with me signed a piece of paper, I guess it was a license, and the whole ceremony was over. Then the celebration, the party, began. All around me, people were eating and drinking. The excitement was contagious, and I had yet to feel the full impact of what had happened.

Except for some young boys in the hall, I was the youngest man there. Everyone else was off in the army. The place was crowded with brightly clothed young girls, middle-aged women, and older men, people who had been waiting for months for any kind of celebration. As I sat at the head of the table, looking down on all the people, old and young, I felt for a minute as if I owned Russia. Here were people celebrating in my honor. It was a feeling I had never known.

As the afternoon wore on, we ate and drank, we drank and ate. There were toasts, toasts to life and health and marriage. Each time the glass would be filled to the rim with the clear liquor that was rushed like a fire through the veins. And each time the glasses were expected to be emptied. Different men stood and raised their glasses, and I was expected to keep pace with them. I felt my cheeks grow hot. The liquor splashed from my glass onto my hand.

From somewhere I heard music. Everything around me was whirling. The room rose and fell, and I seemed to be rising and falling with it. Suddenly, I felt my brother's hands on my arms, and he and some other man were dragging me outside onto the grass. They stretched me out on my back, and the world seemed to spin in a tight circle. "You're drunk," they told me, and I was, sprawled on the grass, unable to move.

They sat with me for a while, but it was clear that I was not going to move, so they stood up to go back to the party. As they were leaving, Moshe leaned over and whispered into my year, "Yankel, don't say anything. We're going to survive through the war. We are going to go back."

I lay on the soft grass that smelled of earth, and Moshe's words ran through my mind. I could not think. My head felt heavy, but still I heard Moshe's words. Intermittently, he would come back to check on me, and again he would tell me, "We're going to survive." His voice sounded clear and sure when he said it. He would pat my head, but I never moved.

Inside, everyone was still dancing and drinking. I could hear the roar of more toasts. And then as I lay on the grass, the alcohol ebbing and flowing through me, I felt a shadow standing over me. I looked up into waves of brown hair. Natasha, Vrublefska's best friend, was smiling at me. She glanced around and then, bending over, kissed me on the lips. Giggling, she ran off.

I lay alone for a while longer, my head in a kind of dull fog. Above me, the trees were spinning, and the sky was rotating into a wide cone. Moshe came back, and then, right after him, Natasha returned and kissed me yet again. It was like a game, first one running out and then the other. I did not want to get up. I knew my head would be pounding, as if someone were swinging at it with a hammer. I knew too that at some point the haze would wear off and everything would be clear. Already, the effects of the alcohol were slowly disappearing. At long last, when I looked up, the sky stood still. Vrublefska remained inside, celebrating, but by late afternoon, she and everyone else were trickling out of the doors. The bottles had been emptied, the food eaten, the celebration was complete.

My brother and the other two men mounted the horses and rode back, but I was allowed to stay with Vrublefska for several days and nights before I had to return. I watched my brother depart, and as I stood, still wobbly, with Vrublefska on my arm, and watched the horses and their riders disappear into the woods, I felt totally alone.

13

Moscow Beckons

I stayed with Vrublefska for three days and nights. Then I returned to Bero-zofka. Marrying Vrublefska was relatively easy, but living with her was not. I would need a special residence permit. I would also have to be transferred from my place of work, and that was something the Soviet authorities were partic-ularly reluctant to do. So, for now, we would be married but live apart. And that suited me fine. I could not wait to return to my brother.

It was close to harvest, and the work was intensifying. Even though dusk came earlier, the days seemed longer and more unrelenting. We spent hours cutting hay. The land was bad, the soil poor and rocky, which made it diffi-cult to work and even more difficult for anything grow. Forests bisected the fields, making any growing space limited at best. I did not mind the hard work. It shortened my time with Vrublefska. It left me free to imagine something different from the world in which I now lived. To keep me going day after day in the fields, I tried to envision the end of the war, imagining that at last Moshe and I were leaving and returning home. But it was more feelings than actual images that raced through my mind. I did not know what would be left. I did not even know for sure how we would leave, and I did not want to think about Vrublefska's reaction when the time came. Gradually, I did not want to think at all. I would numb myself with the mechanical motion of field work, letting my mind become a blank.

Late one morning, Vrublefska appeared at the edge of the field where I was cutting hay. Her chest was heaving, sweat glistened on her forehead. She had ridden to tell me that she was being sent to Novosibirsk. All the doctors from the area were being ordered to Novosibirsk to care for wounded soldiers, who were being brought east by the trainload from the front lines. She would be there at least one week, probably two or more. With that announcement, Vrublefska was gone.

Once she was gone, I felt only relief. I did not miss her. I did not miss having to travel to visit her on my day off. I realized that I didn't care for any of it—I didn't care for marriage, and I didn't care for Vrublefska. She had done everything possible to get me and to keep me, but I wanted neither to be gotten nor to be kept. I felt nothing for Vrublefska. I thought of my quiet, gentle fiancée left behind in Brest, and I wondered how things had ever come to this. I did not lie awake at night and think about Vrublefska the way I had on so many nights thought about my fiancée in Brest. I wanted to survive, I wanted my brother to survive, but I did not want to be married to this woman. It was as if my arms were being drawn and pulled in two different directions, by such strong impulses that eventually I would either be torn apart or I would have to let go.

A week passed and then a letter arrived, not from Vrublefska, but from her friend Natasha, who was living in Vrublefska's house while Vrublefska was gone. Natasha's own house was a nice but somewhat more crowded place in the town. She had to live with her entire family, while Vrublefska had a home of her own. The landlady read Natasha's letter out loud because I did not read Russian. The first few lines said little, but then the Russian woman looked up from the paper and said to me, "This girl wants you to come and visit her." She said nothing more, she just continued to look at me.

I went to see Natasha. I visited her a couple of times and stayed there, in Vrublefska's house, listening to her laugh, having her fuss over me. It was not a wise thing to do. I was a married man, married to her best friend. I was tempting fate, yet somehow I believed that Vrublefska would not find out. What happened next, however, was beyond anything I could have foreseen or imagined.

Vrublefska returned from Novosibirsk, and exhausted, she went to start a fire in the oven to cook or to warm herself. She opened the door and saw freshly torn pieces of white paper. Knowing she had not placed the paper in the oven, she scooped out each piece and painstakingly spread them out on a table, putting them together like a puzzle. What she reconstructed was a discarded love letter, a letter from Natasha to me. Natasha, apparently unhappy with the letter, had ripped it up and stuffed the pieces in the oven, but she had never burned them, so they were waiting, crumpled but still quite legible, when Vrublefska returned.

The letter was bad, but even worse, Vrublefska's neighbors told her that I had been to her house while she was away, that I had visited Natasha. They told Vrublefska, but no one had told me that Vrublefska was back.

On my last visit to Natasha at Vrublefska's house, she had invited me to a party at her family's home. She was only inviting me, not Vrublefska, and, in what was perhaps my most foolish decision, I went. I told myself there would be a lot of other people there, that it was not as if I were going to visit her alone. I went, and there was laughter and drinking, and if there were raised eyebrows, I did not notice them. I was enjoying myself when suddenly, out of the corner of my eye, I saw the hand of the man sitting next to me reach for my neck. He held his palm flat, as if trying to protect me.

There was a cry. I drew back, and only then did I see the glint of a metal blade. I whirled around, and there was Vrublefska, shouting a long string of unspeakable words at me, promising to kill me. Rage had overtaken her entire body. Her face was red, her hair suddenly seemed to have gone wild around her head. She was clutching a knife, and only the strong arms of a stranger were restraining her from lunging full force at me. She was kicking and wriggling and screaming, the knife was thrashing in her hand. I looked at her and ran. I ran with my heart in my throat, my pulse pounding in my head. Even though it was near dusk, I ran toward the woods. I was running for my life.

Once I was under the thick blackness of the trees, I began to collect myself. By a quick grab of a wrist, my life had been saved. If I wanted to live, I knew I should never see Vrublefska or Natasha again. Next time, there might be no one there or willing to save me from Vrublefska's fury—or perhaps even Natasha's.

I ran and walked through the woods listening for the sounds of bears. I did not know what bears sounded like, but I imagined them lurking behind every tree, in every eerie black corner of forest. When I finally returned to Berozofka, I was almost hysterical from the hours of shock and fear. All I wanted to do was find my brother.

I found him and told him. I told him everything. At first, he said nothing. Only in his eyes did I see the disappointment, the anguish. It was too late for anger, but as I looked in his eyes, I realized that suddenly the world was crumbling around us.

In his slow way, a wise way, in the way of a man who knew much more than I, yet who would not blame me because that went against how one treated a brother, Moshe spoke. "I do not think Vrublefska will calm down," he said. "I have always said that we will survive the war together, but now I think the only way for you to survive is to leave. If you stay here, your problems will only increase, but somewhere else you have a chance. This war cannot last forever. One day we will go home. We will be together again."

Leave, all I wanted to do was leave, but I wanted Moshe with me, and now that I was thinking of leaving, I realized that I had no idea where to go. Back to the south? Maybe to try like other refugees to cross the border to Iran and make my way to Palestine. My mind was racing, and at the same time going nowhere. "Moshe," I said, and he started to speak again.

"I think you should try to join the Polish army in Russia immediately. The collective farm cannot be opposed to that, and you'll die here for sure if you don't leave," he said.

Moshe took a breath and continued, "If you survive in the army, you'll be able to make it out of Russia faster. Being with the army will send you in the direction of home, and, who knows," he said, trying to smile, "maybe the war will be over before you have to fight."

Neither of us knew much of anything about the war. News was scanty. Russian radio talked mostly of valor and Russian victories, and whatever else we heard, we only heard secondhand. We knew almost nothing, and Moshe meant what he said more as a comfort than as anything else. But the registering was real. We had seen the posters, even around Berozofka, announcing the formation of a Polish army in the Soviet Union to fight against the Germans. Anyone who could prove Polish origin could join, and I, not as Yankel Pomeranice, but as Kalman Schweitzer from Chełm, could do just that.

Moshe looked at me again. "To save your life," he said, "you'd better leave."

Moshe was right. As much as I did not want to be separated, joining the army offered the best chance for survival. I was scared to death to stay in Berozofka more than another day or two at most. I had hurt Vrublefska too much, and, especially with her influential family, I had no way of knowing how things might turn out. Late that day, I went and spoke to the head of the collective in Berozofka, the same *nayalnik* who had given me my sternest warnings. I told him I wanted to leave for Novosibirsk to sign up with the new Polish army. He released me immediately. To him, I was a problem, and now I would be gone.

The next day, Moshe walked with me to the train station. As we drew closer, I started to cry. I felt the most terrible sense of despair. Here, I had found my brother, perhaps the only other member of my family still alive, and now through my own stupidity we were being ripped apart. We had been together barely one season. I looked at Moshe and broke down. I stood on the dusty road and sobbed and sobbed. Moshe tried to be encouraging. He reminded me that he had always believed we would survive. He promised me that we would find each other again. But we both knew that our futures were far from certain. He was going back to face a ruthless Siberian winter, and I was leaving for what already had been for many Russians certain death.

Once again, I was on a train that would eventually help carry me out of Siberia. But first, I had to travel to Novosibirsk. There, at the station, I showed my documents to register for the Polish army, being organized by the Polish exile Wanda Wasilewska. I did not even have to leave the massive vaulted concrete rail house, nor, I think, did the Soviets want me to. I drank *kipjatok*, the hot boiled water, and waited until they called me. I was placed on a train to Moscow along with some other recruits. We were told that we would be met when we arrived.

The train took its time winding its way west. At each stop, we were besieged by local people clamoring at the windows to buy whatever we had, soap, a canteen, cigarettes, anything. Some of the people on the platform would hold up a bundle of money, tightly tied, with a five ruble note on top and another on the bottom, and tell you that they would give you the money in exchange for your soap or cigarettes. Many passengers obliged, only to discover that they were getting only a five ruble note on the top and another on the bottom. The rest of the bundle was worthless paper. Veteran travelers were used to these scams, but the local people still persevered, because there were almost always new faces on the trains.

After a couple of days on the rails, we emerged from the thick, wooded forests onto a stretch of level, grassy land. We were drawing closer. Moscow was beckoning.

Moscow sits like an island unto itself, spreading out over the great flat plain, which is the only thing vast enough to dwarf the city, a plain that reaches out to the horizon. From the station, we were hurriedly taken along streets only recently freed from the threat of a German siege to a large concrete building now being used as makeshift barracks. We were assigned to a room for several days, where we were examined by a doctor, and if we passed, we would then be weighed and measured for uniforms. The latter turned out to be a completely useless exercise.

At the barracks, we had to turn over our civilian clothing, which was promptly thrown away. I was then handed ten jackets, all too small. The only one that came even close to fitting buttoned as tight as a steel brace around my ribs. The sleeves ended way above my wrists. But to look around, none of the other recruits seemed to be having any better luck. Like the jackets, shoes, when they were available and handed out, were cut so small they crushed bones and tendons. People either hobbled as if crippled or slit the shoes, letting their toes hang out over the soles and touch the ground with every step. If the shoes were not unbearably small, they were so big that paper had to be stuffed inside to prevent the foot from slipping and sliding and blistering as you walked. Some of the recruits tried to swap shoes, but there seemed to be no middle ground in sizes, and nothing seemed to fit.

From central Moscow, we were next taken to the outskirts of the city, to a vast field covered with tents and men, milling about. I had the same sinking sensation that I had when I first stepped out of the station in Taškent and saw the endless sea of refugees snaking like some giant animal across the hot square and the streets in front of the building. I wished I were anywhere but there, even, for a fleeting second, I wished I were back with Vrublefska.

There was nothing on the field except the tents, and I could already feel the air growing cold. Wind would sweep like a vicious horde across the plain, and there would be no escape. Among the tents, I found that people roamed around, aimlessly, with no purpose, no direction, and almost no food. Everything seemed in very short supply.

The tent camp was not like Siberia, but still the conditions were awful. Food, when it was available, took three hours to get and was never enough. There were no bathrooms other than open holes in the camp, and no places to wash. Black, foul-smelling water collected in pools or ran in little eddies through the field. There was a chill in the air and very few blankets. It was a miserable, filthy, lonely place.

Most of the people who had made the journey to join the army expected that, once in Moscow, they would be taken care of. Many of us, including myself, assumed that the army would be efficient. Instead, it was very disorganized. Nothing was taken care of, and things only seemed to be getting worse. As the reality of the conditions sunk in, a number of the recruits managed to desert. Soon, more recruits were deserting than were arriving at the camp, and there seemed to be no end in sight. In the early hours of one morning, some fifty men tried to make a break for it. The new Polish military was waiting. They rounded up the men and marched them out to the edge of the field. Across the camp, recruits were lined up and ordered to the edge of that same field.

The fifty men stood in one long line. Three gunners at machine-gun batteries faced them. There was no trial, nothing, just the rough, guttural shout of an order, and then a split second of silence before we heard the staccato pulse of firing. The bodies crumpled and fell in no particular order as the gunfire sprayed up and down the line. We heard cries too, in no particular order. Some came from men in the instant before they were hit, others from those as they fell or writhed on the ground. And even once the bodies lay on the ground in a tangled heap of limbs and organs and intermixing blood, the gunners continued, aiming their barrels down, to make sure the job was complete. It was fast, and yet it seemed to take forever.

Walking back to the tents, we said very little. We had been warned, and now we were afraid. Except for the very foolish or the very brave, we were here to stay.

And there was something else that many of the recruits, including myself, by now knew. We couldn't afford to be captured by the Germans. It was bad for non-Jews, but a Jew didn't have a chance, and every Jew knew it. Germans routinely shot Jewish prisoners of war, sometimes right on the spot they had been captured. The only way for a Jew to survive was to defeat the enemy. Or die trying.

As the days dragged on, I began to ease into the place. I noticed that there was often more Russian than Polish spoken in the camp. It soon became clear from the way people banded into groups and stuck together that there was a Russian presence as much as a Polish one. Although we were told that the Soviets hoped a "Polish army" would encourage Poles inside Poland to work against the Germans, this was hardly a Polish army. Some of the men were clearly Russians in Polish uniforms. Even quite a number of the army's generals were Russian-born men of Polish ancestry, and some could barely speak Polish. In my own mind, I thought that the Russians must not trust the Poles and that the only way they would allow a "Polish army" was if it was controlled by the Russians. It did not occur to me to think that this army was a means of gaining political control in a region, but then I do not think such thoughts occurred to many of the regular soldiers on either side of the lines.

Gradually, some order was imposed on the chaos that ruled those tents. Bit by bit, recruits were divided into groups and posted to different areas. There was a steady outflow, and one day I became part of it. I was sent along with some thirty or more other new enlistees off to barracks deep in the woods. I believe it was somewhat northwest from Moscow and closer to the Baltics, but I had no way of knowing, and no one was willing to tell us. Our destination was a school where we would learn how to drive. From there, we would likely become combat supply truck or jeep drivers for the army. It was a somewhat daunting prospect for nearly all of us, who, almost without exception, had hardly ever ridden in the cab of a truck and had never pushed a brake or gripped a steering wheel.

We began our training in classrooms where we learned about rules of the road, about how to clean the trucks, and, more important, about the workings of the truck engines. We were also supposed to learn how to handle a gun and how to load and fire artillery.

Each morning, we would walk inside the school building and remove our heavy felt boots. We would line the boots up next to a fire to dry, because the felt was often damp from the soggy cold outside. Then we would take our seats. I remember almost nothing of the instruction. What I do remember took place when the instructor left the room and we remained in our seats.

There would be a momentary lull. Then, suddenly, in one swift fluid motion, one of those felt boots would be snatched and lobbed, sometimes in a high wide arc, sometimes in a straight direct shot, at an unsuspecting student's head. The impact and the challenge did not go unnoticed. The boot would then be hurled yet again at another head or back in the direction of the initial offender. But, this time, the targeting was less sure, and suddenly others were drawn into the melee, as boots flew about the room at lightening speeds. On a number of occasions, recipients even responded with a flurry of fists. It all came to a sudden halt as soon as the instructor returned to the room.

Despite these interludes, our days were mostly filled with preparing for the trucks. Most of us had known combat only when we were fleeing from it, and now we were going to be driving headlong into it. We tried not to think about the future. Inside, I felt adrenaline course through me, unused, shuddering.

At night, we slept head to toe on long wooden platforms that ran along the length of the barracks. One group slept on the bottom, another slept on a rack above us, reached by a series of evenly spaced ladders. I slept on the lower level. And as we slept, a guard walked along beside the platforms, up and back, up and back, keeping watch all through the night.

One night, when it was pitch dark and I was fast asleep, I suddenly felt a soaking sensation, a dampness spreading across me. My eyes opened, I felt my clothes. They were wet. I searched for the source and suddenly realized that it was coming from above, a stream of liquid was running down on to me. The recruit in the bunk above me had wet his bed. Soaked in my bunk, I began to curse and yell. I was cursing the soldier above me, I was letting out a torrent of words with the same swiftness that felt boots flew in the classroom. I was furious. Suddenly, everyone around me was awake, and the barracks guard was running in my direction. The guard yelled at me for making such a commotion, and I responded. I thrust out my foot and kicked him.

He wobbled for a second, leaning dangerously far back, almost falling over. But as soon as he regained his balance, he came at me. I stood my ground. We tussled and yelled until the doors burst open and a band of officers arrived. They dragged me away, promising to make me an example of someone who could not control himself, who did not have the discipline to be a soldier. In raised voices that drowned out the mayhem of the barracks, they promised to court-martial me. "I'm going to shoot you like a dog," one officer hissed.

Suddenly, my mind flashed back to the image of those fifty men lined up in that field. These officers, guns drawn, were promising to court-martial me publicly in the field behind the barracks. I tried to struggle, to break free, but the men held fast. One of the officers began to speak to me, saying, "Do you know what's going to happen to you? You're going to get shot right now." Whether he meant I would be shot for struggling or just shot, I don't know. Now I was fighting to regain my composure. The realization of what was happening had overtaken my anger. I tried to explain what had taken place in the barracks, but mostly I apologized. Over and over, I admitted guilt: "I did something wrong."

Slowly, the tension and the anger began to diffuse. Instead of the court-martial, instead of a pistol fired in the field, they chose hard labor, banishing me to the kitchen for the night to chop wood and go without sleep. There were threats and warnings, but as I was led away to the kitchen, I felt only waves of relief.

I had seen the kitchen before. It was a crude, hot place that served the whole camp area. It was kept running on shifts, nearly all hours of the day, because there was much to be done and little beyond human hands to do it. By the time I reached the kitchen, I must have stank, from my own sweat and from the urine, but I had no opportunity to clean up. The officer swung open the door to reveal the cook on duty, a young woman, maybe twenty at most, alone, except for giant pots and mounds of potatoes. Holding me by the collar, the officer deposited me with the cook and told her to give me an ax and have me chop wood until it was time to line up for the morning instruction. As he spoke, his voice booming, the cook's eyes looked up and met mine. There was a flash of recognition before she quickly looked away. The officer was growing impatient, waiting for her to acknowledge his order. I tried to keep my body still, so my arms would not shake and somehow give away my unease. The cook's eyes opened wide, but she said yes in a cool, clear voice. Satisfied that his orders would be carried out, the officer quickly retreated, back to his own bed and sleep.

Left alone, she and I stood in a kind of awkward silence, each uncertain what we should do. The officer had instructed her to give me an ax to chop the wood, and she hunted around to find one. But once the ax was produced, she put her fingers to her lips, and then she quickly darted out to find one of the camp's laborers. She announced to him that the kitchen had run out of wood. She said she didn't want any trouble for the person who had failed to notice the dwindling supply, and after offering him some extra food, she told him to chop wood and to be quiet about it. She handed him the ax, and he began to chop.

I felt almost paralyzed, but she appeared completely unconcerned about what she had done, and gradually, when I realized that no one was coming to check, when time had passed without any knock at the door, I also began to relax. I leaned against a barrel, and we began to talk, for she and I were friends. The cook was friendly with a few recruits. She was young and a bit flirtatious, and we recruits were young and frequently consumed with thoughts of girls. A number of us, including me, had spent time hanging around near the kitchen to talk to her. But she had often chosen to talk especially to me. Now, I was sitting in the warm steamy kitchen, and she was busily fixing me a meal. The food was wonderful, and, as I ate, we joked and talked, just light conversation, bits of gossip, funny stories, anything to forget about this place. I helped her chop some potatoes, but mostly I sat, not quite believing all that had happened since night had fallen.

When at last it was time for me to leave the kitchen, the cook handed me a salami to take with me. I thanked her and tucked it inside my coat. When I entered the barracks, the assembled soldiers stared at me as if they were look-ing at a ghost. They could not believe I had returned. They expected to find me shot or incarcerated or laboring for days, not simply for an evening. My friends in the barracks crowded around me, eager for details. But their shock over my return was almost erased by their shock when I produced the salami and a knife from my jacket. Quietly, as they clustered around me, I hurriedly cut the salami into big chunks and divided it among my friends. We crammed the seasoned meat into our mouths before heading off to class.

Despite my success, for days, I was afraid that the truth would be discov-ered and that this time my true punishment would be enforced, or something even worse. A week passed, and there was no reaction, no sudden summons. Class, training, everything continued as before, until one snowy morning. On that day, a student arrived at class cradling a large, tightly packed ball of snow. He slipped into his seat, waited a few minutes, and then aimed the snow at another student, drew back his arm, and threw. The instant that the recipi-ent leapt from his seat to take revenge, the instructor arrived. He bristled at the puddle of water on the floor, and, his face growing red with rage, he turned to the student who had thrown the snow and shouted, "If you are going to act like that, I'm going to send you to chop wood for the kitchen all night, just like Schweitzer."

A ripple of laughter rolled through the room, and the soldier, who knew all about my night in the kitchen, replied, "I hope you're going to send me there, such things should only happen to me."

14

Under Fire
at the Front

My first truck was a Soviet-built Zyss One, a lumbering truck whose gears stuck regularly and tail pipe spewed bitter, black smoke. I had heard stories of these trucks and their constant problems with engines, fuel, and fuel supplies. The trucks would suddenly die along the roadway, their gasoline tanks empty, and the drivers would wait, weapons drawn, for the next passing vehicle. At gun point, they would force other drivers to siphon fuel from their tanks. Then at last, the Zyss, its motor sputtering and finally catching, would roar off. Or sometimes it was just the cold and the unrelenting harshness of the Russian terrain that got the trucks. Not every driver was lucky enough to have his truck disabled in friendly territory, and when the engines died among the enemy, the drivers often did too.

I had barely learned the feel of the Zyss at the school, the bouncing, jostling, bruising motion of the wheels rotating over rough, pitted roads, the groaning lurch as the truck fought an incline, and the almost unstoppable speed it gathered racing downhill, when I was shipped out to join a Polish army unit in Russia, right at the edge of the Ukraine.

I arrived and was assigned to a combat supply crew. Our responsibility was to ferry general supplies and usually ammunition from stockpiles in the rear to the front lines. It was a slow process. Many times the truck would simply stop in the middle of the road. Each time the engine died, my frustration grew. It was winter, and the frigid air made every moment until the engine revived torture. I quickly learned that the truck did not respond to curses or even kicking, and I found myself searching my mind for what I had learned in the school, trying to remember everything that I had been taught to do when a truck stops.

The first thing to check was the fuel line, to see if the gas could flow through to the engine. Sometimes the lines would be clogged or twisted. Next, I had to check if the battery was working. I would see if the signal lights still flashed, one by one testing all the cables to find out if any had come loose. Sometimes, it was a quick, easy repair. Sometimes, but not always.

During my first few weeks with the unit, the troops were moving through a rather deserted area somewhere in Russia or perhaps eastern Ukraine. For days, I had been transporting supplies from the rear to the front, driving back and forth along a stretch of empty territory, no houses, no farms, a place other trucks very seldom passed. It was bitter cold, well below zero, and windy, and suddenly the truck's engine began to lose power. I pushed the accelerator to the ground. No response. I could feel the truck straining. The engine sounded worse. It sputtered and then died. I was completely alone. Only the snow stirred around me.

I got out of the truck and propped open the hood. Fuel lines were clear. The battery still worked. I pulled up my collar and tried to make a mask for my face with some cloth. Every time I breathed, the air turned to ice immediately and settled back on my face, stinging my skin. My hands were beginning to lose feeling. My toes, even in boots, were burning in that painful release of heat before going numb. It was then that I found the problem, the filter. The Zyss had an old-style gas filter with a glass cover. The glass cover screwed in over the filter and had to be removed before the filter could be cleaned. But somehow, in the cold, even with the heat of the engine, ice had formed around the glass, blocking the fuel. I had no way to fix the problem. I did not know how to dissolve the ice, but more than that, I did not even have the tools to unscrew the glass cover. I was stuck. It was so cold, and I knew I could not survive for long. My only hope was that another truck would pass by today.

I jumped up and down, trying to stay warm. But I needed a steady source of heat. Then it came to me. Inside the truck was a pail and a small hose, used to siphon gas from tanks of other vehicles when my own tank had run dry. I placed one end of the hose in the gasoline tank and sucked on the other end, just enough to start the flow into the pail. I drained some fuel, and those gallons kept me alive because I used them to make a fire. Several times, the wind blew out the flame, but I hovered over it, protecting it, praying for the rumble of an engine to reach my ears. I waited for several hours, and at last a truck came. The driver knew exactly how to deice the glass cover and fix the filter. He finished in minutes, and I was on the road once again.

Luckily, those lone, isolated stretches, while potentially dangerous, were also becoming increasingly rare as the armies prepared for spring offensives, set to begin long before the actual start of spring. In truth, even though it was winter, the war had not actually ever halted, and in some areas it had barely even slowed. Each morning, we dug the trucks out from under a new snowfall, scraped off the layer of ice that had formed on the windshield, and started the motor to warm the frozen engine so that we could move. Almost no matter what the weather, we were ordered to press on. So each morning, the massive wheels of the trucks compressed yet another layer of freshly fallen snow, and we headed out. It was cold, but not as brutally cold as the previous winter, and the Soviet generals had decided not to draw a winter line and wait. As the battles heated up, I was plunged into the action, where there was no time to think, barely time to react.

In the supply battalions, we almost always worked in convoys, sometimes as few as three, sometimes as many as fifteen. It was a constant race, back and forth, to the heated points of combat. There were only two primary rules: we must deliver our cargo to the line, and, even if we came under direct fire, we must never, under any circumstances, abandon our trucks. If you fled, you fled with your truck.

It was more fear than I had ever known, life always on the edge of destruction. Every moment brought the promise of danger, of a German unit emerging from the woods, a bombing raid, a mine. Inside our trucks, we were not like the men on the front lines, packed together, close enough to hear orders being shouted, to be excoriated to advance, to watch and listen as men crumpled and died. Inside our trucks, we were isolated, never knowing at what moment and from which direction the gunfire would come, falling in a fast, ferocious hail on us. We never knew who would emerge from the woods as we passed. It was an uncertainty different from what soldiers on the front lines clutching their guns faced, but it was a constant, following us, pursuing us at every moment. While the men on the front lines dug in, we drove, our hearts in our mouths and our hands fastened to the wheel.

Even outside of the fiercest combat areas, there was constant confusion. The battle lines changed in a matter of seconds, leaving troops on both sides stranded. The roads were often devoid of signs, landmarks were in ruins, in flames, or completely razed from the landscape. We would head out toward one particular battalion, only to discover another one in its place or nothing at all. Then we would have to return to the field command and begin the journey all over again. Sometimes, en route, the convoy would become lost, and the lumbering trucks would circle around and backtrack, not knowing into whose territory we had strayed. Sometimes, we would drive in and out of the combat areas three times a day, hauling ammunition. Sometimes, it was only once or not at all.

One morning when I was leading two other trucks through a wooded area to the troops, we sped along the road to skirt the action. We had already driven down this very same road earlier in the day and also the day before. Outside the window of the cab, branches bobbed and weaved as the trees rushed past. Ahead of us rose a hill, which meant downshifting and climbing at a slow, lumbering pace. I had a desperate urge to smoke. It was our one great pleasure, the long, slow draw of tobacco into us. Usually, cigarettes were scarce, but they were far easier to come by in the army, which had its own supply, than they were elsewhere in the Soviet Union. Still, even in the army men would do almost anything for cigarettes, even the cheapest ones, half crushed and so bitter they made you spit.

Out of my pocket, I drew a cigarette and a match. I held the cigarette gently between my teeth and, taking one hand from the wheel, tried to light the match. It was a weak match, with only a thin coat, but I knew how to scrape it, firmly, without snapping the stick. There was a quick hiss and the smell of sulfur, but before I could bring the flame to the tobacco, it blew out, leaving nothing but a wisp of smoke. I tried to light a second match and then a third. It was foolish, I could not afford to waste matches.

I decided to pull over. It would take me only seconds to light the match out of the wind. Then, the ammunition and I would be back on the road. I stopped the truck and waved to the other two drivers in the convoy as they passed me, a wave that let them know I was all right. The drivers waved back. The two trucks sped past as I lit the match, ignited the tobacco, drew a long deep breath, and then headed back on to the road. It took less than a minute, but already the trucks were ahead of me. I was in the rear instead of in the lead, and I had to rush to catch up.

My foot was pushing down on the gas peddle at the very moment when I heard it, a sharp noise and then a deafening boom that rocked the earth beneath. Ahead of me, a little over a thousand feet away, were the two trucks, stopped in their tracks, engulfed in flames. The ammunition they carried was like kindling feeding the fire, until nothing but a gutted shell remained.

I hit the brake and wrenched the wheel to turn my truck around. I pushed the gas peddle down until it hovered just above the floor. The engine raced, and the truck seemed to shoot forward beneath me. I was breathing like a sprinter, my feet pushing into the floorboards as if that would somehow make the truck move faster. Behind me now were German gunners poised on a hill. I did not know if they could reach me. I did not know if others were waiting in the woods along the road. Every instant I expected an explosion, I expected to become engulfed in fire and flames. Only when I saw the first outlines of my unit, did my grip on the wheel relax ever so slightly. I drove straight to the officers. Shaking, I told them what had happened. The words came out in a jumble, and even though I tried to hold my arms steady, tremors shook my fingers as I pointed.

There had been almost no time to think, and only now did the full enormity of the morning hit me. But for a cigarette, but for a wind that kept extinguishing a match, I would have been the lead truck, barreling down the road, straight into the sights of the Germans. I would have been among the dead drivers.

Messages were relayed, and by the next morning, a full-fledged battle was underway for control of that hill. And I was again heading down that same wooded road, this time along with nineteen other trucks, carrying ammunition to the front, which had suddenly moved much closer.

As a driver, you weren't just a driver, you were a lookout, a guard, and a mechanic. To survive, you had to learn all the problems that could affect a truck and how to fix them. In some ways it was easy, and there was ample opportunity to learn. I picked up the specifics of engine repair quickly. Only a matter of weeks after I had first been stranded, I was repairing trucks, not just my own but those of other drivers, which made me popular in the unit. It was a good life, or as good as I imagined life could be in the army during a war. Then for about one month, my life changed beyond my wildest dreams. I was transferred from my supply unit with the Polish army to a Russian division, and there I was assigned to be the personal driver for a Soviet general. Each day, I took him wherever he wanted to go, in his jeep.

It was like stepping into a life of luxury. There were no more breakdowns on deserted roads, no more scraping ice and snow and mud off the truck. Now I had a sleek jeep to tend to, one that moved quickly up hill, that seemed to glide along the road. It was a pleasure to care for that automobile. And as the general's driver, I had special opportunities. The general was constantly sending me to pick up supplies for him at the PX. I got things for him and things for myself. He told me I could take whatever I wanted. Here there were cans of food, bottles of liquor, and cartons of cigarettes, things regular soldiers craved and dreamed about. As I ran my fingers over the neatly rolled tobacco, I recalled how, only a year ago, night after night in Siberia, I had pried up the floorboards to pick up discarded cigarette butts.

As quickly and as randomly as it began, my career as a personal driver was over. The general was transferred to another military region. The new officer had his own driver, and so I was sent back to my old Polish supply unit. And, as I had already learned from the days when I drove the general up to the front lines, a new offensive against the Germans had begun.

The army moved forward like a great plodding machine. Troops in the front advanced because there was nowhere else to go. Falling back meant facing the officers and commissars in the rear, men who did not hesitate to turn their pistols on anyone caught retreating. There was no choice except to go forward, but Germans turned the thick forests and hills to their advantage, hiding their forces in the natural cover. Some days, both the roads and the woods ran red. At first, I was shocked by the sight of bodies along the road, headless, limbless bodies, bodies soaked with their own blood. Waves of nausea would sweep over me, and I would quickly turn my eyes. But no one could allow himself to become disabled by the carnage. To do so, one risked becoming part of it.

I stopped thinking about much of anything except surviving, for it seemed that every operation lost not just soldiers but also drivers and trucks. There were no clearly marked lines and sides. Some days it seemed we were passing through a collection of small, violent skirmishes, which only collectively became a full battle. These days were the most dangerous, partly because the shooting was random and partly because German forces could be lying in wait between Soviet forces. Stretches of open fields were the worst because they offered no cover. In the woods, while it was easy for the enemy to hide, it was also difficult for them to see you coming from far off. They could not easily train their sights and follow you, the reaction had to be instantaneous, and, in a second, it was possible for anything to go wrong.

I had arrived in one small, nondescript town, the kind soldiers passed through or stopped over in every few miles, towns that were merely clusters of houses emerging from fields or woods. I was part of a convoy of about fifteen trucks, arriving on the heels of a large battle. The trucks and their drivers were gathered, awaiting orders from the field command. We were standing around, smoking, when someone saw them, German soldiers, several thousand feet away, advancing through the woods. We had been told that the battle area had moved, but the lines changed so often that the information could easily be wrong. All we could see were the uniforms of the Third Reich, moving swiftly through the shadows of the trees. We did not know how many men were there, but several units could easily be concealed amidst the thick, dark trees. We did not know their strength, but neither did they know ours. An officer ordered a driver to take his truck and head for the main highway, where he could flag down Soviet tanks. The rest of us waited, wondering how long before the Germans caught sight of us.

It seemed like an eternity before the driver returned, and with him came two tanks. Almost as soon as they came into view, the tanks began firing into the woods, barrage after barrage of shells. They ripped through the air, letting off clouds of smoke and bright flashes when they hit. We listened for the thunderous return, for the deadly rain of German shells and bullets to sweep down on us. But there was nothing. The tanks ceased firing. Perhaps it was a trick, a ruse to cause us halt, so that the Germans could move their artillery into position. We stood with our trucks, breathless, still awaiting orders, with no idea where we might run to safety.

At that moment there was a flutter of white through the trees, and cautiously, tentatively, some fifty German soldiers, ragged and scruffy, emerged from the forest, their hands raised above their heads in surrender. One man waved a piece of torn white material. In the heat of battle, the soldiers had been left behind on the Russian side, and they were wandering through the woods, searching for their unit. They surrendered to fifteen truck drivers and two tanks. Had they walked our way only fifteen minutes earlier, however, they might well have taken us.

This type of confusion was constant. Survival was more an act of chance or luck than of planning. An order that sent you east instead of west might mean death. An accidental wrong turn might save your life. War was random, and all the more terrible for its randomness.

In addition to supplies, I sometimes ferried officers to the front lines in my cab. They said little, and I said little. There was nothing pleasant about the trip. I was always on edge, not knowing what they might do if I made a mistake or somehow violated a regulation. One morning, I was carrying two officers with me. We rounded a bend, and suddenly the sound of gunfire pierced the air. Bullets and shells seemed to be flying from all over, falling like a great metallic rain on us. I heard them denting the side of the truck, but I could not see the Germans who were firing them. The enemy was hidden, but where? A shell exploded on the road, cutting a crater into the dirt and rocking the cab with its impact. I wondered if I should turn back or, if immediately behind the bend, we would be cut off. Ahead, no one was yet in the road. Behind me lay the unknown.

The officers looked panicked. We were easy targets, like sitting ducks inside the cab, and they knew it. Rather than turn around or push forward, they had other plans. They told me to slow down. As the engine slowed, the sounds of gunfire crackling in the air grew more deafening. The officers, in their gray-green coats and squared-off hats, opened the door and jumped to the ground, as the truck continued to roll slowly. They shouted at me, reminding me that I was under orders to stay with the truck. They landed on the ground, slightly unsteady, but after a few seconds regained their balance and, pistols drawn, started to run toward the woods to hide themselves in the thick bushes that ringed the forest.

For an instant, more than anything I wanted to follow them, to be free of the truck, to run for my life. But I could not, except with the truck. I knew the officers could shoot me on the spot if I abandoned my truck. Or, even if I survived, they could shoot me later if I was found without the truck. I pushed the gas peddle, trying to regain some momentum, and I watched the officers through the mirror as they ran, heading back along the edge of the road. Then, suddenly, first one and next the other fell, shot by the Germans. They had only gone a few hundred feet back toward the woods. I escaped with my life, inside the truck.

Being in the army meant always being prepared. We often slept in our clothes, ready to be awoken and moving within a minute if the order came. Sometimes, at night, the officers themselves would instruct us not to get undressed, leaving us to sleep the fitful sleep of men waiting for the grating pulse of gunfire or the thunderous explosion of artillery.

Many of the men in the battalion, indeed in this Polish army, were in their thirties and forties and used to war. They had been soldiers in the Polish national army who were captured in 1939 by advancing Soviet forces and sent to Soviet jails. They were released only to join this new Polish army. The other soldiers were mostly Jews, not all of them Polish, who had joined as a way to fight the Germans and also as a way to leave Russia and return to their homes. Whether these Jews were Poles or Czechs or some other nationality, nearly all had fled to the Soviet Union to escape Hitler. In our battalion, the Poles stuck together and the Jews stuck together, with a few exceptions. The drivers, Jews and Poles, had shared routines of field ration meals, truck cleanings, and jokes—mostly told in Polish but sometimes in Yiddish or Russian. We pined after women and after better-fitting clothes. And sometimes, along with other men in the battalion, we went bathing.

Even in the bitter cold, many of the younger men would wash when we came to a creek. It became a ritual, something that reminded us that we were still alive. As a group, we would race, fully clothed, down to the bone-chilling water. Only at the water's edge would we pull off our coats and slip out of our shirts, still leaving them tucked in, hanging down out of our waistbands. Barechested, we leaned over the creek and doused ourselves with the water. Some men even waded partway into the water, which might carry chunks of ice that had broken off from larger flows. Then, just at the cold seemed about to siphon all feeling from our limbs, leaving them completely numb, we would leap from the water and start running in the frigid air, across a field or snaking through the trees in an adjoining wood. Each man's skin tingled as the cold air swept against his damp skin. We could feel the hot red blood rush through our limbs as we ran. Clouds of steam rose from our bodies as we moved. We ran single file, and, in motion, we looked like a train, releasing one long column of heat into the atmosphere. We would keep moving for about a mile, until our skin grew warm and we could laugh at the cold. It was as if when we bathed, we washed and burned off all our fear, and all the feeling numbed by war, for a few glorious minutes, returned.

In the winter months, the army generally commandeered houses in small towns, and that was where we stayed. Families were moved in with other families, and we took over, sleeping in their beds and on their floors. In the Russian sections, there was little resistance. But not so as we moved farther into the Ukraine. Many Ukrainians had collaborated with the Germans, welcoming them into their land, joining with them against the Russians. Now, it was the Russians' turn, and they reaped revenge. They shot to kill, they raped, they raided and destroyed. In one small town, I watched a wounded Russian soldier, hobbling on crude crutches, beat a Ukrainian to death for being a collaborator with the Nazis. The Russian grasped one crutch and, leaning entirely on the other, delivered blow after blow, as the Ukrainian lay writhing and screaming on the ground. Again and again, I heard wood smash against bone, a whack followed by a dull thud.

Some of our own men also died like this. Some died on mined roads. Others died fixing bridges under fire. One thing was certain, the carnage was continuous. We moved forward at the cost of rolling over our own.

Many of our most vicious encounters took place at bridges, or rather the remains of bridges, which had been destroyed by the Germans to prevent our forces from advancing. In one spot, a battle was raging along the banks of a small river. Russian and Polish soldiers were ordered to build a temporary bridge out of barrels so that we could cross with our supply trucks to reach other troops that had already broken through farther downstream. The barrels had to be lashed together with chains and wires, and then steel plates were run across the tops, so that tanks and trucks could roll across the water. Wave after wave of soldiers worked building that bridge, and wave after wave fell, their dead and wounded bodies carried away by the water. It became very abstract, man after man moving from the shoreline into the water, laying a foot or so more of bridge, and then dying, or dying before he ever had a chance to reach the edge. We lost many men this way. Sometimes, the Germans were still shelling the bridge as the first trucks moved across, and we would feel the sudden awful tremors as shells exploded around us. Sometimes, we drove right past bodies of men who had been alive only an hour ago.

15

A Long, Narrow Mound

By summer of 1944, the tempo of the war had changed. On June 23, three years and two days after the Germans had launched their all-out assault on the Soviet Union, the Soviet army began an offensive to drive the Germans back across the border, back into Poland, back as far as they could be pushed. It was hot and humid. Clouds of mosquitoes rose from the soggy wet land. Tires sunk and stuck in the mud. Sweat beaded on our brows and ran like small rivers down our backs. This was completely unlike the bitter cold that sharpened your senses and made you push forward simply because motion would make you warm. This was a heat that drained your strength, that exhausted you before the battles began, that filled your lungs with thick, damp air. The cold of winter was horrible, but so was the heat, in its own way.

The offensive was in full swing, and we were driving forward, into the area I had fled some three years ago. It was odd to see recognizable terrain, to hear familiar names of villages, even if they were still off in the distance. But even odder was the fact that I had become an officer. I had been promoted not long after my return to the unit and made an officer in the supply company. Not a high ranking officer at all, but an officer nonetheless, and I was placed in charge of overseeing twenty trucks.

Whatever needed to be moved, we were the ones to move it. We carried ammunition, gas for tanks and trucks, foodstuffs, even army field kitchens to keep up with the troops. Food was a constant problem. Sometimes, during a battle, we took foodstuffs from towns or remnants of towns as we passed, searching barns, cellars, storehouses, fields, wherever we could think to look. While it had been worse in the heart of the winter, when there was nothing in the fields except snow and we had only some canned goods, even now the rations, along with whatever we could find in towns and fields, were barely enough. Also, the Germans had been there first, and as they pulled back mile by mile, they took any supplies with them. Or they burned what was left behind, a tactic the Soviets had used in 1941 in the hopes of slowing the German advance. Now Soviet troops were returning, looking for sustenance in a land that had known nothing but war and occupation for nearly three years.

The Germans were faltering, though to us, as the summer began, they seemed far from collapse. The goal was to force them back across strategic rivers. They had already abandoned their positions along the Dnepr River, and now, farther west in the Ukraine, the Pripet River posts were also falling. The next major river in the region was the Bug. A forced crossing would further cut communication and supply lines and limit their natural defenses. Cornered, the German troops fought using not just all-out attacks but also skillful small assaults, meant to harass or disable us. On the ground, it seemed like an endless flurry of gunfire, which produced constant fear and constant loss. Mostly, we were powerless to stop it. It was more unpredictable than the fierce cold in Siberia, which usually took the sick or the weak. Here, the end could come for you anytime, any morning on any day could be your last. Again and again, some of us escaped with our lives while others did not.

We tried not to think about these things. But stuffed in our pockets, pressing through the cloth into our flesh, were documents, sometimes even letters and names, which we carried so that others could identify us afterward. As we cleaned our trucks or ate our food, sometimes we talked about what we would do once the war was over, but it was usually in general terms. We did not talk too much about our lives or homes. There was no point. It was not good to get too close, and it was never good to know too much, although it was unavoidable. We did become close, and then one by one we were ripped away. We tinkered with the trucks to keep them in running order, sometimes making repairs with rags and string. When there was a lull in the action, we waited for things to start up again. When there was action, we hoped for the next lull, and we hoped it would come quickly.

I struggled to keep the trucks running and the officers happy, to move the supplies on time. Our battalion had been given a fleet of GMC (General Motors Corporation) trucks from the Americans, which were far more reliable and easy to care for than the Zyss. But still there were always problems, missed communications, broken-down vehicles, lost battalions, every conceivable type of delay. We had just finished a long stretch of ammunition supply runs when the order came to move a field kitchen and bakery that were now back some ten miles from the troop lines. Eight trucks were sent, and accompanying us in my cab was a Polish officer. We followed a main road, worn with tank and truck treads, pitted and scarred from shelling. Gullies had formed around the small craters left from grenade and shell explosions.

A single-lane road led off to one side, and along it I noticed little garden areas. Several nice wooden houses, with weathered trim painted in fanciful designs, were clustered together. Gates stood in front of the yards, gates leading to driveways and what looked like garages. Then it struck me that these houses and garden areas were still relatively intact, not a looted, smoldering wreck sitting just off the main road. It seemed to be a good sign. The area had likely been bypassed. The houses rested in a wooded area that had never been cleared, and threading along the edge of the woods was an empty field, presumably used as a pasture for animals or even for crops, at least in peacetime. The kitchen was in that field.

Suddenly, gunfire. By now, I knew the sound all too well. Up ahead, the lead trucks had already taken the brunt of the blow and were shooting up in flames. A gasoline tank exploded, like a bomb detonating, sending up a plume of fire and smoke. I could think of nothing but getting off that main road, for, as long as I was on the road, I could not risk taking the time to turn around. Overturned trucks blocked the road in front. Around us, everything was in confusion. There was the sound of shelling and a thick black smoke. Then I remembered the houses. I turned and headed down the small, single-lane road.

I needed space to turn the truck around. Almost without thinking, I backed into a gate, splintering it apart. I gunned the engine and the tires rolled over the wooden boards and up into the driveway. But that had given me the room I needed, and I turned the truck around. Then I looked out of my window. I could see Germans with machine guns, their gray coats and helmets visible in the daylight, running toward us through the woods. Their eyes were obscured, but the ends of their noses and their chins protruded from under their helmets. They were firing their rifles and racing for the exit back to the main road, racing to cut us off. They had taken over the kitchen area and were waiting to ambush us. As I backed up the truck, I suddenly thought that more Germans could be in the sweet, innocuous-looking wooden houses behind us. I shifted gears. It seemed to take forever until the mechanical levers changed over and dropped and clicked into place. The soldiers were rapidly advancing through the woods. They were racing to be in close range, to cut us off, perhaps to capture the truck. Otherwise, they could have simply aimed a shell at the gasoline tank and been done with it.

I was racing these soldiers, not knowing if they had already cut off the road going back. My hands and feet were shaking. This was about as close as I had ever come to so many of the enemy, close enough to glimpse outlines of faces, beards, and skin. My foot was trembling, hitting the gas peddle with a jerky motion, up-down, up-down, up-down. I was afraid of over-gassing the truck and flooding the engine, but I wanted to go fast, to go very fast. Slowly, in what seemed an eternity, the truck began to build speed. We reached the main roadway only seconds before the Germans, and we turned, the sound of gunfire echoing behind us. When we were out of direct range of German fire, with only the sounds of shells echoing in our ears, the officer next to me threw his arms around me, hugging and kissing me. For today, at least, we had escaped death.

As the gunfire grew fainter and then subsided, I looked up and down the road. Only then did I realize that out of the eight trucks sent to collect the kitchen, just my truck and one other had survived. Everyone else had been burned alive.

The army was making progress. We were coming through the northern reaches of the Ukraine, through places that had been occupied by the Germans for nearly three years. Now the Germans were retreating, in some cases simply fleeing, leaving behind ammunition and supplies. We were chasing them as they had once chased us. It was like a second great blitzkrieg, only rolling west. And with it came the inevitable destruction. Roads were pockmarked with craters, giant gaping holes that could take out a wheel or an axle. Convoys rolled past scorched fields and burned-out houses, some little more than embers. We watched other houses, caught directly in the battle, erupt before our eyes into bright, hot flames. Animals, the few that remained, howled as their barns ignited. When the wind blew, soot and smoke wafted over us, blackening our skin.

It was in the villages, however, where we began to see our first glimpses of full-scale destruction. Town by town, we uncovered the devastation wrought by the Germans. Its signs were everywhere. We saw the remnants of ghettos, invariably the worst buildings on the narrowest, most dilapidated streets, where Jews were forced together to live like animals in overcrowded sties, while local families and soldiers confiscated their homes and possessions. Now, the rooms were empty and silent, looted of all but the most meager reminders that people had lived there. Sometimes, we might find a broken dish, a dirty rag, a child's ribbon. But there were more than just the remains of violence, there were also the stories, awful, unbelievable stories.

Away from the eerie stillness of the ghetto, residents would point out the places where the Germans exacted public revenge. We heard stories of atrocities, of how, for the death of one German soldier, one hundred people would be forced, in the middle of winter when the temperature was well below zero, to undress, stand stark naked, and be sprayed with water, which would quickly turn to ice on their skin. They died as human icicles. And if they didn't die fast enough, the Germans opened fire on them with machine guns. Or sometimes, the Germans simply lined up the people in the square and machine-gunned them, row by row by row. We listened and we heard, but despite everything, it was hard to believe, hard to picture, hard fully to imagine.

What was far less forthcoming were stories telling how many of the people who died were Jews, how often they were the ones on whom the Germans exacted their revenge. And few people now spoke of the mass graves outside some towns where Jews had been machine-gunned to death or the winding train lines that passed from town to town where those who escaped the initial mass killings had been herded into sealed wooden cars and carried to concentration and extermination camps like cattle to the slaughter.

It also soon became clear that a wrath and fury had been unleashed that was not satisfied with the destruction of the Jews. Roving bands of Poles and Ukrainians, who had once rounded up their Jewish neighbors, now, in the final months of the war, had turned on each other with a vengeance. Several times, we entered small Polish cottages in Ukrainian territory to find their owners nailed to the wall, spikes through their wrists and feet, throats cut in the most brutal kind of savagery. Often these dead Poles had married Ukrainian women. The Ukrainians, believing that the Poles were polluting their people, had sought revenge and quite literally crucified their neighbors. We only saw the eerie, silent aftermath, when the body barely seemed like a body and the thick red blood was dry, brown, and crusty, but even then it turned my stomach. The horror of opening a quiet door on a quiet plot of land and finding such violence cannot be described.

Then, too, our soldiers brought their own type of destruction. They raided homes for whatever they could find, and they tore through bedding with knives in search of hidden food or booty. They scoured barns. They raped young girls and women. They continued a pattern of plunder that had begun in the Crimea with the German retreat and that would intensify as they pursued the enemy across Soviet soil and back into Poland.

As we drew nearer to Poland, my unit cut a wide swath some ten miles above Olyka, the town where I had left my brothers and sisters three years, what seemed like several lifetimes ago. I had already seen so much devastation, but I could not help holding out hope. Surely, not every town could be the same, I told myself. Surely, some places escaped. One thing was certain, I could not pass so near and not go.

I knew I did not have much time as I approached one of the senior officers in the company, not quite certain what I would say, dreading in my heart that he would say no. In a jumbled confusion of words, I told him the story of my brothers and sisters fleeing first to Brest-Litovsk and then to Olyka. I told him how I had gone to invite them to my wedding as the Germans attacked and how I had left, running through the night. He looked at me and listened. I did not know whether I had made any sense. I did not know what he would say. He looked at me again and pointed to a jeep. I could borrow the jeep to go to Olyka, but I had only a couple of hours at most because the company was on the move. Even as it was, I would have to race to catch up with them again. If I found my family, he would try to help me arrange a leave later. He did not mention any other possibilities, but they hung there, in every unspoken word.

I grabbed a map from my truck, got in the jeep, and began to follow the signs, signs for larger towns nearby, for junctions, for rail lines. I drove at breakneck speed, the jeep practically riding on two wheels around corners and bends. Passing by me was ravaged countryside, fields that had not been planted, forests charred from bombing runs, bombed-out roadways scarred with tank treads. Even where a crop had been planted or a cluster of houses, with brightly painted shutters and gray concrete walls, looked out on the road, it could not dispel the exhaustion and waste that had settled over the landscape. The longer I drove, the more I preferred to concentrate on the road, letting whatever stood alongside pass by in a series of incoherent blurs. Also, thinking about what was immediately in front of me prevented me from thinking too much about all that lay ahead of me.

I did not recognize the roads around Olyka, but I remembered everything about Olyka itself. It was as if I had carried an image of the town, frozen in my mind, for just that moment when I would need to find my way through it. Instead of being lost, I knew exactly where to go.

Before the war, Olyka was a quiet place, with tidy streets lined with single-family homes. Flowers grew in front of the houses, in the back, people raised vegetables and even fruit trees. A beautiful square stood in the center of the town, a place for people to gather, and a place where every Wednesday farmers from the lush surrounding countryside would come to the *targowy*, a Polish word for farmers' market, to sell cattle, goats, chickens, crops, whatever they raised and grew. Then the farmers would buy supplies from the local merchants. They would leave with shoes, material, nails, pots and pans, whatever they needed. And every three months, a huge market, called a *jarmark*, was held. Hundreds of farmers would come with livestock and crops and baskets of rich ripe fruits and grains, even sweet-water fish. Everything smelled fresh, and the abundance was overpowering. That was the Olyka I remembered, that was the Olyka where I had visited my brothers and sisters. It was the only Olyka I knew.

Now, the streets were still there, but many of the homes along them had been destroyed. I saw giant holes torn in roofs and houses, which were little more than piles of rubble. Sometimes, the owners had tried to shore up a sagging wall or patch a hole, even using stacks of hay or bundles of tree branches to keep out the elements so that they could go on living there. Many of the town buildings were far less lucky. They had been burned by the Germans. Where churches, a synagogue, even what I think had been a town hall or a museum had once stood, there were now little more than scorched remains. There were almost no flowers, grass grew in thick knotty tufts, and the sounds of wagons, of joy in the streets, were nowhere to be found.

I drove straight to the house of a Polish woman, a friend of my sister Esther, who also knew Ytzel, Srulke, and Genia. Why I expected her to be there now, after all the fighting, I do not know. But she was there, in her house, sewing or washing or some such thing. When she came to the door, and I introduced myself, in my army uniform, she was speechless. She just stood there, sucking in air. She looked at me as if she were looking at a ghost.

Several long seconds passed, and then she invited me in. I told her I had come to look for my brothers and sisters, and I asked her what had happened to them. Until that moment, I still held out hope. There had always been a chance. After all, I had escaped.

"When the Germans came, it was very hard," she said. And then I knew, I knew but I did not want to believe. I had heard so many stories, stories of horrible things, but I had not been able to bring myself to believe all of them. Now I could not escape them. Now they were no longer stories, now they were my family.

The Polish woman told me how in the early days, right after the Germans reached Olyka, they had rounded up a large group of Jews and had taken them to a field outside of the town. And there, in that field, at the edge of a ditch, they had divided the Jews into lines and shot them, firing each volley on a fresh line. And all the while the Germans were firing, the people in the town could hear the gunfire echoing from far away. The Polish woman stopped speaking. I asked her, "What about my sisters Genia and Esther, what about my brothers Ytzel and Srulke? Tell me." I was pleading.

"Those three, Genia, Esther, and Ytzel were among those Jews taken by the Germans to that field," the woman said.

Genia too, Genia who had fled from Lvov thinking she would be safe in the countryside.

"But Srulke, what about Srulke?" My voice was shaking.

She went on. She told me that the remaining Jews were herded into a ghetto in the town. The woman said she knew my brother Srulke was among those who remained. The woman paused again. Srulke had escaped from the ghetto one night. He had been hiding in the area, perhaps in barns or in fields. But he did not get far or stay hidden long. Some Polish people brought him back to the Germans. It was not just these people or Srulke, the woman explained. The Germans paid a reward to anyone who brought an escaped Jew back to the Germans. When the ghetto was liquidated, Srulke was shipped out along with all the others, on trains, in windowless wooden boxcars. The Nazis had said they were taking the Jews to be workers, but no one who was taken had ever returned.

I had ridden on those very same train tracks when I arrived in Olyka. I thought of Srulke going off alone, and my eyes filled with tears. I knew there were camps where the Germans took the Jews, camps where terrible things happened, things worse than anyone could imagine. Maybe even still, perhaps Srulke had survived, I thought. I could not bear to think otherwise. The Polish woman did not know, there were many rumors, but few facts, very little that anyone could be certain was true. She offered to show me the grave of my sisters and my other brother.

It was not a grave with stones to mark each individual resting place, rather it was just a roll in the field, a long narrow mound that took the form of the ditch below. Someone had arranged a few loose stones to indicate the spot, but there was nothing to recall anyone who lay there. I stood over the burial spot and looked down. Already, grass was growing. I looked around the place and then again at the grave, which held hundred upon hundreds of men, women, and children, from the very old to the very young.

There are no words to describe how I felt. I don't know if anyone can ever describe such a feeling. Underneath me were my sisters Genia and Esther and my brother Ytzel. In my mind, I saw their faces, but now, all around me there was nothing. Why did I survive if only to come here, if only to have this waiting for me? I wanted to fall to the ground and claw away at the earth. Or to be swallowed up by the soil itself. But instead, I just stood there, under the warm sun, and cried.

The tears came, and they did nothing. It was a misery I had never known. As much as I had heard, despite the many awful stories I had been told as the army pushed west, I had not been able to believe that so many terrible things could really have happened, I had not been able to believe it until I was actually standing there, on the ground where my brother and my sisters lay. All my tears could do nothing for their suffering, all my tears could do nothing at all. I had come back to nothing.

I knew I had to go back to my unit. Already, nearly two hours had passed. I did not want to be separated from my unit, and the longer I waited, the more difficult it would be to find the battalion. I did not necessarily want to go back to the war, but at least in the unit there were people I knew. It was a place for me to be. I did not want to stay in Olyka. I said almost nothing to the Polish woman as I left. I got back into my jeep and began driving. As I passed small towns and houses clustered into villages, I realized that the destruction had not been confined to a few towns, that the atrocities had not happened in only a few places, but that in almost every town something terrible had happened, that terrible things had happened in these woods and in these fields. I felt a deep emptiness reach into me. It was like sinking into blackness, where everything seemed very far away. Over and over, I tried to remember my family, my brothers and sisters as they were. Along a stretch of road, I again broke into tears.

It was late afternoon when I returned to my unit, lumbering along one of the main roads, preparing to make camp. From my expression, I'm sure it was not difficult to figure out what had happened. That evening, I told my friends. More than half of the men in the unit were Jews. They looked at me with anguish, the anguish of others who have left families and friends behind, who also do not know what awaits them when they return. I gave back the jeep and told the officer what I had found. He shook his head slowly as I spoke. He said that it was terrible, that he knew these things happened. There was nothing else to say, no comfort for such a loss, a loss many men knew could become their own. The next morning, once again, we were moving forward.

We were struggling, but now the Germans were collapsing. Unlike the previous winter, when each mile seemed to be gained only by scraping our way across half-frozen land, through woods infested with German soldiers, and roads lying squarely in the sights of enemy artillery, this time the gains were larger, and the miles fell more quickly, if not necessarily more easily. The battles and confrontations fused into one long struggle of gearing and regearing, of hauling supplies in anticipation of action or in response to action. The territory passed by in a blur, as if seen from the window of a high-speed train. Villages became indistinguishable, one region merged into the next. Each day, we woke to the heat of the air and the heat of battle. These things never changed. Otherwise, time rushed past until it was punctured by an incident, something so striking that it would fix itself in the mind and stand apart from the daily tumultuous onslaught of conflict.

It was just a town, somewhere along the border between the Ukraine and Poland. It was a small, ordinary town, and we stopped there only briefly on our way west. Outside of the town were acres upon acres of flat fields and farms, except in one field, where there was a mound, maybe fifty feet in diameter and about two feet high, high enough to notice. Did we suspect something when we first saw it and ask questions? Or did someone from the town, a survivor tell us? I do not remember which came first, only that we were told.

When the Germans had come three summers ago, one of the first things they did here, as in Olyka, was to round up all the Jews in the town. It was not a very big place, so there was a manageable number of Jews. The Germans loaded the Jews on the back of flat carts and trucks and carried them out of town to this spot in this particular field, where a small ditch cut gently into the earth. The Germans ordered the Jews to disrobe, to remove rings, watches, anything of value. The Jews did so, we were told. Then the Germans lined them up along the edge of the ditch, they lined up old men and old women, pointing at their slack bellies and breasts with rifle butts. They lined up mothers carrying children. They lined up young men in their prime and children still in school. They lined them up in neat rows and then positioned gunners at machine guns. The gunners fired into the rows, and the bodies, dead and half-dead tumbled into the ditch. As one row fell, another was ordered to move up. Mothers covered their children's eyes and ears. Men began to pray. The gunners kept firing, round after round, until each row had been decimated. But not everyone had been hit, and not all of those who had been hit were dead. Some had only been wounded when they fell in. Some had been missed entirely, but either the German SS ordered them to jump in the pit or they fell in, out of shock and fear.

It was summer, and there was concern about the spread of disease from so many bodies, so the Germans ordered that the bodies be buried immediately, as they lay in the ditch. But the bodies had completely filled the ditch, so any burial would have to cover them with a small mound of earth. The local residents, mostly Poles, were detailed to do the burying. And as they began to shovel the earth onto the bodies, they could see a few legs and arms moving, hear the muffled sounds of people calling out to one another in pain. They kept filling in the ditch and covering the bodies with shovel after shovel of earth, and still, here and there, arms and legs kept moving. And when the bodies had been covered with dirt, so much dirt that the limbs and heads and hands were no longer visible below, they said, the mound of dirt itself kept moving.

I thought of my brothers and sisters, of the way each of them had moved his legs or her arms. I thought of them still moving.

16

Return to Radzyń

We came across more and more mounds. Some had been dug up by the retreating Nazis to remove all trace of what they had done. The rotting corpses buried below were exhumed and burned in giant fires until nothing remained except bits of dry white bone. A few times, however, we came across fresh mounds, the sites of exterminations carried out in the final moments of retreat.

Some of these mounds, I later learned, covered the bodies of slave laborers, usually Jews, who were forced to carry out the task of obliterating all traces of even more heinous Nazi crimes.

I do not remember exactly when we crossed into Poland. There were so many borders, Soviet and Polish, from before and after the wars. The land looked the same, fields and forests, which would gradually extend into purely flat farmland, running straight out to the horizon. Even now in the midst of war, people in this region, as in the others earlier, had tried to plant the land and cultivate, but seeds were almost impossible to come by, and artillery fire and advancing armies cared little about plowed and seeded fields. For the most part we stayed in the neglected countryside, skirting cities because they were dangerous, often filled with small pockets of Germans, and also because the fighting had left the cities even more devastated and almost nothing of value remained. I remember driving through one spot and seeing signs for Chełm. I thought of the Schweitzers, Kalman and his wife. I thought of my document, which he in death had given to me and which had given me life. My heart felt heavy, but I had also since learned that there were far more grisly ways to die than simply chopping wood in the Siberian cold. I thought of the Schweitzers, and so many memories came flooding back. But we were moving fast, and within a day Chełm was only another place we had left behind. The objective was to press forward, and that was all.

We were moving on a long, broad front, which meant it was easier to ferry supplies forward to the front lines because the supplies themselves were no longer miles back. It also meant that we were closer to the action, that what the troops came upon, we came upon almost immediately afterward. And so it was with the city of Lublin, which fell on July 24. The city fell, and the Germans retreated, lifting their reins from the surrounding countryside. For us, it was a confirmation that we were at last fully inside Poland and that in time, town by town, it would be freed. I think I had as much hope as anyone for victory and peace, even after all I had seen. The Americans and British were pushing from the west, we were winning in the east. But the farther we advanced into Poland, the more the exhilaration of victory was tempered by the discovery of atrocities. Each town, each village had some new story. Until we crossed the border, the incidents had always seemed local rather than part of a larger, more insidious plan to wipe out an entire people. Only inside Poland did we see firsthand the full horrendous scope of what Germany had done, did we understand that Hitler had made good on his promise to "kill the Jews." Only in Poland did we come upon such places as Majdanek.

Majdanek was a Nazi concentration and extermination camp located outside of Lublin, liberated by the Soviet army. It had a sordid, ugly history, some of which I learned during those days, some later. Originally built to house prisoners of war—5,000 Soviet prisoners died of starvation and exposure inside its walls in the fall of 1941—Majdanek became the final destination for more than 130,000 Jews deported from Poland and across western Europe in 1942 and 1943 alone. Sixty-percent of all arrivals, mainly women, children, the sick, and the elderly, were shot or gassed upon arrival. The rest labored in the camp until their time came. In November of 1943, the Germans killed 42,000 Jews interned in Majdanek, 18,000 were machine-gunned in a single day in a nearby woods. The SS called that day, November 3, 1943, the "harvest festival."

By March of 1944, only 612 prisoners remained, and they were forced to exhume the bodies buried in the forest and burn their remains so no proof of the massacre would remain. When Soviet troops arrived to liberate the camp on June 24, only a few hundred people remained alive. The first troops saw them in their rough striped uniforms and emaciated bodies. Soviet photographs recorded them and the camp on film. We saw those photos and so did the world. But when my unit entered the camp to see this place, the survivors had been removed for medical care. Only the dead remained.

Lying along the roads leading to and away from Majdanek were bodies.

They were not the bodies of soldiers felled in the heat of battle. They were the striped-cloth clad bodies of prisoners, of Jews, gunned down as they ran from the camp in the final hours before it fell. They were thin and hairless, and their clothes were little more than rags. Some had died with their eyes open, frozen, in a look of incomprehensible agony. Others had begun crawling after they were shot, finally collapsing onto the arms and legs that had dragged them from the road. Still others had just crumpled, dying where they had last stood.

At first, we did not see much to mark the place from which these corpses had fled with their last vestiges of strength. There was only a thick high wall, strung with barbed wire and a substantial gate. Inside, were rows of low, single-story buildings, arranged in long precise lines with a dirt area in between. There were tire marks and ruts, signs of churned ground. Small bits of ash drifted along the open area and banked a bit against the buildings. Doors to the buildings had been left open. Other Soviet and Polish soldiers roamed about wearing dazed expressions on their faces, but almost no one spoke. And then I heard it, a cry, a wail, not high-pitched, but lower, deeper, the sound of a man being overtaken by tears.

Through the doorways, in the buildings, with my own eyes, I also saw it. One room had piles of shoes, shoes rising in a high mound like grain, hundreds, perhaps thousands of shoes. Some had very poor soles or no laces. Some had tumbled down off of the pile and landed on the floor, where they still lay, isolated. All were small. They were so small, those shoes, I could have fit two in my palm. I stared at those lonely mangled little shoes, baby shoes, for a very long time.

There were other piles, piles of more shoes, regular adult shoes. They were heaped together, all shapes and sizes, some worn right through the sole, some with fine women's heels, some where the leather was so strained and cracked it looked like an old farmer's weather-beaten hands. The Germans had collected tens of thousands of such shoes from their victims but seemed to have found no use for this collection of soles and leather. So the shoes had remained in their storehouses, piled one on top of another.

There were still other smaller, more compact piles in Majdanek, piles of human teeth ripped from the gums, the white enamel eaten away by an ugly brown. There were piles of hair, coarse and fine, light and dark, sometimes separated, sometimes not. And piles of glasses, lenses cracked, frames bent and broken.

I could not look at another pile. I was gagging, my stomach was rising up inside me, tears were filling my eyes. My throat had closed, and I was choking in my own breath. I practically ran from those rooms. But there was still another room, a sooty black place. What I saw in there, I could not believe. One wall was filled with ovens, ovens where hour after hour, Nazi workers, some of them Poles whose families farmed the lands around the camp, opened the little iron doors and slid bodies, already shrunken and contorted from the gas chambers, into the flames to be cremated. Even now, the scent of death clung to that place, the bitter, acrid smell of burning flesh and hair. I could not think about those ovens. To have never known that such things existed and then to stand before them, as bits of charred bone and flesh still lay inside, is such a complete horror, a horror without words. All around me, men were crying like babies, and I too was sobbing, even my skin was crying tears. Now, for the first time, we were learning the truth of what had happened. Now for the first time, we knew.

I went back to my battalion. Again, I passed the bodies, cut down along the road. I was so weak, so devastated, I could hardly move my muscles. My reaction was one of complete numbness. There was nothing to say. I got out of my truck and sat down on ground. I did not move for a very long time. Images from the camp kept flashing through my mind. I found myself going back over every inch, trees in the distance became gnarled, disjointed bodies, steam from a pot over a fire became smoke from an oven. When I closed my eyes, I saw those piles of small shoes, so many shoes, so many little children taken from their mothers. They took the children from their mothers, and they killed them. And they kept the shoes. Even when I slept, I saw the shoes. It was unrelenting.

Slowly, I began to ask myself if, when I came upon them, I would kill Germans.

I was not a combat soldier, firing at troops through the forest, through the camouflage of trees. I was certainly prepared for death. I watched it and passed it every day. But I was not trained for killing. If I killed Germans, it would likely be up close, in a town, in a place where I would be able to see them. I went over and over it in my mind. I could not rationalize simply killing Germans for revenge, killing them not because they themselves had done something, not because you could prove that these individuals were the ones responsible for these terrible crimes, but simply because they were Germans. Somehow, as angry, as hurt, as pained as I was, I could not bring myself to kill people and families in towns. Some soldiers did. For them, these towns, or towns like them, had nurtured the men who had tried to destroy an entire people spread across many nations, the men who had already killed their families, their neighbors, their friends. They wanted an eye for an eye. For me, however, it was too late. The killing could ease nothing in my heart.

As we pushed farther into Poland, something else began to happen. Poles began to enlist in our army. Sometimes they came up to the officers in towns, sometimes they simply found us along roads, but they joined, calling us and the Soviets "liberators" who had at last freed them from the Germans. One new Polish soldier I remember in particular. This Pole, who was maybe twenty-six years old, was fast becoming a "big man" in the battalion. He was willing to do any job, follow any order, and thank the officer for giving it. He scrubbed his truck until it looked much cleaner than the other trucks, and when he was given an order, he snapped himself into a salute and answered, "Yes sir." While the rest of us had fought and struggled for close to a year, he was only now appearing, eager to please, trying to prove, it seemed, that he was somehow better than we were. None of the other drivers liked him. We didn't trust anyone who was so nice to all the officers and who made such a big show about it. While he might have been considered a model soldier, we felt his attitude was a bad sign, not a good one. But we just couldn't put our fingers on it.

As a result of his enthusiasm, the Pole was even made responsible for a few trucks, and when he gave orders he screamed and yelled and even raised his fists at the other men. And he got his way. One night, however, all that changed.

Early one evening, after we had been hauling supplies all day, I was one of the last to return to the camp. It was a requirement that, no matter how far you traveled or how much you had done, you had to clean and wash your truck thoroughly when you returned. That evening, however, I could not find my brush to wash the dirt and dust from the truck. I looked and looked, but it was gone. The Polish man's truck was parked nearby, so I opened the cab door of his truck and began to look for his brush. I thought nothing of it. We all borrowed supplies from each other all the time. My brush had probably been borrowed by another driver.

On the floor, where most drivers kept their brushes, I found only an envelope with a letter. I could not understand how anyone from Poland could receive mail through the Russian-Polish army inside Poland. I was curious, so I pulled out the envelope and the letter. I could not read more than a few words of Polish, but I saw some words I recognized—something about Germans. An odd feeling came over me. Suddenly, I had become very suspicious about this big, blustery guy who talked all the time about driving the Germans out of Poland. Quietly, I slipped out of the cab. I had already forgotten all about borrowing the brush. I shoved the letter into my shirt and wandered back over to my truck. I opened the engine and pretended I saw something wrong inside. If the Pole or anyone else had seen me, I didn't want to arouse too much suspicion. I looked around and saw another driver, one of my closest friends in the unit. He had fled to Russia when Hitler first attacked Poland. I trusted

him. I motioned to him, and he came over, and it was then that I pulled the
letter from my coat. In a whisper, I told him that I had found the letter in the
cab of the Pole's truck. My friend knew Polish, and he was equally curious
about this new Pole. In hushed, breathless words he read the letter out loud.
It was a letter from the Pole's family, a letter telling him that the Soviet secret
police had been given his name by the Polish underground when the Soviets
occupied the town and that the Soviets were looking for him. His family im-
plored him not to contact them, that they would find him. Some of the references in the letter were vague, to disguise them, but to us they were still quite
easy to understand. It was all suddenly very clear. The Pole had enlisted in
the army to avoid being shot as a Nazi collaborator, although no doubt each
day in his truck he was searching the roads for some friendly Germans to spirit
him away to safety behind their lines.

We both looked up, not knowing quite what to do. We were Jews. Already,
on Polish soil, we had felt the hostility, the hostility that not even five years
of war and millions of dead could erase. We worried that if we showed the
letter to an officer in our own company, we could become the victims, not this
new Pole. But we had to show the letter to someone. We decided to carry the
letter to the main Russian headquarters, five miles away. Officers there were
intent on catching collaborators. Pretending we were testing the truck after
repairs, we started the engine and then roared off down the road. We gave
them the letter, and that letter destroyed the Pole. Within two hours, military
police appeared at the camp. They would not listen to his loud protestations.
They simply grabbed his arms and dragged him away. We said nothing and
only stared at him as everyone else did, wide-eyed.

He was not, however, the only such Pole. A surprising number of Nazi
collaborators enlisted with the advancing Polish and Russian armies to avoid
being revealed as collaborators by their neighbors when these same armies
came through their towns. Some even managed to seek out units in other regions to avoid passing in the vicinity of their former homes. For me, it was
an odd irony. Just as Poles had turned in their Jewish neighbors and even their
Polish neighbors who helped Jews when the Germans first came through, now
Poles were turning in still more neighbors to the Russians. And the Soviet
soldiers showed the collaborators little mercy, even less than they showed the
Germans. Most often, collaborators were tried and shot on the spot. The
Russians were particularly hard on Ukrainian collaborators, but the Polish
collaborators were not far behind.

Our first month in Poland, despite the rapid retreat of the German army,
was a tense time because of the fast-paced battle, the uncertain dividing lines,
and the constant threat of spies ready to give us away. The Polish people themselves in the small towns often welcomed us, crying at the sight of the Polish
eagle emblazoned on our hats, kissing us, saying we were sent from God to

liberate them. Many people shared whatever they could with the military, even though the Germans had left them with almost nothing. But in town after town, I knew that if the people had realized I was Jewish, everything would have been different. The same people who watched and cheered as their neighbors were forced into ghettos and marked with the star of David were now rejoicing over the arrival of Jews, but this time the Jews were concealed in Polish uniforms. And there were also those moments when I felt a warm grip grow cold, when people turned to stare as I spoke my name, Kalman Schweitzer, the name of a Jew.

I wish I knew who or what created this anti-Semitism, this mistrust. Why did some nations and peoples save Jews and others hunt them down? Why only several hundred miles to the north in Denmark were things so different? Why were the Poles so different? Why did things come to this? Why, why? it rings like sobbing in my ears.

It was summer, and we were sleeping in the forests and in the fields. The nights were warm, and we did not need the shelter of towns. I was glad. In towns, you could never be certain that you would awake alive the next morning. Roving bands of underground Polish fascists, collaborators still at large, even trapped German soldiers and resettled citizens, all were still lurking in the war-ravaged countryside. I had, however, long ago vowed not to be afraid. If you gave yourself over to being frightened, you let your enemy become stronger, and you risked falling straight into their hands.

My main duties during this period were to lead convoys to train stations, where we picked up provisions, wheat and rye that would be milled into flour, jugs of cooking oil, crates of dry milk, many times we did not know what it was. We simply ferried the goods from one spot to the next. In August, it was freshly dug potatoes, the first of the harvest.

From Lublin, we had moved north, and now we made camp in a wooded area near a main road that led to a secondary road into the small farming community of Bialka and then on to Brest. I knew that road. So many days, as a boy, I had walked along it in the cool hours before dawn. Bialka was one of the small villages where I had gone peddling with my father. It was where we usually purchased chickens. And sitting just off of the main road nearby was Radzyń, my home.

The first night in that camp, as the trees shielded us, creating a canopy of darkness, I felt pure panic. I was desperate to know what had become of my parents. At night I closed my eyes and saw mounds in my sleep. I would wake with fear in my heart. I also feared any stranger who wandered into the camp. I feared he or she would recognize me, would call out "Yankel" and give my whole life away.

Then the order came. We were to head out along the road to Bialka, the road to Radzyń, to pick up potatoes. How could I pass by without stopping? How could I not go? And yet how could I go?

I made a deal with one of the drivers. I told him that I had friends in the area and that I wanted to see what had become of them. It was late afternoon when he dropped me off at the edge of Radzyń. I told him I would meet him the next day in the fields along the road. He waved and sped off, and I was left completely alone.

Even in the fading afternoon light, I could see the rubble along the streets, buildings gutted, perhaps looking just as they had looked after that first German raid. But unlike many towns and villages that were reduced to little more than smoldering cinders and the outlines of walls and floors, Radzyń seemed to have survived the bombing raids and occupation. I looked down the street and knew exactly where I was, only a short distance away from the Obremskis' house and from what had been my home. I walked back, remembering. I saw the house that had belonged to the Graboevitzs. Empty. The Shumleks'. Empty. I saw the nearby house, where, as a child, I had hidden in the cellar, covering my ears during a terrible storm, as lightening cracked the sky and thunder shook the foundations. I remembered the pounding in my heart, how I felt so very scared. Now I was too old to run to a cellar, draw my body into a ball, and cover my ears.

I could not bring myself to walk to the back, where my family had lived, so first I knocked on the Obremskis' door. Neither Mr. Obremski nor his brother was in evidence, but Vladec and Romek were there. So was their sister, Yerke. They did not cry out in joy, but only let out a gasp of astonishment. They looked at me in my Polish army uniform with the eagle on my cap, and then they let me in. As I stepped in the hallway, everything looked as I remembered it, the long hall with two apartments, one on either side for each family.

Vladec, Romek, and Yerke were too amazed to say anything beyond a greeting. I did not wait. I asked them about my mother and father. Each one looked at the other. I was alone with them. They were alone with me. Finally, Vladec shrugged his shoulders ever so slightly and spoke. He told me about being ordered to take my parents out to the field. He told me how my father had refused to dig a grave. He told me about how the Germans had shot my father first and then my mother. He told it in a very abstract way, as if my family had not lived for years behind his family, as if he had not seen my mother and my father nearly every day for his entire life.

"We are so sorry," Yerke said. And from the way she parted her lips and showed her teeth, I could see that she was lying.

"When the Germans came, it was terrible. We all hated the Germans." Again and again that night, all of them would tell me how much they hated the Germans, they who had collaborated, who had helped the Nazis round up their neighbors just because their neighbors were Jews.

After hearing the story, I could not bring myself to ask Vladec about his family, about Mr. Obremski and his brother, but I did ask Vladec if any Jews from Radzyń survived.

"Six," he said. He listed names. One was a child of a tailor, another a butcher, a third I knew from the weekly bath, the other names I recognized, I had heard them all.

"Take me to my friends," I said. "I want to see them."

"I don't know where to find them," Vladec answered. "Besides, it is almost dark now. Tomorrow I will make some inquiries, tomorrow you can go."

I had no choice. It was almost dark and still dangerous to be out on the streets. It was too big a risk to try to find them. I would have to wait. Silently, I glanced around the house, with its modest bedroom, kitchen, and a small eating and sitting area. I remembered it as a well-kept place, with ordinary furniture and curtains, but all in good condition, with clean windows and flowers in the yard. Now it was shabby and worn. It looked as if it had aged thirty years in five. Window panes were cracked, the furniture soiled, everything looked slightly unkempt and unclean. Where there had been flowers, weeds now ran wild. Shingles had come off the roof. It was a sad place, and I dreaded every moment until dawn.

Vladec offered me something to eat and gave me a bed to sleep in. But I did not dare close my eyes and drift into sleep. I was carrying a machine gun and a pistol with me, and all night I sat up in the bed, my back pressed against the headboard. I held one weapon in each hand, my finger on the trigger, pointing at the doorway. My palms were damp and clammy. My arms ached, but I held them still. Sometimes, I would close my eyes for a moment, but just as quickly, I would force them open. Through the darkness I kept both eyes fixed on the door, not knowing whether or when someone would burst into the room. My pulse quickened at the slightest sound. I was afraid of dying in that bed, the bed of my former landlord, of being murdered only a few yards from what had been my home.

Dawn came, and I was exhausted but still awake. I got out of bed and discovered that Vladec had already gone out. When he returned, I told him again I wanted to be taken to see my friends, the Jews who survived.

"I cannot take you," he replied. "Last night, they were killed. Some Polish fascists found them, and they were killed."

I sat down. I could feel my face growing hot, my throat closing in. Tears came to my eyes. Six people who had survived five years of Hitler's rule killed in one night by their own Polish neighbors. To survive for this. To survive to die.

My heart ached, but I would not cry in front of these people. I would not give them the satisfaction of seeing me weak. I hated them. I hated them for what they did, and yet I also knew that they had most likely saved my life by keeping me in their home last night. Or maybe they were just afraid that killing a Polish army officer, even a very low-ranking one, would bring them problems.

From that moment on, all I wanted to do was leave, to run. Suddenly, Radzyń had become a very sinister place. I wondered who was lurking behind every corner. I felt nothing but fear around me. I did not want to walk around. It was like a long, slow cut with a knife to see the streets, the faces, the faces of those who had stood silently by while so many died.

Standing on the street, I watched some hunched women, scarves tied tight around their heads, walking with their market baskets. I thought of the row of Jewish butcher shops and the butchers who took turns slaughtering cows so there would not be too much meat or too little. I thought of the lines that formed each Friday, and of all the storefronts that were now empty, of all that was no more.

I left the Obremskis, and only for a moment did I walk back to the shed that had once been my home. I peered through the soiled windows, which my mother had worked so hard to keep clean, into the empty space. It was too much. Quickly, I walked out toward the street, only glancing back once to see the outlines of the roof and the attic above our rooms, where, among the rafters, I had raised pigeons.

I remembered sneaking up to the attic, shimmying up the wooden walls and pulling myself into the narrow space where the birds nested. There my twelve-year-old hands found the round, speckled pigeon eggs. Each day, I would check on those eggs, hoping against hope that they would hatch. And when some did, when those little birds opened their mouths and squawked and sputtered, I felt as if I had been present at a miracle. I wanted so much for the pigeons above our home to live. I worried about them during storms. I left bits of grain and nesting grass for the birds. I listened for their soft cooing sounds. And now I knew that in Radzyń, as in thousands of other small towns, neighbors did not feel for neighbors even the slightest bit of what I felt for those birds.

17

The Wait
for Warsaw

I waited several hours for the driver on a field at the edge of the road. I wanted to be there early, because I did not want him to arrive and start calling out my name. When he did arrive, laden down with potatoes, almost nothing was said. He asked if I had found my friends. I answered no, and we sat in silence as we rode back, the potatoes shifting their weight around each curve. At the camp, everything was unloaded, the potatoes sent to the kitchen, and no mention was made of my absence. Our unit did not stay long in this camp, and I was glad. The fields, the flowers, even the air seemed bitter now. Even the brightest greens were tinged with death.

We were moving northwest, rolling over long fields and winding streams, toward the Vistula River and Warsaw. The Germans were still in the capital, and we were preparing ourselves for a bloody assault. In less than two weeks, we had gone from Majdanek to the Vistula. We had moved across the countryside at almost lightening speed. It was as if the Germans were a carpet, being rolled up before our very eyes. But, when our unit reached the southern Warsaw suburb of Okeçie, everything halted. The advanced stopped. We cleaned trucks and rifles. We walked over to the river and craned our necks to see upstream. We watched clouds of smoke drift along the banks. We listened to the distant sounds of explosions ripping the air. Day after day, we watched and waited, and we did nothing.

Warsaw was burning. Poles, knowing the Russian army was approaching, had launched an assault on the occupying Germans. Many Jews, survivors of the Warsaw ghetto uprising some sixteen months before, had joined them. They fired on German soldiers and tanks, they battled inside the city. For sixty-three days, they fought the Germans to liberate Warsaw, while we waited on the banks of the Vistula.

The troops were restless, and the rumors flew. Much of our information was little more than half-truths. We had heard about an uprising in the ghetto that was crushed, and we wondered if the ghetto had risen up again. We wondered why the Russians did not attack, why we did not attack. We saw the smoke, and it could only mean that inside the city Poles and Jews were dying. We were the Polish army, yet we did nothing. Weeks elapsed. Then months. Only one man could be behind this decision, could have ordered an entire army to stand still as a city went up in flames under complete control of the enemy. Joseph Stalin. Everyone agreed that it could only be Stalin. As summer gave way to autumn and autumn gave way to the snowy, bone-chilling cold of winter, we sat, restless, on the banks of the Vistula. Day after day, night after night, we could not understand why.

We were helpless on that river bank, near Warsaw and yet so far removed from the turmoil inside. On the days when the wind blew north, the city seemed very far away.

More and more after Radzyń, I simply wanted to survive. Even when I got a bit of shrapnel in my hand from a mistaken shelling, I would not let the doctor operate. I was too afraid. I decided I would rather live with the pain than risk having someone cut into me when I was so alone in the world.

I did, however, still hold out hope that Moshe was alive in the Soviet Union, that after the war we would once again find each other and embrace as brothers. Most of all, I did not want Moshe to return to Radzyń alone.

But surviving depends on others. Your survival must be something that is in their interest as well, it must hold some benefit for them.

I had already learned that from an experience with my watch, from the watch that I no longer owned. I had won the watch in a bet. It was a silly bet with another soldier. We bet on how many kilometers are in a mile, and we bet in watches. I knew the answer, so I won the watch. About that time, a second soldier in the battalion began to bother me. He was a big burly Polish guy, in his thirties, and he made my life miserable. He picked on me constantly, calling me names, shoving me, mocking me. It reached the point where I was afraid he would take a gun and kill me. Several times, he would race his truck straight toward me, turning the wheel away only at the very last second. He terrorized me until I was on the verge of tears. I did not need to fear my own camp in addition to combat. Finally, I could not take it anymore, but I did not know how to end this ordeal. In desperation, I asked, "What do you want out of me?"

The bully just stood and stared. He stared at my arm. Within seconds, I unbuckled the watch and gave it to him. After that, he left me alone.

When I was a driver for the general and was able to buy whatever I wanted from the PX, then, too, I had doors opened and options. I was always popular because I could get some extra cans of meat or bottles of vodka, a good

pair of gloves, whatever was needed, whatever was desired. Those were easier days. I needed a way to bring such days back again, to be able to make
people happy. And then my opportunity came.

I was an officer, and I was good with numbers, so the battalion officers sent
me to oversee the loading of freshly harvested rye onto twenty trucks. The
rye was then supposed to be taken to a mill to be made into flour. The whole
transport was a rather lengthy procedure. First, the trucks had to be weighed
on a scale. Then, they were driven a little more than a mile to a train station,
where they would be filled with grain. From the train station, we drove them
back to the scale, where the trucks and their contents were weighed. The difference in the weights determined how much grain each truck was holding,
and based on that, the officials calculated how much flour to expect from the
mill. It was a very direct process, except that on the way to the train station,
the trucks passed through a thick woods.

I had one or two soldiers waiting in that woods, and together we took the
heavy snow chains off the trucks. We soon had it down to a rhythmic routine,
uncoupling the chains at just the right spots, dragging them away in unison.
Next, we removed the extra fuel tanks, and we left everything underneath the
protective cover of the trees. One by one, the trucks lumbered off to be filled
at the train station and then went back to the scales for their second weigh-
ing. We did this with one truck, and then another, and then another after that,
and no one was the wiser. If I managed to leave five hundred pounds of chains
and fuel off the trucks, then I had five hundred pounds of extra rye.

The rye was of no use to me. I was merely in charge of delivering it to a
mill, where it would be made into flour and each bag would be collected by
the military, down to the last kilo, according to their calculations. To the mill
owner, however, I knew the rye would be of immediate value. The war had
left the farmland devastated, and what little was harvested was quickly confiscated by the military.

In the lead truck, I raced to the mill. I found the mill owner. He was a burly
man, with a thick sloping back and arms that looked like hairy tree trunks. I
took him aside and told him that I had an extra 225 kilos of rye, or about five
hundred pounds beyond what was listed on the order form. Before my eyes,
his face turned white. His hands trembled as he held the paper. I could almost hear his heart beating. The stakes were high. If we were caught, the army
officers would have no compunction about shooting both of us. It was a gamble. I had rolled.

"What do you want for it?" he asked.

I told him. I wanted watches, salami, vodka, diamonds if he had them, although to many soldiers at this point in the war, food meant more than any
precious gem. The miller did not even try to bargain. He did not hesitate. "I
will get them for you, right now," he said, and we concluded our deal. It was

a good deal. Bartering the flour on the black market, the miller could get far more than he ever gave to me. As it was, I left with half of my truck filled with foodstuffs, liquor, and small luxuries.

On the way back, we stopped the trucks in the woods to gather up the chains and the fuel. I gave each man a sip of vodka and a thick slice of salami. Then I brought out still more food, and we ate. We had a feast off of the proceeds from that rye. And each man knew that a full bottle of vodka would be waiting for him when we returned to camp. Once we were back with the battalion, I did not drink. I sat up all night in the cab of my truck making packages. I gave every officer a package. I gave packages to soldiers who wanted to send something to their wives. No one cared where any of the stuff came from or how I got it. Now, officers were coming to me, wanting me to get more. "Kalman, can you find a bottle of cognac?" they asked. And I did. I traded bottles of vodka, I traded jewels. I found people who wanted my things and who had other things. I gave because I wanted to give. I kept making packages out of the back of my truck, knowing that it was good to share, knowing that survival depended on sharing. Once, a general had taken me out of a line of men who were being sent to a battle on another front. He did it because I was able to trade whatever we had to get more supplies for him. He spared me. Perhaps such things could happen again.

The smoke had stopped rising from Warsaw in October. Almost every day, we would walk to the river and look over at the different spires, the rising and falling skyline that still remained, and wonder why we did not move on Warsaw. October ended, November came and went, and still no order to attack. Day after day we sat on the banks. Soldiers wondered out loud where they could get some more vodka or more women. But inside everyone wondered when this would end. The order did not come until January 1945. By then, I had spent six months of my life on the Vistula.

We fought the Germans for several days from outside the city, guns pounding against the old walls, bombers screaming across the sky. All around the city, Poles had already destroyed roads and rail lines to slow German resupply and then German retreat. But whatever destruction we had seen outside paled against what we found along the boulevards and back alleys. Even in the cold, we could smell the burning and the dying.

When my unit entered Warsaw, the fighting was still going on, house to house, street to street. We moved tanks through narrow, old streets, and we hauled load after load of ammunition, especially artillery shells. We made our deliveries, and we also left with a full cargo, a human cargo of wounded soldiers crowded into the backs of our trucks. They lay moaning, their faces twisted with pain. Some waved the feeble remains of limbs, as if trying to shake loose of the agony.

Medics would run from body to body, bandaging, unrolling yards of white material, which would turn red in seconds. Then we carried the wounded back through the streets to a central point, where they would be loaded onto stretchers and hauled away, into long corridors inside makeshift hospitals. Almost every driver had wounded in his truck. And after we had unloaded them, we loaded more boxes of ammunition on top of the pools of blood.

During our runs, we drove past the charred remains of the ghetto, which was nothing more than rubble, piles of incinerated wood and stone. Still, we searched for surviving Jews, looking, asking. We found none.

I later learned some two hundred Jews survived, but we did not see them. We saw nothing but blood in the streets, heard nothing but the thunder of guns. The days inside Warsaw condensed into little more than a blur punctured by desperate cries. Our trucks were choice targets for German snipers lurking in doorways and windows. Each ammunition load was like a slow-moving, short-fused bomb. A few trucks and containers did explode, rocking the streets, sending tremors through buildings and through our hearts. We did not spend much time in Warsaw. As soon as the city was reasonably secure, the bulk of the army was on the move again, racing after the Germans.

The Germans were fleeing. They were abandoning cities and strongholds. Sometimes they made a pretext of holding on, sometimes they simply packed and ran. And we followed, we followed them into towns and to the outskirts of cities. We followed them along train lines and, perhaps most important, to the rivers, where they had to cross and fall back farther.

But even as the Germans were driven back to the borders of their homeland and beyond, they fought like cornered animals. You could see the wild desperation in their eyes. They now risked not just losing but losing everything. The bloody, vicious war that we had known in Russia, in the Ukraine, driving into Poland, returned.

At the end of each day, the carnage littered the roads and fields. During my early days in the army, I had thought about death almost constantly, but watching hundreds upon hundreds of men die, I felt the shock and the horror a little less each time. Slowly, those who survived became hardened. Slowly, we no longer realized what was happening. After bloody battles, men sat on corpses to eat their lunch. A number of times, I ate my rations next to the dead. The land was choked with them, there was nowhere else.

I stopped thinking about dying, I only hoped it would not happen to me.

We had moved 170 miles in nine bloody days, over half the distance from Warsaw to Berlin, largely because our troops were relatively fresh and supplies were close at hand. Communications had improved, and the Polish underground regularly disabled German-controlled rail lines and bridges, as well as their communications. Western Poland collapsed like straw in the wind, and in February, we found ourselves near the Oder River, the gateway to Berlin.

But the speed with which we had advanced suddenly came to a halt amidst the February rains and mud, which disabled trucks and tanks and exhausted soldiers as they slogged westward. Some days the mud was sticky and wet, others it froze rough and hard. When we moved supplies, half of the trucks broke down, wheels spinning, engines expiring, everything consumed by the mud. We spent two months in the mud, traveling up and down along the Oder River, waiting while men and matériel were moved into position for what would be the final drive, toward Berlin.

As we ferried troops and supplies, moving into new areas, even into places that were part of Germany, we usually made camp in local towns because they provided an immediate source of shelter and food, both in short supply during the winter. The previous winter, we had also taken over towns, but then we were in newly freed territory, now under Soviet control. Here, we did not know when or where we might find our enemies.

Sometimes, the soldiers would first go house to house checking for Germans. But if the town was already secure, the process became one of selecting a house or houses where we could stay. At times, half of the town would be evicted from their homes and forced to move into the houses of relatives, friends, or neighbors as soldiers sprawled on their beds and rummaged through their cupboards. Other times, we stayed in the homes with the families. A town could find itself hosting a whole unit or only one man. If a truck broke down, you could be forced to stay over in a village until another truck passed or some type of help arrived. I spent several such nights in houses, in small towns, lying awake the whole night, afraid of stray German soldiers or roaming bands of Polish fascists, like the ones in Radzyń, who would willingly slaughter Soviet and Polish soldiers or Jews and then vanish back into the night.

Many of our own soldiers trusted no one. Even when we collected milk from the villagers in the mornings, we made a resident drink from the pail first. If he refused, we spilled the pail. We knew of soldiers who had died from poisoned milk, part of a futile effort by the locals to dislodge their new occupiers. We might have arrived as the liberators, self-proclaimed or otherwise, but no one had been able to free either side from fear.

Especially the local women. Many times I would enter a house and go room to room to make sure it was secure. When I got to the basement, I would see them, cowering in the corner, their eyes open wide. They would cringe like small frightened animals in the semidarkness, clutching each other, until they saw something in your face that reassured them you would not drag them from their hiding place, rip their already torn skirts, and ravage them. Of everyone in those towns, the young women and girls suffered the most.

What can I say about young men in their teens and twenties who have been away from home for months or years, who know that tomorrow or the next day or the day after that, they will be moving out again, who know they will not go to jail for rape? It was awful. It was awful to see those girls and the look of terror in their eyes, to hear their mothers, half-hysterical, throwing themselves in the soldiers' path, pleading "take me instead of my daughter."

The Soviet army had strict rules prohibiting soldiers from raping and abusing civilians in the towns we took over. The army did not want to get a reputation like the Germans, who were known for their atrocities. But there were rules and then there were men. Many said they were taking their revenge for what the Germans had done to Russian women. Later, I heard stories of American GIs who wooed German women with chocolate. The Russian soldiers would have none of that. They saw what they wanted, and they took it, quickly and brutally.

In the villages, driving in my truck, I could hear the screams of women being raped. One time, in one nameless, ordinary town, I heard the most horrible wailing. I slowed and looked and saw a drunken Russian, with a gun pointed at ten naked women. I raced in the truck back to the military headquarters, and the officers sent some men to arrest the Russian with the gun. But, mostly, nothing ever happened to the soldiers, and the much touted rules were ignored. Some men who had ethics before they became soldiers kept them, many others lost them, and still others never had any at all.

During these months, we lived a life of fear and contradictions. We were afraid, and yet we were surrounded by constant suffering. People in the German and Polish villages were starving. They clustered around our trucks begging for food. Some approached us on the street, clutching our arms, imploring us with their eyes. They had no fuel to heat their homes, no gasoline to power trucks and buses. Their stores were empty. They were a defeated people, and they, too, were afraid.

I had food in my truck, pounds and pounds, boxes and boxes, and I gave it out in some towns. I gave it out not knowing about the people, not knowing what they had done, but only because I knew what it was to be hungry, so hungry day after day. If you have food and you see people hungry, how can you hold it back? Before me were simply people like all those I had seen in one place or another for almost four years, the old and the young, women and children.

They lived in clean houses that had neat, if worn, yards. They were polite, and many spoke as if they had attended school. And yet I knew that from some of these houses and yards came people who had committed horrible, heinous crimes. Again and again, I asked myself how this could happen. A person must have an animal inside him to do what some people from these towns did, to kill children by dropping them in barrels of boiling water and scalding them alive, to rip babies from the bellies of pregnant women, to make old Jews race on their hands and knees like horses in a derby. Where in these tidy places were the seeds planted that would one day become such beasts? I wondered even as I handed bundles of food into outstretched arms below.

Some soldiers did not like the fact that I shared food with Germans and would even be friendly to them. And perhaps, in retrospect, it was not wise. Perhaps the Germans in the towns were using me to protect themselves, figuring that knowing and being friendly with a soldier would give them some extra security. Another soldier in the unit, a friend of mine, yelled at me for associating with Germans. He did not associate with them, he hated them, and he shot them.

One of our jobs was to guard ammunition stockpiles. Our orders were to yell "halt" three times, then shoot into the air, and only after that shoot to kill. Many times I yelled halt, I even shot into the air. But I never had to kill anyone. When it was his turn to stand guard, my friend did not yell "stop," he did not fire into the air. He just shot, and he killed. If a German man passed by, he shot him. Sometimes he fired randomly at people in the streets. I tried to reason with him, but he would not listen. And he was not the only soldier to spray bullets over civilians.

If I had known which of the people in the streets committed crimes, I would have been the same way. But I could not hate, I could not kill people solely because they were German, even after all the things that we found.

In one small town, not far from one of the small Nazi camps inside the German border, my friend found boxes of jewelry with Hebrew inscriptions while searching a house. He found wine cups and seder plates. He found things that had been in people's homes, people who were no more, homes that had been lost years ago.

He dragged me by the arm into the house and held the skillfully crafted pieces before my eyes. "Here, these are the things I found among your so-called German friends. This is what they have in their homes. Perhaps these are not even their homes, perhaps these Germans have merely taken them from Jews."

He was shaking, and his face was red with rage. These Germans had stood by while horrible, unspeakable things happened. I realized they knew. How could they not with so many trainloads of people clicking and clacking across the rails of Europe, and the trains always returning empty? They helped themselves to people's homes and to their things. They did not trouble themselves with the loss of so many lives. I looked at the cups, the plates, the carefully rendered letters from a language born three thousand years ago. I stood there convinced. Yet I could not bring myself to point my weapon at people on the streets, even the people standing before us, and squeeze the trigger.

The other soldier wanted to shoot the Germans in the house right there. He said this was not the first house, that he had found other houses with hidden Jewish things, with paintings, with lovely old items handed down for generations. He had drawn his gun, but I would not let him shoot. Instead, we took the residents to the military headquarters. As we left, we both knew that this was not the first such town or the first such home to have these things. Nor would it be the last.

18

Final Assault

The order came in mid-April to begin the final assault on the Germans.

We broke through, and they fell back, taking whatever they could with them. Perhaps they still believed they would be protected by some magical wall as they drew back closer and closer to Berlin. But we pursued them, and no wall went up, no defenses appeared. The German army and SS had no choice but full retreat.

Again, we were plunged into the heat of battle, racing from one location to another. The names and places blurred, only events stood out.

Early in the campaign, we reached a German SS stronghold along a river, which the SS was in the process of abandoning. The river was a wide rushing body of water, a place where I believe some wealthy Germans had country homes. The SS had fled the site in a train, which managed to travel only a few miles, maybe even less, before it halted. The train tracks ran right up to the bank but could not cross. The twisted metal remnants of a bombed-out railway bridge still bent over the water, but the tracks themselves led nowhere except to the current and rocks far below.

Several trains had halted along that bank, and the Germans ran from these trains to the river, where they boarded small boats as the Soviet and Polish forces shelled from the shore. Our soldiers were feverishly raising towers along the banks so they could fire down on the boats from above. The sound of gunfire and the smell of smoke choked the air.

We were bringing supplies up from the rear when we spotted what appeared to be an abandoned train. At first, we were cautious as we left our trucks to examine this train, its engine suddenly silenced, doors opened, everything stopped in mid-motion and giving off an eerie silence except for the artillery thunder from the shore.

Right away, we imagined an ambush. Cautiously, we climbed the steps, weapons drawn. At the very least, a straggler or a saboteur could be waiting inside. But there was nothing, just a breeze blowing through the open doors. The floors were littered with trunks and suitcases, no doubt meticulously selected and packed, only to be abandoned. We opened them.

Sometimes we had to use knives or axes to break the locks. But when we raised the lids, we looked in on piles of treasure. Crammed inside were silver candlesticks and platters, rolled up canvasses covered with rich oils, glittering diamonds, some still in their settings, others ripped from rings and brooches and pendants. There were chains and bracelets. There were chalices and plates like those we had found at the house, painstakingly inscribed with Hebrew letters and Hebrew words.

There were mounds of gold, worked into every conceivable shape and form. And there were other trunks stuffed with human fingers, fingers chopped off of hands, some with the knuckle removed as well. And now here were these appendages, jumbled together, lying across each other in the most bizarre fashion, fingers where the flesh had all but rotted away, exposing the flinty white bone beneath, fingers still wearing rings. There were wedding bands, thick and thin, and decorative rings with stones and precious gems. There were rings that must have been passed down for generations. And now, in this trunk, in this train abandoned on a river bank, they still clung stubbornly to these pieces of human hands. I turned my head away and felt my stomach heave up inside. I was revolted.

Other men cried out in horror as they too broke locks and discovered human bones. By now, however, there were more than a hundred soldiers, Polish and Russian, inside the train. Trunks and suitcases were lying open everywhere, exposing a vast supply of loot and plunder.

As we went through the different cars on the train, we also found some suitcases already opened, perhaps by Germans who stuffed their pockets as they fled. I could not believe that in the whole world there could ever have been so many fine things. I don't remember who was the first among us to take diamonds, silver, and gold, but soon we were all filling our pockets with small items, stones, a few pieces of jewelry. Some men even folded their jackets into bundles to carry the treasure. If we did not take it, the next soldiers through would, and even so there would be plenty left for them. For months now, ever since we had reached Warsaw, soldiers had found and confiscated local and Nazi stockpiles for themselves. Among the ruined towns, they had found riches.

I ran back to my truck and unscrewed a door panel, filling the empty space with glittery diamonds and heavy gold. If I ever survived the war, I thought, I would have gold. I would go home with gold.

It did not take long before several high-ranking officers arrived at the scene.

They ordered us off the train and locked the doors. We quickly headed back to our trucks and drove farther down the river bank. Many times though, in my mind, I have returned to that train and seen the endless array of jewels and paintings, silver and gold. But even more clearly, I have seen those severed fingers and their rings.

Not just the SS men but thousands in the German military were on the run from the Polish and Russian forces. For several days, they had flooded the roads and railways in the area, streaming west, almost the way the refugees had streamed east four and six years earlier as the then-fresh German forces bombed and blitzkrieged across the countryside.

Not all of the Germans had managed to escape, however. Some were still hiding in homes and villages in the area, and so, although we were with a supply company, we found ourselves under orders to help clear towns, to check houses one by one. We had checked houses before when we had taken over towns. Then, the inspections had been largely a precaution, since most Germans had fled the areas long before we arrived. But now, the threat was far more immediate and real. Stranded German forces were holed up in houses and barns. Under each window sill, behind each entryway lay a potential trap. A few men in my unit rode everywhere with their weapons cocked.

We went house to house, many of which were empty, opening the doors with our guns. Some doors were unlocked and could be nosed open with the gun barrel, but others were shut tight, and we had to pound on the doors with the heavy wooden handles of the guns. One man would pound on the door, the other would stand behind him and cover him. It was not a very good system.

I was in one village, pounding on one door, when the force triggered the gun and it went off, shooting a soldier standing behind me. The bullet entered his chest and left a gaping hole. Blood soaked his entire coat. There was nothing anyone could do. These accidents happened, they happened often, but the system didn't change. And there was nothing you could do about it. Every day, more people died, and every day you wondered why it wasn't you.

My crew found only a few Germans. What we did find was gold, gold in banks, in private homes, gold hidden by the Germans in almost every conceivable spot. We found more oil paintings, some still in frames, many others simply rolled up. We knew nothing about paintings. Some had bright colors, some dark brooding ones. There were scenes of the countryside and of people in fancy dress with high hats and feathers. Mostly we did not bother with the paintings. But everyone went after the gold.

I took a heavy suitcase, a nice one with double lining, and I carefully emptied my pockets of the gold, placing each piece inside the suitcase. I had already selected the place to bury it, near a deserted little house in a Soviet-occupied German village. I dug a good sturdy hole, buried the suitcase, and covered it thoroughly so that nothing would show. Then I made myself a little marker. With this suitcase and the stuff hidden behind the panel in my truck, I figured that if I survived, I'd have something for my entire life. I was not alone. Throughout the war, thousands of people buried things, especially Jews being driven from or fleeing their homes in the early days. They buried things with the expectation that they would return. But instead it was often new families who moved into the homes, Poles, Germans, and others who dug in the yards and found the treasures.

When the war ended, I went back to the town, right to the spot. I dug, but I could not find the suitcase. I kept digging. I went to other spots and dug again. Nothing. I couldn't find a trace. I have no idea what happened to the suitcase. Maybe someone saw me and dug it up right afterward or maybe it is like the bags of sugar on the collective outside of Alma-Ata, missing, confined to the ground for years, if not for eternity.

I lost the gold and jewels in the side panel of the door too. Before the end of the war, my truck was hit by gunfire, and I was forced to abandon it, running for my life. Ultimately, I came away with nothing. Some soldiers must have gotten rich, but I was not one of them. Right through the final weeks of the war, I kept finding riches and then, just as quickly, losing them.

In those last weeks, we were closing in on the heart of the German army, and they were in a full, all-out run. They were leaving everything behind and fleeing for their lives. We kept coming upon the remains of their presence. We found more stashes of gold, silver, and jewels. Nearly all of us were carrying some of these remains in our pockets, and those who weren't were looking for them.

I had some new jewels in my pocket, but one night as I slept in the woods, with my jacket rolled up under my head, they disappeared. When I woke up in the morning, I reached into my pockets, more out of habit than anything else, and I discovered that everything was gone. I searched the ground around me. Nothing. I had felt the gems before I had fallen asleep, and it seemed that someone had lifted them from the exposed pocket during the night. Now they were gone.

But even those who did succeed in keeping the riches they carried away had no guarantees. Several weeks later, a friend of mine in the unit was shot and killed during a skirmish. Whenever someone was killed, we were under orders to remove his documents and hand them over to the officers in the headquarters. They kept lists of the dead, notified families, performed whatever official paperwork was necessary. I found my friend after the skirmish. I had seen him fall. As I reached into his pocket to retrieve his document, I felt a piece of cloth with a hard center. Slowly, I drew out the cloth. It was a hand-kerchief, tightly knotted. I undid the knot and pulled back the cloth to reveal a handful of glittering diamonds, burning like fire in the sun. Right then, at that second, as I bent over his body, those diamonds meant nothing. They were simply hard and cool, like his skin. For all their value, they could do nothing to save him.

Many soldiers died in these final weeks of war. All the way into Berlin, the fighting was fierce. Once we had reached the city, the troops were forced to fight from street to street and house to house, for ten long days. Around us everything was destroyed, streets, buildings, homes, all had been reduced to rubble. Day and night, the artillery pounded away. The bombing and shelling were constant. Even when we collapsed with exhaustion into sleep, often an exploding shell would shake the ground beneath us, jarring us awake.

Rumors flew. We heard that the Germans were surrendering, that their leaders had fled, that the fighting was intensifying, and finally that Hitler had committed suicide. We did not know who or what to believe. We were sweaty, shell-shocked, and tired, so very tired.

Suddenly it was over. On April 30, 1945, Adolf Hitler did commit suicide, and on May 2, the last Nazi garrison in Berlin surrendered to the Soviets. Every soldier celebrated. Vodka flowed. Men shot their weapons off into the air, and no shells exploded, no one shot back. We had survived.

But we were not set free. Both the Soviet and Polish armies remained on alert, supposedly because Stalin feared an American attack. Officers passed on rumors through our garrison outside of Berlin that each man in the Polish army would receive a piece of land in Poland, land I now assume would have been confiscated from landowners. I was not interested in any land. I did not know what I would do with it. Truly, I did not want to stay in Poland, although I did not know where else I might go.

Many men did believe they would be given land, but they still wanted desperately to return to their homes now, not later. Even the rumored promise of land could not hold them in the garrison. So, although we were still on alert, soldiers were granted ten-day furloughs. Every Pole and many Jews tried to go back to their own hometowns. But I had already returned to Radzyń. I knew all the Jews had been killed. If I returned to Radzyń again, I would only see my enemies.

For anyone who was thinking not of returning to his homeland but of deserting and heading into one of the Allied zones or perhaps going to the United States, there were dark rumors that had been circulating for months, rumors that would give any man pause. Ever since we had crossed into Poland from Russia, these rumors had moved through the ranks. The stories had a special meaning to Jewish soldiers. They were told and retold until sometimes they blended one into another.

We passed on stories about a boat loaded with Jews that was refused permission to dock first in Cuba and then in the United States. With no port to go to, no country willing to receive it, the boat turned around and began heading back to Germany. Once the ship's course became clear, we were told, the Jews on board jumped off the decks, drowning themselves in the dark, cold Atlantic rather than return. In truth, there was not one boat, there were many boats. There were Austrian Jews who had been refused permission to enter Finland and who threw themselves overboard as their ship began to return to Germany. There was the *St. Louis*, a boat carrying over eleven hundred German Jews, which was refused permission to dock first in Cuba and then in the United States and eventually returned to western Europe. And there were the refugees who drowned in boats escaping to Palestine.

There was also a second story, equally troubling. This story asserted that the U.S. embassy in Switzerland had known about the Nazi concentration camps at the beginning of the war, had known what the Nazis were doing to the Jews. According to the story, the embassy cabled President Franklin Roosevelt, who responded that he didn't want to know about what was happening and that the embassy was never to raise the issue again. We had no way of knowing whether this story was true, but the more it was told, the more it was taken as the truth. It was a story that lent an ominous tone to the nation that many of us knew solely for its rich supplies of trucks and food.

I listened to these stories, looked around at men who had spent months and years of their lives fighting a grueling war, and wondered how I would begin to reclaim whatever was left of my life.

One of my friends in the unit, an officer, was heading to Łódź, a city in central Poland that had become a headquarters for Jewish survivors in the region. Stefan was almost ten years older than I and a mid-level officer, but we were assigned to the same battalion and over months of combat had become good friends. There was a lot of camaraderie among Jews in the army, and the closeness only increased as we saw what had been done to our people, to the places we had called home. Regardless of rank, one Jew almost never looked down on another, and Stefan was no exception. Many nights, we would meet by the trucks and wander off to sit on a bench, maybe share a drink, and talk. We talked about surviving, about discrimination in the military, about being hated simply because we were Jews. The Polish officers didn't approve very much of friendships between senior officers and much lower ones, but Stefan didn't seem to care. Sometimes when I passed him in the truck, he would motion to me to slow down, and we would arrange to meet later. In Stefan, I had found a friend.

Stefan was determined to go to Łódź. He was hoping to meet someone he knew, and he convinced me to come along. "Maybe you will meet someone you know, Kalman, maybe you will find a relative," he said.

I wanted to go. I also wanted to hope, and yet finding someone might only create more problems. Anyone I knew would know me as Yankel Pomeranice, not as Kalman Schweitzer. Even Stefan, after all these months, did not know my real name. It was not that I was afraid to tell him. I was simply worried that in an unguarded moment he might call me by my real name, and that, in the army, would cause all sorts of problems. After all, I had escaped from a work camp in Siberia, and I did not know if they were still looking, even now, for Yankel Pomeranice.

I agonized, but at last I decided to go. Only my brothers Moshe and Luza and my sister Serke could still be alive, and if I found them or someone who had seen one of them, what would it matter if my name was at last known?

We requested to go to Łódź on furlough. After a short delay, the request was granted, and we went. I do not remember how we got there, probably a combination of truck and train. It was already summer when we arrived. What we found was a blackened and bombed-out city clawing its way back to life.

Łódź had been a transit point for deportations to death camps, and, in its most run-down district, the Germans had established a closed ghetto for 160,000 Jews. Only 725 apartments in the whole area had running water. Now, however, this scene of desperation had become a scene briefly filled with hope. People, many of them Jews, flocked there looking for families. I do not know, however, how many ever found someone.

But some survivors did find other people. As we were arriving in the city, I watched a group of Jews converge on one man. He had been a Jewish collaborator with the Nazis in a concentration camp. He had overseen the killing of children, one man joining the group told us. Now, in Łódź, Jewish survivors from the camp had recognized him. They set upon him and beat him right in the street. They delivered blow upon blow until he died.

Łódź was a gray place, a devastated industrial city once again under Polish administration but inside the Soviet zone and largely under Soviet control. It was a place marked by frustration and despair. Stefan and I found a room to stay in, something relatively easy for two men in Polish uniforms who had fought alongside the Russians. Then we went to look. I remember it was a Friday afternoon.

In the central part of the city was a large brick building that had become a headquarters for Jewish survivors. People flocked to that building from all across the region. Inside were long white sheets hanging on the walls. Above each set of sheets was a letter and underneath were the names of people and families who had survived the war. Survivors added their names, scrawling in the margins of the sheets in the hopes of being found. Stefan looked under the letter of his last name. He saw many names, but none from his family, none that he recognized. He saw no one.

"Kalman," Stefan said, turning away from the long white sheets, his voice husky with emotion, "why don't you look?" Still, he did not know my real name, still I was too uncertain to tell him.

"Why should I look?" I asked. It was a question to which I already knew the answer.

"I know two brothers and one sister could still be alive in Russia, one brother I left in Siberia, how would they have been able to come here? I know everyone else has been killed. I know where everyone is. There is no reason to look."

At that moment, I had tears in my eyes. Suddenly, standing in that room in the midst of so many names, living names, I knew for certain that I had lost over half of my family, that I was alone. Inside that brick building, everyone looked like little children after a fire or some catastrophe, calling out and searching for their parents. In that building, in Łódź, we felt like little children, wondering where is my mother, where is my father, where are my sisters, my brothers, where is anyone? Even being able to find someone from your hometown was like finding a relative, you wanted so much to believe that someone was still left, that you were not so completely alone. But Stefan and I had no one.

We left the brick building together, not caring if we lived or died. We had no one in the whole city to talk to, no one to say anything to, not now, perhaps not ever. Life seemed so empty, so without meaning. We decided to get a bottle of vodka and sit down somewhere and drink. And perhaps we would get another bottle, and another one after that, until we could think no more, until all feeling was gone.

We had only walked a few steps from the building when I heard a sound, a sound coming from very far away. Above all the noise on the street, the rolling of carts, the chatter, the footsteps, and the shoving, I heard it, this very faint sound. It was the sound of a voice, and it was calling "Yankel," my name.

I stopped walking, and I said out loud, "Who's calling me?"

Stefan turned and looked at me. He thought I was losing my mind. "Kalman, I don't hear anything." He said it very gently.

"No, someone is calling me." I was sure. I kept hearing the name, over and over, a soft voice growing stronger, calling it in the Yiddish way, "yanKEL," not the harder-sounding Polish "YANkel." It was my name.

I had not moved since the first sounds reached my ears, but now I turned around, and I saw a woman running toward me. I saw her skirt swirling around her legs, her hair coming undone, but I could not see who it was. She kept running and calling.

Then suddenly, I thought my eyes were playing tricks on me. The woman was coming closer. I gasped. Stefan was holding onto my arm. I could barely speak. "That woman, she looks like my sister, but I saw her grave. I saw it in Olyka."

And then into my arms came Genia, alive and in my arms.

19

The Sewers of Lvov

Genia and I embraced not like a brother meeting a sister but like two people who had escaped from their own burials. In the seconds that my sister Genia and I held each other, I realized that we were not the only ones in tears, people around us were also sobbing. There must have been a hundred people on that section of the street, and I heard them stop, and then I heard them cry.

The next thing I knew, I was lying in a hospital, returning to consciousness, with Stefan's worried face bending over me. My sister was also in the hospital. From the shock and the excitement, we had both passed out, and since we were already weak, especially Genia, we were taken to the hospital.

Genia had been told that I was killed in the army. Even in Łódź, even on that very street where we found each other, she had no proof that I was alive. All she had was a feeling, a force inside her that told her I was near. She felt that force, and she began to call out my name. It was at that moment that I heard her voice.

I told Genia my story or as much of it as I could manage. I told her about Moshe, and I told her about my visit to Olyka, to the grave, the grave I had been told also held her. At first, I was filled with hope. Perhaps the Polish woman had been completely wrong, perhaps none of our brothers and sisters had died in that grave. But soon my hope, like so much else, disappeared.

As I was fleeing east, Genia had headed west, back to Lvov, where she had already married a man whom I had never met, a man named Shumiel Weinberg. Not long after her return, she gave birth to a daughter. But I knew none of this in those few frantic days we were together in June of 1941 in Olyka.

Genia had fled to Olyka from Lvov the day the Germans attacked, and she had come alone. In our few hours together, I barely noticed anything, except that with the passing of each hour, the Germans were undoubtedly drawing closer.

Afterward Genia almost never spoke of her life between the German attacks, she seemed to find the entire period too painful to recall. For me, those years have always remained unexplained. In anyone's life, so many moments remain a mystery to others, even to those who love them.

I do know that once Genia returned to Lvov in 1941, she was trapped inside the city. The closed, censored world of the Soviet zone had left thousands of people unprepared. No one knew what the Nazis would do under occupation, and only in summer of 1941 did they begin the first wave of their "Final Solution."

In Lvov, the destruction began immediately. On June 30, when the Germans overran Lvov, bands of Ukrainians roamed the city setting fire to Jewish homes and shooting Jews on the streets. Some Jews were even less fortunate. The Ukrainians dragged them to prisons, where they were tortured before being shot.

For the survivors, however, the ordeal was just beginning. Within months, the Germans had herded Lvov's Jews into a ghetto. It was not until much later that I learned the details of life inside the ghetto, the cramped living space, the filth, the forced labor, the random shootings, and the mass killings that led ghetto residents to carry cyanide pills so that they, not the Germans, could choose their own end. For Genia, it was not the ghetto that was so awful but what preceded it. Before Nazi forces closed the ghetto, Genia and Shumiel gave away their daughter, their only child, to a Ukrainian family who promised to keep the girl until the end of the war. They did not want to carry their dark-eyed daughter, who still took only the most hesitant baby steps, into the oppressive uncertainty of the ghetto. So they gave her to this family, along with money for her safekeeping, on the promise that she would be kept and raised until her parents' return, a day that both families knew might never come.

Genia could barely speak about the child, about those days. What happened did not all come out then. Rather, her story came forth in bits and pieces and fragments over time. Not all of it ever fully came out. Some things she was not willing to relive. I can only imagine what she thought as she watched German military and Ukrainian police round up Jewish children in the ghetto in March of 1943, tossing them by their fragile limbs into trucks, shooting some of children as they hauled them out of homes and hiding places. Here was everything she had feared, and yet what did she know about the fate of her daughter on the other side of the thick rolls of barbed wire that marked the edge of the ghetto? Perhaps she still hoped for her daughter, and perhaps that was what sustained her as she and Shumiel descended into the sewers of Lvov on the night of May 30, 1943, as the Germans began their final liquidation of the ghetto.

Genia told me that it had all been arranged. For weeks before their descent, a group of men, including her husband, had been preparing a sewer tunnel to become their home. They had begun by digging a shaft from the cellar of a house in the ghetto. They had spent weeks on their hands and knees picking and chipping away at a thick concrete floor using only forks and spoons. Only when the men had made a substantial indentation in the floor did they dare to use a pick and a chisel to reach the soft earth beneath. Next, they dug a shaft through the earth, reinforcing its sides with boards. Finally, they reached the heavy limestone roof of the sewer chamber. Descending into the narrow shaft, they chipped and scraped away at the limestone until they had broken through to the vaulted maze of tunnels below. When the time came to hide, they would descend through the shaft and into the sewers.

Helped by three Polish sewer maintenance workers who discovered the shaft and decided to aid the group, after the group promised to pay the men in return, the band of Jews found a closed off tunnel that could serve as their "home." The group cleared silt, filth, and debris. They tried to remove the rats. They built benches and stockpiled supplies throughout the adjoining sewer tunnels. When the night of the liquidation came, Genia and her husband and eight others descended through the shaft onto a ledge alongside the dark rushing Peltew River that flows under Lvov. They were not alone. Hundreds of people had climbed down into the sewers, not through carefully constructed tunnels but through manholes and any other openings they could possibly find. Now these people crowded along the narrow ledge above the river, many slipping, even in an hysterical panic jumping into the fast-moving water below, where they drowned or were carried out of the tunnel into the open air as German soldiers waited for them on the river banks, with brilliant spot lights and submachine guns.

Genia and Shumiel held on, reuniting with the rest of their group, and a sewer worker named Leopold Socha. Although Socha had agreed to protect them only in exchange for payment, he continued to protect them long after all the money and any jewels were gone. Their carefully constructed shelter had quickly been occupied by others now hiding in the sewer, and in the early days, the size of their own group had grown to seventy. Socha, however, could not provide food and shelter for seventy. Ultimately, somehow twenty-one people, including two children, were selected to follow Socha to a hiding place. Genia and Shumiel were among them.

Their first "permanent" hiding place was a damp, cold spot under a church and near public bathrooms, whose waste flowed past them throughout the day. The Polish sewer workers brought them food each day, mainly bread and potatoes, which were cooked on a small kerosene stove. But having survived thus far when so many others had died was no guarantee. In addition to the daily threat of discovery, conflicts had developed among members of the groups. Shumiel and his friend Weiss found themselves in conflict with another family, the Chiggers. In a small space where fear, filth, and isolation were inescapable, problems multiplied. All Genia said was that one day her husband, Shumiel, and two other men, one named Weiss and the other a man named Itzek Orenbach from Łódź, left the sewer for the outside world. Shumiel left behind his wife, Weiss left behind his mother, and Itzek Orenbach left behind a brother named Chaskiel. The bodies of the three men were found by another member of the group several days later. They had been shot, presumably by the Germans, the moment they emerged from the sewers. Genia was now a widow, and, unknown to anyone else in the group except her husband, she was expecting a child.

Shortly thereafter, the group was discovered by other sewer workers, who opened a manhole above their hiding place. One member of the group struck a sewer worker with a shovel, giving them some extra minutes to flee through the tunnels and away from their hiding place. There was a quick succession of three other hiding places, and finally Socha led the group, now numbering only eleven, to a storm basin, which was to be their "permanent" home. Genia, trying to disguise the growing baby under her clothes, crawled through a succession of narrow pipes to reach the hiding place.

In this new place, they built benches to sit on, which at night became a communal bed. The basin's ceilings were so low that no one could stand up straight. Every Friday night, however, one of the women, Chigger's wife, lit candles provided by Socha and said the Sabbath prayers.

Genia became the cook for the group, making a chicory and cocoa blend ersatz coffee in the morning, which they drank with a slice of bread. For lunch, Genia usually made potato soup by frying onions and then adding potatoes and water until the contents had been boiled and could be mashed. Chaskiel Orenbach raved about her cooking. Genia did not have to describe to me how she made the soup. I had tasted it or something like it many nights. It was what we ate growing up in Radzyń.

Only when Genia was close to delivering her baby did she tell any of the women, confirming what some had begun to suspect. Socha found a clean towel and a pair of rusty scissors, and the group waited for the moment. The baby, a boy, was born during the evening in late September or early October of 1943. Genia did not make a sound during the delivery, she merely gripped, tighter and tighter, another woman's hand. The baby was healthy and whole, but its cries threatened everyone. That same night, its life was extinguished beneath a rag. "It was agreed by everyone, unanimously," Genia said.

Nothing more was said about the baby. The group continued on in their dark, daylightless world inside the storm basin. An older woman, Weiss's mother, succumbed to the conditions and died. Winter came and the ten remaining survivors seemed no closer to the end of the war and freedom. Socha continued to bring them food and bits of news. Genia continued to make her soups, the heat from her cooking melting the snow on the street above, which aroused considerable curiosity and which Socha explained away by citing the effects of steam from heating pipes.

The winter dragged on, largely uneventful except for recurring illnesses that weakened everyone. But then there came a single, terrifying day, a day that, for Genia, would become one of her worst memories. It happened one Sunday in March. A torrential rain caused a flood in the streets. And the water was rapidly rising in the portion of the sewer built just for that purpose—the storm basin where Genia and the others were hiding. The water rose as high as their chins, their heads were trapped in an air pocket against the ceiling. One of the children begged a very religious man in the group to pray for the water to stop. Above in the city, inside a church, Leopold Socha was also praying for the people in the sewers. Like a miracle, Genia remembered, the water stopped pouring into the basin's chamber, and gradually it began to flow out into the sewers, leaving them soaked and muddied, but still alive. Night after night though, Genia would wake in terror, still feeling the water rising, soaking her, splashing into her mouth and nose, placing her only seconds away from drowning.

Through the remainder of March and all of April, May, and June the group waited in the sewer. They were waiting for the Russians. Socha brought them news of Russians advances and setbacks. Then, in early July, the group heard the sounds as the Germans prepared to fortify the city. Socha had already increased the group's number by one, having added a Russian soldier named Tola, supposedly a wounded prisoner of war scheduled to be deported to Germany, but soon many thought he was a deserter from the Russian army. The soldier had fallen in love with Socha's sister-in-law, a nurse, who had pleaded with Socha to protect him. So now Tola and the Jews huddled in the storm basin listening to orders being shouted and fortifications being constructed above. The building was followed by explosions as Soviet artillery began shelling the city.

The constant sounds above them, even the crunch of soldiers' boots on the street, made the group fearful. They believed that even a slight sound would give them away. From then on, they spoke only in whispers. In mid-July, Socha, who had come nearly every weekday to check on the group, made only one visit. Already, food was scarce, and they had little if anything to eat. When Socha made his next visit, he said the Germans had retreated quietly one night, leaving behind bands of Ukrainians. Many Ukrainians had collaborated with the Germans throughout the war, and now they were free to attack anyone, local Poles and even a few surviving Jews who had emerged from hiding. They attacked anyone who might bear witness to their actions as the Soviets arrived. Socha delivered that news, and then he was gone. It was the last time that Socha crawled through the pipes to reach the group in the sewers.

On July 26, just as Genia was fixing coffee, they heard a voice from the street calling to them to wake up. It was Socha. His next words were, "You can come out."

Within minutes, these survivors and the Russian deserter crawled through a storm pipe to daylight. Covered with filth, stinking like the sewer beneath them, and nearly blind in the sunlight, one by one those who had survived emerged into the world As Socha exclaimed to a few bewildered Poles, "These are my Jews."

For Genia, it was the first time in almost fourteen months that she had been able to stand up and see the world above ground.

From the moment she emerged from the sewer, Chaskiel Orenbach stayed by her side. Perhaps they had been drawn together in the sewer when Genia lost her husband and Chaskiel lost his brother in the same attempt to escape. I do not know. I only know that the two had grown close in the sewers and that for months Chaskiel had constantly complimented Genia's cooking. But even though she was now free, Genia was despondent. She had lost her husband and a baby son, and her daughter's fate was still unknown. It became too painful. Genia and Chaskiel moved out of the apartment block that they shared with the other sewer survivors into another part of town. Together, Chaskiel, who had been in business in Łódź, and Genia began to work to save money to try to buy back Genia's daughter from the Ukrainian family.

While the war dragged on in the west, Genia and Chaskiel made contact with the Ukrainian family. A rendezvous was arranged where Genia and Chaskiel would hand over money under a railway bridge in return for the little girl. They were cheated. The family grabbed the money, and the little girl was not returned.

Still, Genia would not give up hope of finding her daughter. Not long after, as Genia and Chaskiel were riding on a train, Genia spotted a woman with a little girl from her window, a girl she thought looked exactly like her daughter. The two leapt off the train at the next stop and made their way back to the site, but the little girl was gone. For several weeks, Genia knocked on doors throughout the surrounding towns, looking. She asked hundreds of families about the daughter she had lost. Nearly a month passed as she searched, her body still weak from the long ordeal in the sewers, so much so that sometimes she would have to sit down on the ground for long intervals to rest. Yet, after countless hours of going house to house and street to street, Genia did not find any trace of her daughter.

Lvov had become a nightmarish place, the city where she had survived while the rest of her young family was destroyed. While the Soviet front had stalled, while she still held out hope of finding her child, Genia was able to live in Lvov. But she could not live there anymore. Chaskiel was from Łódź, and they planned to marry. So, not long after Łódź was liberated early in the New Year, Genia and Chaskiel boarded a train and traveled west, to what was to be their new home. When Genia found me on the street, she was already married and living in Łódź with Chaskiel. She was trying to put some of her old life behind.

Not long after we had revived, Genia and I were released from the hospital, and along with Stefan, who at last knew my real name, we returned to her apartment, where I met Chaskiel. I soon learned that on the floor above Genia and Chaskiel lived another woman from Radzyń who had survived. In fact, a number of Jews from Radzyń, some who had fled to the Soviet Union and even a few who had survived the Nazi concentration camps, were now in Łódź. Suddenly, I had found a bit of my home.

Our first night together was a Friday night, and I watched Genia place the candles on the table, with the same graceful movements I had seen my mother make. She lit the wicks and recited the blessing, which was never quite finished that night. It was lost amidst a rush of tears.

That night, for the first time in four years, I sat down to a Sabbath meal. We ate Challah and fish and sipped wine. It was an evening of joy, wonder, and misery, all at the same time. In the face of destruction, we had survived. But our family, our community had been shattered, so many we loved had died.

Stefan and I stayed with Genia and Chaskiel. Although I had found my sister and Stefan had found no one, grief did not drive a wedge between us. Instead, we became closer. We had a shared memory of survival and loss. Now Stefan was, to me, like another member of my family. We had quickly become inseparable.

Little more than a day or two had passed since we had arrived at Genia's home before Stefan and I began talking. I was asking, "What are we going to do now? We have to go back, our time is almost up."

My brother-in-law, Chaskiel, was also sitting in the room. He began to laugh and said, "You're not going back. Enjoy yourself, eat some more, and we'll talk about it later."

We looked at Chaskiel, but he just continued to laugh and smile and said nothing.

Within a few days, we learned just what Chaskiel meant. One afternoon early in the week, he announced, "I will arrange it so that we will be out of Łódź before your ten-day furlough is over. The time has come to leave."

Chaskiel knew this perhaps better than we did. Like Lvov, Łódź had been decimated during the war. The city was largely in ruins, its once thriving Jewish community, one of the three largest in Poland, was now all but gone. Although bombs no longer fell and piles of dead were no longer carted away each day, the city was also, in the mid- to late summer, still not at peace. Soviet troops and their Polish allies maintained a firm grip on Łódź and its citizens.

As Chaskiel spoke, Genia looked startled. So did Stefan and I. But Chaskiel continued, completely undeterred. He was very direct. He was not asking us what we wanted to do. He was instructing us what we were to do. "We will head to the west, to the American zone," he said. "I know some people who are part of a group that smuggles Jews to the American zone."

That was the end of the discussion. It was decided. Now it would simply have to be arranged. I felt a wave of relief come over me. Ever since I had crossed the border and returned to Poland over a year before, somewhere deep inside me, I had wanted to leave. My parents had been murdered on this soil. My brothers and sisters had been forced from it, only to be murdered themselves or helplessly to lose those whom they loved. Everywhere I looked, on the streets and in homes, I saw painful reminders of all that was no more.

I saw orphaned, emaciated children and single men and women, each one the only member of his or her family to survive. I saw rubble and ruin. And even here, whenever I looked at my sister, I saw in my mind this beautiful girl who would not let my mother fetch water from the stream, I saw her running from house to house, banging on doors, crying for her child. Perhaps in another place, my mind would not flood with those images. Perhaps in another place, that brooding look of pain would be eased from her eyes.

So now yet again I was preparing to run, not from any imminent danger but from the further breaking of my heart.

20

Two by Two, We Were Free

The next few days passed as if they were a dream. It all seemed so unreal, finding my sister one day and deciding to escape almost the very next day. Chaskiel began making all the arrangements, and I paid almost no attention. For once, I was not afraid of discovery. Nor was I alone and on the run.

In fact, I felt a great sense of relief. Once the decision to escape was made, Stefan had told me, "I do not want to stay another night in this graveyard." To me as well, Poland had become a place to which no one willingly returned.

Chaskiel completed the arrangements quickly. He said very little about how our exit was to be organized and who was organizing it, but I believe we fled with the help of the Brecha, an underground group that smuggled Jews out of Poland. We brought whatever money we had and a bit of food with us. Chaskiel managed everything.

Our greatest challenge was to leave Łódź. We had no documents and no travel permits to head south. Even to buy train tickets we needed papers, but Stefan and I had none except for our army papers, which would only permit us to return to Berlin. Stefan and I especially needed to ensure that we left no trail behind for any authorities to follow if they came looking for us.

But the Brecha had a plan.

On a morning early in the week, we left Genia and Chaskiel's apartment for what was to be the very last time. We took nothing with us, except for a photograph or two. Genia might have had a piece of jewelry. Everything else was left in its place, just as if we intended to return. We walked down the street and boarded a streetcar to take us to the edge of the city. At first, the car was crowded, but gradually as it drew closer to the end of its route, the passengers thinned out, until only a few old women and men remained. Throughout the ride, I barely glanced at the streets and buildings as we moved by, one block blending into the next. I was leaving, and yet somehow, I think in my mind I had already left, long, long ago.

We climbed down from the streetcar and headed in the direction of a wooded area, where the remnants of Łódź gave way to a wilder, forested space. Somewhere inside the woods gradually spreading before us was our first destination. We, however, tried to appear as if we were simply heading out for a midday stroll, Stefan and I in our Polish army uniforms, Genia and Chaskiel in the most fashionable dress they could muster. Chaskiel carried a picnic basket containing four workmen's outfits that, when worn, would make us look like laborers heading to a new job. Once on the run, these clothes would serve as our disguise.

We wandered along the dusty roads and pathways laughing, trying to act at ease. Then, at the marked point, Chaskiel turned toward the trees, and we followed him, walking coolly into the thick dark forest, moving farther and farther under its cover until we disappeared.

We knew there was very little time. Chaskiel handed out the bundles in the basket. To avoid attracting attention, even of any animals, we spread out, each one of us looking for a secluded spot where we could change clothes. I was walking a bit to the left, already anticipating the moment when I would unbutton my uniform and don the simple laborer's clothes that I now carried in a bundle under my arm. In a way, the precautions seemed silly. Who else would come upon us in this thick woods?

I took off my cap and began to unbutton my tight-fitting uniform jacket. I dropped the jacket to the ground and slipped on the loose, billowy laborer's shirt. The cloth was rough, but the cut felt easy and loose. Already, inside, I felt free. I held up the pants.

Suddenly, I heard the crack of a twig and the crunch of a step on the forest floor. The sound came from the left, too far over for it to be Stefan, Chaskiel, or Genia. I stopped and froze. I heard another step. Someone was walking toward me.

"Run . . . run . . . gather the clothes . . . leave the clothes . . . just run." Thoughts fired through my mind, but my body stood perfectly still. Then I saw the figure in plain view, and my face turned white.

Coming towards me was a Russian army officer.

I could see stars on his uniform, marking his rank. And now, here at my feet, lay my Polish army jacket and cap, the eagle insignia already covered with leaves from the forest floor. They had found me. We were all about to be caught trying to escape. Somehow, someone had uncovered the plan, and our entire group had been set up.

I told myself to think fast and started to devise a story to explain, trying to weave the bits and pieces into something plausible. I did not move. The officer, tracing his route through the trees, looked at the ground and then looked up, directly at me.

But even once he saw me, the officer kept walking. He only turned and looked at me again and, pausing slightly, said, "Don't be afraid, I'm going the same way you're going."

I stood dumbfounded, trying to comprehend what he had just uttered, trying to realize that I was safe, that this man was also running away. I watched him move farther into the trees. I could barely see his outline among the trunks, but if I trained my eyes I could see a small glint from the red stars. I saw him pause and then bend over. He was undoing his jacket. He was also changing clothes. I stared in disbelief, not a muscle moved. I watched until I heard Stefan calling my name.

The sound of his voice propelled me into action. I rushed to switch my pants and then grabbed up the clothes that had been left on the ground. They would be deposited elsewhere, perhaps used by others. All I knew was that they were no longer a part of my life.

Stefan was calling me because he had found the trucks that were waiting for us nearby. Genia was sent to one truck for women, Chaskiel, Stefan, and I were sent to another. We climbed into a crate inside. The crate was solid, but the slats had about two inches of space between them, enough, I realized, for air. Once we were secure, several men covered the crate with potatoes. The potatoes hid the crate, but they also allowed air to filter through for the journey. And they were very obvious, no one would want to dig through a truck loaded down with potatoes. I felt the lurch as the trucks set off.

It was a bouncy, awkward journey over roads that seemed as if they were little more than muddy ruts. We were tossed from side to side, our bodies becoming bruised as they slammed into the rough wooden slats of the crate. We tried to hold on to anything that might slow the motion. It was no use. Above us, the potatoes rolled and thundered, sliding like an avalanche, first cascading one way and then another. Even with the intermittent airflow from above, the crate grew hot and sticky. The motion was nauseating, and the air smelled stale. My head throbbed with the sound of colliding potatoes.

In the crates, time moved very slowly. I believe our journey was no more than a couple of hours, but we saw nothing of it. We did not know the direction. We did not know the roads. We only knew that at some moment, it must all come to an end.

It did. Suddenly, the truck jerked to a stop. We waited, barely breathing, trying to make out a few words from the muffled voices up front. We felt the door slam as the driver got out of the cab, and then we heard noise alongside. Someone was climbing up onto the truck. For a few seconds, all was still. Then

we heard a thumping noise above us. Someone was poking through the potatoes. We tried to flatten ourselves against the floor of the truck, expecting that
at any moment the potatoes would be thrown off and the crate exposed.

At that moment, however, a voice spoke to us, saying we would be out in a
few minutes. Those words were like a great blanket of reassurance. We waited the interminable minutes while the potatoes were shoveled off above us,
and the crate was at last exposed to light and air.

We emerged, sore, cramped, bladders bursting, miserable, and still not yet
free. But there was no time to waste. Together, we were about twenty people
along with one or two guides from the Brecha who blended in with the group.
Since most of the escapees did not know each other, no one seemed quite
certain who was a guide and who was actually fleeing. Aside from Genia,
Chaskiel, and Stefan, I did recognize one man among us, the Russian officer
from the woods. Once he nodded at me and I at him in a kind of tacit acknowl-
edgment, but we did not speak. No one in the group spoke. We did not want
to attract any attention, especially by speaking Yiddish.

Before we left the trucks behind, our guides handed us brooms, heavy, straw
brooms, the kind used by maintenance workers. We passed them among ourselves, until each person had one. We looked like a maintenance crew, like the
old women who before sunup each morning don kerchiefs and smocks and
draw heavy whisk brooms across the streets and through the train stations.
Clutching our brooms, we walked, almost marching, along dirt roads. We
walked what seemed like a number of miles through the late afternoon light,
until we reached a small wooden train station. It looked old, weathered, and
largely ignored. I did not even bother to read the name hanging above it, if
indeed there was one hanging there at all. We proceeded to march up the side
of the train station and onto the platform. Uncertain, a few people in the group
began to sweep in a slow, hesitant motion, as clouds of dust rose into the air
and the rough straw scraped across the concrete. The leaders told them to wait,
and we all did, for what, however, we did not know.

Then, one by one, we heard a slow, rumbling sound. The tracks quivered.
It was a train. We could see it growing larger in the distance, its black body
trailing a long white plume.

The train was a collection of freight cars, and it ground to a slow halt at
the station. The door of one boxcar in the middle was slightly ajar. Quickly,
clutching our brooms, we entered a boxcar, like a crew ready to sweep out
whatever remained inside. But instead of pausing to wait while we cleaned,
once we entered the car, the train started up again and began to move along
the rails. The heavy side door was pulled closed and latched.

Although we did not know for sure, I believe that several people on the train
and perhaps another in the station had been bribed by the Brecha to let us on
board. Both the train and the station had appeared absolutely deserted. And

now that we were in the car, no one came to check. Sitting in silence on the dark, hard floor of the boxcar, we let the motion overtake us. Outside, dusk was falling.

We were leaving our homeland, most likely forever, without so much as a single glance. The border crossing would be made in total darkness. We would probably feel nothing, except for the hesitant breaking of the cars, a pause, and then the slow acceleration as we entered Czechoslovakia. Within minutes, Poland, the place we had been raised, the place we had once called home, would be completely gone.

Exhausted, many of us slept that night in the safety of the train. I remember several points during the night when the train slowed and stopped, any-one of them could have been the moment of our crossing.

Even after we crossed the border, it seemed that we kept riding for a very long time. As the hours lengthened and light appeared outside, filtering through the cracks in the wood, we knew that by now we were heading west. Of all the wooden boxcars that had crisscrossed Europe, we had survived to ride in this one, and no dark rough car had ever seemed sweeter.

We got off the train sometime in the afternoon somewhere in Czechoslova-kia. Two Czech guides were waiting for us as we exited the train that ground to a halt near a small station. Upon leaving the car, we threw away the brooms into a deserted area and were instructed to begin walking. We walked for a very long time, largely along trails and small rural roads, avoiding any major thoroughfares or towns. Night fell and we continued, a bit more slowly, part-ly because we were exhausted and partly because we could see very little in front of us. I thought of my first night walking alone, six years ago, of the inky black shadows that had emerged from smaller paths onto the road and of the sliver of moon that had hung overhead, guiding my way.

By now, we were all very tired, and yet we could not rest. We had to move at night, out of sight of the Russians. We did not ask how much farther be-cause we were afraid of attracting attention with our speech, but we all looked up at the fuzzy veil of stars over our heads and wondered.

I do not know how many miles we had walked or how late into the night it was when the guides stopped us inside a wooded area and told us we were at the Austrian border. We were less than a quarter of a mile from the Ameri-can zone. In whispers, they gave us our instructions. We were to be divided up into groups of two, and we would cross into Austria in these groups. The guides motioned, and at that moment I saw a small, wooden bridge, maybe a hundred feet long, extending like a thin finger from Austrian soil to Czech. An American soldier was standing guard over the bridge, the guides told us, so we had to move quietly. We could not be caught sneaking in. They did not tell us the penalty. They left that to our imaginations.

Noiselessly, one by one, we removed our shoes, exposing our swollen, tired feet. We walked out of the woods in our groups of two and onto the slope that led down to a dark river below. Above us, the moon cast a pale, soft light on the open space. I emerged with Stefan. Genia and Chaskiel were following right behind. I looked across the bridge. It was wide enough to accommodate a truck, perhaps one coming from each direction, but it was still relatively small. The American soldier was sitting on the left side of the entrance to the bridge. Even with the entire right side clear, I could not understand how we would pass unnoticed. But there was no time to waste. Stefan was tugging at my arm, and together we began to walk. As we drew closer, I could see the soldier's head and fist resting against the barrel of his gun, his other arm was curled around it. The soldier did not move. He was asleep.

Silently, clutching our shoes in our hands, walking on our toes, we crossed that bridge underneath the stars.

Two by two, we were free.

21

Salzburg

Once the last of our group had crossed safely onto Austrian soil and into the American zone, we sat down on the damp ground, our knees weak and bodies drained, almost unable to believe we were actually free. Hesitantly, I turned my head to look back over at the bridge, wondering if the American soldier at the other end was actually asleep or was merely acting, keeping his eyes closed and pretending to hear and see nothing. For a second, I began to worry that as we sat, soldiers would suddenly converge on us and force us to cross back to the other side of the bridge. But all around us, the world was still and dark. We could not hear another human sound.

Even now, however, there was no time to savor our liberation, no time to lean back and actually let freedom sink in. When they left us on the other side, our guides had made it very clear that our journey did not end with that bridge. We now had to follow a roadway that led to yet another train station and yet another train that would carry us farther west, to a United Nations' displaced person's camp. There, we would at last find refuge and be able to rest. In hushed voices, with light taps on shoulders, we roused each other and began to walk again. Sure enough, less than a mile away were tracks and a station and a train. We climbed on board. No one stopped us or asked us about our destination, and we were too exhausted to care. At the first light of dawn, the train pulled out of the station. We covered the rolling green land of Austria in a little over a day, and I barely noticed any of it. I was sleeping.

The train made several stops as it pushed west. I dimly remember the sounds of whistles and the calling out of names. But little mattered until we reached the city of Salzburg. I had been so overcome with my own exhaustion that only at this moment did I realize my sister Genia was desperately ill. Her face had turned gray, her body shivered and burned. She was lying in her seat, barely conscious, and moaning. Frantically, Chaskiel and I motioned for a conductor. Someone in the station called for an ambulance, and Genia was carried off the train, as Chaskiel, Stefan, and I followed anxiously behind.

Genia was hospitalized immediately. The war, the months in the sewers, the half-starved aftermath, and finally the strain of loss and even of escape had taken their toll. Her body was wracked with infections and inflammations. Chaskiel, Stefan, and I sat on benches in the hospital, waiting for word. We had been there a little more than half a day when a representative from one of the Jewish relief organizations appeared. Somehow, the agency had heard about us and had arranged for a place to stay. We were too exhausted to comprehend all that was going on. Willingly, we went with a relief worker to Parsch, a Jewish camp for displaced persons in Salzburg, located on the outskirts of the city, in a district with the same name. It was the fall of 1945 when we arrived at Parsch. I believe it was around October, although I was never aware of any precise date, more just the chill in the air and the fading color of the leaves. In Parsch, we were given an apartment in a brick building, as well as food and clothing. I remember some three hundred to four hundred families lived in these brick apartments, near the streetcar tracks. Day and night, we could hear the whistle and clack of streetcars passing by. That is almost all I can recall from those early days. My entire life and Chaskiel's were consumed by Genia's illness.

Each day, we took turns traveling back and forth to the hospital to sit with Genia. She had been transferred to a special hospital connected to the camp, but that only shortened our travel time, not our vigil. We held her hand, we talked to her, as her eyes receded into hollows and she lay too weak even to speak. The doctors could not pinpoint any one ailment. Instead, they told us she was suffering from a wide number of diseases. One doctor said, "As far as I can tell, she has almost everything listed in a medical book."

I was sick with grief and could hardly bear to leave my sister's side. She was all I had left in the world. I did not know whether anyone else in my family was still alive. I gripped her hand and pleaded with a God somewhere not to let her die.

While Genia struggled in her hospital bed, Stefan was preparing for another journey. Within days after arriving in Salzburg, he had enlisted in the Haganah, the fighting force determined to liberate Palestine from the British and to establish the state of Israel. From the moment we left Łódź, Stefan had wanted to go to Palestine, and less than two weeks after we arrived in Salzburg, he was given that chance. A transport was leaving for Palestine from one of the area transit camps. In addition to Parsch, the DP (displaced persons) camp where Chaskiel and I stayed, there was another camp, Riedenburg, on the opposite side of Salzburg, also named for a district somewhat on the outskirts, away from the center city. Riedenburg was a transit camp, a place for Jews and other refugees who were merely stopping for a few days or weeks in Salzburg on their way to somewhere else. I watched Stefan pack what little he had, mostly a change of clothes issued to him in Salzburg. When he had finished and was ready to depart, Stefan hugged me, we cried, and then he was gone. Once in Palestine, he became a general in the Haganah and died in 1948 fighting in Israel's war for independence. But at that moment in 1945 when we parted, neither of us could see our futures. I only knew that I was losing my one remaining dear friend.

I began to devote even more of my days to Genia. Almost every waking hour I spent with her or searching for things for her, a bit of food that might tempt her, a flower in bloom. I stayed by her side for hours on end, until Chaskiel came to be with her. Some days, we spent longer stretches sitting with Genia. Other times, we would even take turns for shorter periods several times a day. It seemed, however, that nothing could be done for Genia. She was not regaining her strength. She could not keep food down. In desperation, I asked one of the doctors if anything would help her. He suggested chicken soup. I was speechless. Thinking that perhaps I had not heard him or understood him, he repeated himself. He was serious. I nodded and walked out of the hospital. From that moment on, my life was consumed by one activity. I had to find a chicken for my sister.

I went into the neighborhood around Parsch and asked anyone I could find where I might be able to buy a chicken. Even though Salzburg was a city with a population of around a hundred thousand, not counting refugees, it still had farmers within its borders, in addition to those who worked the fields outside. One man gave me the name and address of a farmer who might have chickens. This farmer lived on a street in the same section of Salzburg as Parsch. It was only minutes away. I wasted no time. Buttoning my jacket against the chill fall air, I started out toward the chickens.

The man who owned the farm was named Hans Miedel, and he was there when I arrived. As I looked around, I saw that he had not a farm but more like a small plot for growing vegetables and a coop with a fenced-in area where he kept some chickens. I walked toward Hans Miedel, preparing to introduce myself. He straightened up when he saw me, and I began to speak in my halting German, learned on the front lines of the war. It was cold outside, and as I was explaining my story, Miedel invited me in. The house was a small place, quaint, but certainly not luxurious. Unlike the bleak brick apartments at Parsch, though, it had the air of a home.

Two women were sitting inside, knitting. One was an older, stately women, and the other was a young woman with wavy hair. She rocked as she knit, resting the wool against her round belly. Hans Miedel introduced me to them as Frau Pfeifer and her daughter, Sylvia. I began to repeat my story to all of them, the story of my sister, and why I had come in search of a chicken. At first they said nothing, they simply listened as the words poured from my mouth. But as I spoke, I looked into their eyes and saw in each pair a deep sympathy. They were looking at me with compassion. Surprised, I almost stopped speaking midsentence, and as I continued on, my throat tightened. Standing in their living room, I was overcome.

It was clear to me that Sylvia and Frau Pfeifer lived with Miedel. But I did not ask any questions. It was a time when people lived wherever they could. Miedel told me he would be happy to give me a chicken, but I would have to come back at dawn the next morning, when the chickens were in their coops and one could be easily caught. I knew Miedel was right. I knew from the days when I used to go with my father, before dawn, for the chickens.

The next morning, I was up before the first light. Only the faint glow of a few street lamps guided me back to Hans Miedel's home on Gaisberg Strasse. When I arrived, he was waiting for me, and so were Sylvia and Frau Pfeifer, bundled in big, bulky coats. Together, we selected a lovely, plump chicken. I took out my money, what I had been given as a refugee stipend, to pay them, but they refused it. They would not accept one penny for the chicken. Suddenly, I felt upset, even angry. I did not need pity or charity. I wanted to pay them, because it was right and also because I wanted to be able to come again for another chicken. If they would not take my money now, I knew I could not return. I held my money out to them, and still they would not take it. My face turned red with shame. I wished I could walk away, but I also was desperate to get a chicken for Genia. Finally, we reached an agreement. I would not pay for this chicken, but I would pay them if I came again.

They smiled at me, and I smiled at them, looking from face to face, until my eyes came to rest on Sylvia. When I had arrived yesterday, my greatest interest was the chicken, but now I found that Sylvia was also occupying my mind. Just looking at her touched me. Her face glowed with an expression of kindness and warmth, and deep inside me I felt my heart stir. I looked at her, and my heart began to beat faster. Welling up inside me, I felt a sense of love.

Hans Miedel and Frau Pfeifer invited me to return to visit. They said they wanted me to come back and tell them how my sister was. Miedel gripped my hand as if he meant it. Sylvia blushed as they spoke. I nodded and thanked them, and as I walked away, I turned my head back, ever so slightly, to catch a glimpse of that lovely young woman with the warm smile and long wavy hair.

I took the chicken to a kosher butcher and made the soup in the little kitchen in the red brick apartment back at Parsch. I chopped and boiled and strained, trying to prepare it just the way I remembered my mother and my sister Genia had prepared it. But as I worked, thoughts of Sylvia crept into my mind. Although that morning I had seen her for only the second time in my life, and only for a few moments, I longed in my heart to see her again. I conjured up images of her face, her smile, her hair. And then suddenly those thoughts would be replaced by others. Almost angrily, I would ask myself, "How can I think of her when she is Austrian and I am Jewish? It is only a dream, a stupid dream."

The soup was still warm and swimming with the tiniest threads of freshly cooked chicken when I brought it to Genia. Her eyes filled when she smelled the hearty, comforting smell, and she smiled a weary smile when I raised a spoonful of the broth to her lips, with its distant but familiar taste of family and home. Slowly, Genia ate a bit of the soup. The next day, she was able to eat more. I was overjoyed, and I knew that I would have to return to Hans Miedel's and purchase another chicken. Late that afternoon, I followed the streets back to his farm to make arrangements for the purchase. As I was leaving the farmhouse, Frau Pfeifer invited me to come back a few nights later for dinner. Sylvia was standing off to one side. It was all I could do not to look straight at her. I said yes immediately.

When I came for dinner, I brought a gift of liquor and canned goods. Salzburg had special distribution centers for refugees in the DP camp, places where we were able to get food and other supplies. While we had relatively easy access to those things, for many citizens of Salzburg, a bottle of liquor or a can of meat or vegetables was difficult to afford, sometimes even to find. Frau Pfeifer and Hans Miedel were thrilled by the gifts, and it was clear to me that they had tried hard to fix a nice supper. Just to be a guest left me feeling overjoyed. For the first time since I had arrived in Salzburg, I walked into a home, sat down with a family, and ate a meal that had been carefully prepared. Suddenly, the endless hours at the hospital and the long, lonely stretches of wandering aimlessly through the apartment at Parsch, pacing from one side to another, vanished in my mind. I believed that anything was possible. I spent almost the entire evening talking with Sylvia. It was already about the beginning of December, and together we sat close to the fire, fending off the chill in the air. For a few hours, I forgot about all my loneliness, all my problems. It was as if I had entered a little corner of paradise. Everything was so friendly and so easy, I could scarcely believe that this night was real.

I went back once again to visit, and it was then that Frau Pfeifer invited me to eat Christmas dinner with them. I accepted and offered to bring some liquor to the celebration. Genia was still in the hospital, and I longed for some company and the sight of Sylvia as much as anything.

December 25 arrived. I dressed, took the liquor under my arm, and started out toward Hans Miedel's. As I walked, a million thoughts began to rush through my mind. I started to wonder why they would invite me, a Jew, to celebrate Christmas with them. With each step, I was imagining different possibilities when suddenly it hit me, the liquor. They wanted me to come because I was able to bring liquor. The more I thought about it, the clearer and more certain it seemed. They didn't really want me at all, I thought, they just wanted the liquor. A powerful feeling of hurt flowed through me. I was almost at Gaisberg Strasse.

For ten minutes, I stopped and stood, in my best clothes, out in the street, looking in the direction of the house. Then, tears filling my eyes, I turned around and left. But, as soon as I drew close to Parsch, the loneliness overwhelmed me. I thought of Sylvia. I so wanted to see her again. I turned around and started back. Three times I walked to Hans Miedel's. Three times I could not bring myself to knock on the door, and each time I walked back to Parsch, certain as I left Miedel's street that they only wanted my liquor, yet wanting so much to walk into Miedel's home whenever I saw the first bricks of Parsch. Finally, after the third trip back to Parsch, I was so cold and exhausted and upset that I could not think of walking back to Miedel's again. I was alone inside the apartment. Chaskiel was still at the hospital with Genia. I sat in a chair and poured myself glass after glass of liquor, until I had drained much of the bottle. Then, wearing all my clothes, I lay down on the bed and fell into a drunken sleep.

When I woke the next morning, my head ached and my stomach felt raw. My clothes were wrinkled, and I was still alone. Suddenly, instead of being upset, I felt embarrassed. I had to go to see the family and explain. Slowly, I made my way to Hans Miedel's. Frau Pfeifer opened the door and gave a cry of relief. She practically pulled me inside and offered me tea. Then she and Sylvia gently scolded me. The three of them had waited for me for hours, she said. They did not know for sure where I lived, and they had worried that something had happened to me. Sylvia was especially upset. I told them I was embarrassed to come because I could not find any liquor. "We didn't care about the liquor. That doesn't matter at all," she told me. "We just wanted you to come."

Her every word sounded so sincere, and inside I felt so ashamed. Frau Pfeifer offered me some of the food from the dinner, and I ate it. Miedel and Sylvia came in to sit with me, and both asked me to come back again. I looked at them and felt as if I were looking at a family of my own.

Gradually, I began to divide my time between Genia and Hans Miedel, Frau Pfeifer, and, mostly, Sylvia. Genia was getting stronger. After some three months, she was going to be released from the hospital. She would be going "home" to the apartment in Parsch, home with Chaskiel. At Parsch, there were many people like Genia and Chaskiel, people trying to learn how to live as normal families again—or in some cases for the very first time. But in Parsch, everyone was also waiting. People were waiting to leave for the United States, for Palestine, for Canada, for wherever they could go and, ultimately, whatever nation would accept them, with no one quite knowing where he or she belonged.

For many in Parsch, including myself, the search for relatives who had survived continued. That winter, I started going to the transit camp in Salzburg whenever a new transport arrived from the Soviet Union. I had not given up hope that I would find Moshe, Serke, and Luza alive. I went once or twice a month, depending on how frequently the refugees arrived, and asked for my brothers and sister, asked if anyone had seen them or heard their names.

It was also about this time that life in Parsch became far less pleasant, in part because of one man, a Polish refugee named Saul Stabitski. He was a large, muscular man who lived in the camp. I do not know what had happened to him or his family during the war. I only know that he hated all Germans and Austrians and that he experienced fits of rage. At regular intervals during the month, he would board a trolley and pick fights with people in the car, unleashing his fists on the passengers one by one, until perhaps as many as ten men staggered off the train, bruised and bleeding. Whenever these incidents happened, U.S. army military police, m.p.'s, would come to search the camp. Even in the winter cold, every resident of Parsch was forced to line up on the main street that ran through the camp while the m.p.'s searched for the perpetrator. We had to line up again and again because the police were never able to catch him. One time, I heard that Stabitski had hidden under a blanket on a bed while the police searched room to room, and still they were unable to find him.

This was only one part of the seedy side of the world after the war. Under the clean, white snows covering Salzburg that winter, an entire world of deception and black marketeering thrived. Former Nazis reinvented their lives, con-men preyed on unsuspecting residents and refugees, smugglers and black marketeers became rich passing goods back and forth across the borders of Switzerland, Austria, and Germany, while many local people just tried to get by. The war might be over, but there was still a brutal struggle to survive. That winter, I had my first glimpse of this other world that was lying in wait.

Also, early that winter, Sylvia's baby came due. I had suspected that she was pregnant on my first visit, and when I returned for dinner I was sure. Not long after that, Sylvia told me that the baby's father was a man named Karl Strausse. She said that he had been a pilot and that he had been killed in a plane crash in the final weeks of the war. Although he had only been dead a short while, Sylvia did not speak of him in warm, loving tones. Her voice sounded distant and matter-of-fact. I was so surprised that I did not ask exactly when he had died. I did not even ask if Sylvia had formally married Strausse. He was dead, a baby was due. Knowing more would not change either fact. It was almost like an unwritten code, no one wanted too thorough of an examination of their wartime lives.

I did know, however, that Sylvia had been taken out of a college when she was just seventeen to work as a secretary in the regional SS headquarters in Linz. Day after day, she saw the Gestapo drag people in to be interrogated. Jews, Italians, Ukrainians, Russians, people of all nationalities and faiths were brought to the building. Sylvia's voice would falter and tears would come to her eyes when she talked about the suffering. She told me about prisoners who, as they were led to rooms on the third floor, would break free and hurl themselves over the stairway railings, fall three stories, and land on a hard marble floor, desperate to die rather then spend another minute with the Nazis. Crews would come like clockwork and remove the bodies and scrub away the blood. At night, Sylvia went home and cried, terrified as she walked along the streets that someone would notice her, would piece together why she was crying.

Sylvia started putting pieces of bread in the pockets of her coat and slipping bits each morning to the prisoners being held near the office. Her heart pounded as she covered the bread with her fist. If she was caught, she would certainly be arrested. She might easily have been sent to a work camp or worse. She might have been labeled a collaborator and killed. Each morning, when she arranged the bread in her pockets, she knew this morning could be it. She was trapped, but the people brought in for interrogation were often as good as dead. Once the war ended, some of those prisoners who had survived came forward to testify how Sylvia had risked her life to give them food when they were detainees.

Sylvia had worked for my enemy, but she was not my enemy. Every pain I felt, she felt as deeply. Between us, there was no war.

Instead of seeing less of her, I spent more and more of my days with Sylvia, waiting for her baby to be born. When the baby came, Hans Miedel drove us to the hospital in his small van, which burned a foul smelling fuel and was used to haul chicken feed. I visited Sylvia every day while she was in the hospital. I brought her flowers and admired the baby, a boy Sylvia named Waldamir. Until the doctors allowed her to return home, I spent hours with her, leading the nurses to think that I must be the baby's father. I was very conscious of their smiles at me and their glances when they thought I was not looking, glances of shock and horror at the sight of me, a Jew, with this lovely blonde Austrian girl.

This was, however, a happy hospital story. My other one was not. Genia's recovery was proving quite difficult. Sometimes, it did not seem she would recover at all. She had been released from the hospital and had returned to our apartment in Parsch. But the release had become mostly an illusion. Within two weeks, she was back in the hospital. Thus began a process that continued for over a year. Genia would leave the hospital, come home, fall ill, and have to be hospitalized again. Through these frequent setbacks, she struggled to set up her temporary home and get on with her life, her life with Chaskiel.

Genia's constant illness left me drained. More and more, I found an emptiness creeping into my days. Sylvia's life beckoned, offering hope and a respite.

As I came to share more and more of Sylvia's life, I gradually stepped into a world far removed from anything I had ever known. Over the last seven years, I had fit into many worlds. Once again, I found myself fitting in. I had indeed become a survivor.

Sylvia's mother, Elsie Pfeifer, had been married to a writer and had given birth to two children, a little boy and Sylvia. Herr Pfeifer wanted his wife to leave the children with their grandparents and to travel with him around the world. But Frau Pfeifer had no desire to leave her children, and she divorced Herr Pfeifer, vowing never to wed again. When I knew her, she maintained an apartment in Linz and divided her time between Linz and Salzburg. She cared deeply for Hans Miedel, but she would not marry him.

While I knew about Frau Pfeifer and Hans Miedel, in the beginning, I knew far less about their neighbors. Across from Hans Miedel's farmhouse was a hotel and guesthouse frequented by the Austrian chancellor. I would often see police and motorcycles stationed outside and hear music and laughter wafting over from the hotel, which I learned owned Miedel's tiny farmhouse and farm. On the same street was a grand villa, which was now chopped up into three apartments, one on each floor. The villa belonged to a man named Hesse, who had owned a textile business before the war. Hesse and his family, including three grown children, now lived on the villa's first floor. On the second floor of the villa lived a bachelor named von Royce. He claimed to be a baron, descended from Austrian nobility, and he liked to while away his hours over drinks in nightclubs. On the third floor lived a woman, about thirty years old. She was German, or at least she said her ancestors were German—she called herself a "Volksdeutsche"—and she would often come downstairs to visit. No one had known her in Salzburg before the war, and she did not discuss any part of her past. She paid her rent each month to Herr Hesse and talked only about the present and the future.

Gradually though, over many months, I got to know these people who made their home on Gaisberg Strasse. I knew Herr Hesse's son, who had been a banker in Poland before the war. I met Herr Hesse's two beautiful daughters. I went to cafes and wine cellars with Herr von Royce. But mostly, I spent my time with Sylvia.

Spring was arriving in Salzburg. Flowers were blooming in window boxes, and each street seemed to have a small square with flowers arranged in colorful designs. At night, I could stroll through the streets and listen to the sounds of music coming from beer gardens and wine cellars. Yet even amidst the beauty, there was still an air of anti-Semitism. I would get looks on the street. I would feel awkward and alone, but as I met more people, I could ignore whatever I felt. Salzburg in the spring and summer was a magical place.

It was all so new that I did not mind being poor, and I could forget that I was adrift in the world.

But not everyone was poor. For some, the black market offered if not instant riches at least the prospect of enough money to feel secure. It provided for the German woman who lived in Herr Hesse's villa and also increasingly, it appeared, for my brother-in-law Chaskiel. After the war, jobs were scarce, especially for refugees, and buying and selling became one of the only ways to make a living. It was easy to become involved in an enterprise that offered limited risks and the chance for large rewards. So, when the German woman in Herr Hesse's villa asked me to help her sell some items, cigarettes, cognac, sugar, and canned goods, such as turkey and pineapple rounds, on the black market in return for a share of the money, I agreed. This woman seemed to have an endless supply of basic goods and luxury items. And with no way to make a living, with no jobs available anywhere, I was relieved to have a chance to help her sell them.

I soon discovered that there were many people with things to sell. One afternoon, Herr Hesse took me downstairs to the basement of his house. In the dim light, I could make out maybe a hundred or more boxes stacked on the floor. Hesse opened up one box, which was brimming with handkerchiefs. Before the war began, Hesse had salvaged these handkerchiefs from the textile factory he had owned. He managed to keep them hidden through the entire war. Now it was time to sell them. Hesse told me each box was full of handkerchiefs, and I quickly realized there must be about a thousand handkerchiefs in that one box. Then Hesse offered me a deal. He named his price for a dozen handkerchiefs and told me to see if I could sell them. Anything I made above his price, I could keep for myself. If I could sell these dozen handkerchiefs, then I could come back and he would give me more.

I took him up on the offer, and I started selling the handkerchiefs. I sold them in the refugee camps and in a couple of areas nearby. Some of the refugees bought handkerchiefs from me and then started reselling the same handkerchiefs at a higher price. I said nothing. People were eager to buy the handkerchiefs, and I had a chance to make a bit of a living. Over the months, I sold dozen after dozen, until the whole supply was gone.

The more I looked, the more I began to see of this underground commercial world. People sold whatever they could get their hands on. Even American soldiers sold supplies from their PX on the streets. But while some people sold surplus, others sold treasures. A woman who lived above Frau Pfeifer in Linz had a large collection of jewels, which she parted with, one by one. Sylvia and I saw her elaborate box when we went to visit Frau Pfeifer. I remember my eyes opening wide at the sight of so many sparkling gems.

When I next visited my sister, I told her and Chaskiel about the woman. Chaskiel was intrigued, so much so that he actually wanted to search her apartment to see what she had. He even proposed that he would come to Linz when I was there and that I should leave the downstairs door open for him to gain access to the apartment house. Looking back, that request was like a final cut that severed our relationship. Increasingly, I had come to be uneasy about my brother-in-law. I did not like to be around him. It was far more pleasant to spend my time with Sylvia. Little things, like his off-hand remarks or the way his eyes shifted when he spoke, made me wary. I looked at Genia, sweet, kind Genia, and I wished that she would be free of Chaskiel. Already, a plan was brewing in my mind. I had met an American soldier from Brooklyn, the same place in the United States where my mother's sister and brothers had settled. This man was an officer, and he was Jewish. He promised that when he returned, he would take out an ad in the newspaper looking for my relatives. They can sponsor you to come to the United States, he told me. I received a letter from the soldier when he returned to Brooklyn. He was going to place the ad, and he told me he would write as soon as he had any word. At night, I dreamed of finding my mother's family, and I dreamed that Genia and I would leave Chaskiel and head to America.

Not long after Chaskiel made his remark, I told her of my plan. I told her that we should run away and try to get to the United States, that we should run where Chaskiel could not find us. Genia looked at me and said nothing. Then, firmly and slowly, she shook her head. She was not going to leave Chaskiel. For better or worse, they were husband and wife. And Genia was expecting a child.

Instead, not long thereafter, it was Chaskiel and Genia who left me. Together, they moved to another DP camp in Bergen-Belsen, West Germany, near the site of a Nazi death camp, but also now a gathering place for refugees, especially Polish Jews, many of whom were waiting to go to Palestine. Chaskiel had some friends in this part of Germany and pushed Genia to leave Austria. They invited me to move with them. I declined. Nothing could induce me to go to Germany. I could think of nothing waiting for me in Germany, and even more, I could not bring myself to leave Sylvia. They packed and left. I stayed behind in the apartment for a month or more. The loneliness was almost unbearable, and I decided to take Hans Miedel up on an offer he had made. I left the confines of the camp and moved into a room in Hans Miedel's farmhouse, the same house where Sylvia lived. By now, it was more of a formality than anything, because I spent most of my time at the house anyway. I had been in Salzburg more than one year, and in bits and pieces, my life had changed.

Moving in with Hans Miedel and Sylvia only amplified my feelings of poverty. I had no way to make a real living and was completely dependent on others. I began to sell more things for the German woman in Herr Hesse's house, and she in return began to invite me, Herr von Royce, and an American army officer, a colonel or perhaps even a low-ranking general, to her apartment for dinner. I quickly learned how she always managed to secure so many staples. The American officer arrived carrying a huge box of foodstuffs, cans of turkey and pineapple rounds, bags of sugar, bottles of liquor, and other little luxuries that he had gotten from the PX. And when Herr von Royce and I excused ourselves to have a drink in a local nightclub, the American officer always seemed to stay behind.

This German woman was luckier than some other women. A number of women in Salzburg, no one knew for sure quite how many, whether it was merely a few or some larger number, had turned to prostitution as a way to survive. Salzburg had special zones and locations where prostitutes could work, in an effort, I suppose, to protect against violence and the spread of disease. But often young women would try to work illegally on their own. They mainly serviced soldiers, especially American GIs, who paid with script, the money used by the soldiers. Although script was not U.S. dollars and could not be legally exchanged in Austria for other currency, script was still bought and sold on the black market. It could be exchanged legally in Switzerland, and many people crossed over the border to convert it into hard currency. Hans Miedel had a little outbuilding, a shed really, that he rented to an illegal prostitute, a young woman maybe sixteen or seventeen years old, who had a steady parade of American soldiers come to her door. She received piles of script, and she was constantly trying to change it on the black market, right up until the moment she was caught by the police. Then we learned the money she had changed was only half the story. Hidden behind loose boards in the walls of the shed was another thousand or more dollars in script, which she apparently had wanted to keep secret from everyone. Each week seemed to bring some new revelation about this dark, seedy world.

I was not proud of that world or of my place in it, but for now it was my only place, until the government of a nation an ocean away decided otherwise.

The American officer had placed the ad, and three of my relatives responded. They wrote that they would sponsor me to come to the United States. To me, they were writing that they would give me a future. We sent letters back and forth across the Atlantic for years, and I learned that one of my cousins was a doctor, a successful surgeon in New York, and his wife was related by marriage to the wife of an American entertainer named Danny Kaye. Along with another cousin, they sent me some packages and money, but most of all, having promised to sponsor me, they began the endless paperwork that would hopefully one day lead me to the United States. Now I only had to wait. Almost every month, and later every two weeks, I wrote the U.S. embassy in Austria trying to get more information. Each year, the United States would let in only a certain number of refugees, and I knew that I would have to wait. I only hoped that it would not be too long.

22

This Is America

My year in Salzburg quickly stretched into two and entered a third, with no end in sight. I had spent six years waiting for the war to end, and now I was spending half that much time waiting for my life to resume after the war. I was, however, not alone. Refugees waited for years to receive visas to emigrate.

Nineteen-forty-eight began rather inauspiciously. It started out with my face cut and bleeding, the result of a fight on New Year's Eve at a night club called Silvester on the Danube River. Sylvia and I had gone there to celebrate the New Year. There was a big crowd, including a group of refugees. One of them, who was drunk, insisted on dancing with Sylvia. She did not want to dance with him, and when I told the guy no, he hit me. We fought, exchanging several bloody, bruising punches before we were separated. It was yet another reminder that tension was everywhere, and it did not bode well for the new year.

But I was wrong because this was to be an incredible year, a year of great fear and great joy. I turned thirty that year, and only six days after my birthday in May, the state of Israel was established. Jews in Salzburg rejoiced, while across the border, Czechoslovakia joined Hungary, Poland, East Germany, and Romania in ushering in a Communist government. So much was happening in the world, and yet for me, so little seemed to have changed.

Salzburg remained a devastated city. There were almost no jobs to be found, and the black market continued to flourish. Smuggling cigarettes across the German-Austrian border became a popular way to make a profit. The cigarettes moved in trucks and were sometimes hidden under the folded-down seats of cars. Inside Austria, the cigarettes commanded far higher prices. Even U.S. military men joined the smugglers. Everyone was looking for a way to make some money.

But something else was also happening in Salzburg. Bit by bit, old, ugly hatreds once again reared their heads. Pro-Nazi groups had started to meet in secret around the city. People who had hidden their past at the end of the war were once again surfacing. Or sometimes they were simply being flushed out. That was exactly what happened on Gaisberg Strasse one afternoon when the American OSS (what would later become the CIA) came for the German woman who lived on the third floor of Herr Hesse's villa. They banged on her door, and when she opened it, they arrested her for war crimes. The Americans had been searching for this woman for months, and all the while, she had been living here, under an assumed name, even carrying on with an American officer. We were told that she had been part of the Nazi SS in Warsaw and that there she had been one of the people who oversaw the killing of Jewish children in the Warsaw ghetto, one of the ones who watched as children were dropped alive into vats of boiling water. She had fled before the city fell and had found refuge in Salzburg.

When I heard the news, my body began to shake. I thought I would vomit. I had eaten in this woman's apartment. I had sold supplies for her on the black market. She had lived in my midst. I felt such rage at this world where traitors were allowed to live concealed lives. I wondered if there was anyone I could truly trust.

For weeks, I could not bring myself to set foot inside Herr Hesse's villa. Even though he and his family and Herr von Royce had always treated me well, had acted as my friends, I could not help wondering about their pasts and what might have happened to me in a different time and place. Many Jews in Salzburg, people I knew from the camps, were angry with me over my friendships with Austrians. They did not approve of how close I had become to Sylvia. Many saw me as having fallen for the enemy. And after the German woman in Herr Hesse's villa was exposed, even I began to doubt what I had done.

Sylvia tried her best to reassure me. She reminded me of the people who hated the Nazis. She reminded me that we were all struggling together to rebuild our lives. She made Hans Miedel's house into a home, where we ate together and laughed together. We spent hours playing with Waldamir, who was now walking and speaking his first words. We went to operas and musicals, which, for a few hours, carried us away to another time and place. Sylvia even made sure that we did not spend all our time in Salzburg. Together, we went again to visit her mother in Linz, and on several afternoons we left the confines of the city and hiked through the mountains. One time, we came across a farmer selling sandwiches, and we had just enough money for one sandwich, even though we were hungry enough to have eaten two a piece. Gradually, in these small ways, my suspicions receded. I was even able to enjoy the company of the Hesses and Herr von Royce again, to go the wine cellars with them and laugh and sing. They were particularly friendly to me after the incident, perhaps to protect themselves. I didn't ask any questions. To some degree, I felt at their mercy. It was as if, even three years after the shooting had stopped, we were all still in hiding.

Still, very slowly, the cloud that had appeared over Salzburg receded. But then something else happened, something that rekindled all my feelings of fear.

Ever since she had moved to Bergen-Belsen, my sister Genia had written begging me to visit. She had given birth to a daughter, Yona, and she asked me to come to see the baby. At last, I relented and decided to go. Visiting Genia was a difficult proposition because I would have to travel not only into another country but also into an entirely different military zone. Salzburg was under the control of the Americans, while Bergen-Belsen was under British control. I would need a special pass to go from one zone into another, and I had heard that people caught trying to cross between zones without the correct documents were denied immigration visas. My plan was to travel to the border and then to apply for the documents there.

I crossed with relative ease into Germany and then boarded a train that would take me to the meeting point of the two zones. Near the city of Frankfurt, I began to talk to a man seated nearby. After only a few words, we discovered that we were both Jewish, and we promptly switched to using Polish, believing that no one on the train would understand us. I told him where I was going and why, until he interrupted me midsentence, his voice excited. My sister Genia was this man's next door neighbor. He knew both Genia and Chaskiel and could almost complete my sentences when I spoke. Meeting this man was like a miracle. Quickly, I told him that I did not have the correct documents to cross into the British zone and that I was going to try to get them at the zone border. He told me not to worry, that he had a pass to travel between the zones. He reached into his pocket and handed the document to me. "I have to get off the train for business, but I will take another one back to Bergen-Belsen late this afternoon. Tonight, I will come to the Orenbachs' house and get the document back."

I was so excited that I accepted immediately, not thinking about how I would cross back into the American zone without a document. The man got off soon after, leaving me all alone on the train, with the document. Only minutes after Genia's neighbor had left, another man got up from his seat and walked over toward me. He sat down, and he began to speak Polish. In a low, threatening voice, he told me to give him money or he would have me arrested. I looked at him and said nothing. I pretended to be calm, while inside I felt nothing but panic.

"You have a false document," he said. "You came from Austria and are now in Germany with a false document. I'm going to have to call the police and have you arrested."

Struggling to keep my wits about me, I tried to challenge him, asking him who he was and where he was from. With a glint in his eye, he told me that he was Ukrainian and that he understood Polish very well. Then he told me again to give him my money or he would call the police. I knew immediately that he was another refugee, but knowing that did no good. I was not afraid about having the document, but I was afraid that if this Ukrainian did call the American zone police, they would not let me go to the United States. I did not want any trouble from this man. I had the equivalent of fifteen dollars in my pocket, and I handed it to him, hoping that would be enough. It was not.

He demanded more money, but I did not have more money. I was wearing a small ring on one of my fingers, and I pulled the ring off to give it to him, but he did not want the ring, he only wanted more money. "I know you have more money," he told me. "If you do not give it to me, I will summon the police."

I was growing more and more afraid. He refused to believe me, and I was very worried that he would start making a bigger scene and attract the attention of all the other passengers. Even now, people were turning their heads to look at the two people speaking this foreign-sounding language. My only hope, I realized, was to get off the train.

I told the Ukrainian that I had more money but that it was sewn into the lining of my pants. I would have to take off the pants and rip them up to retrieve the money, and the only way I could do that was if we got off the train. He agreed. We got off the train at the next stop. Right away, behind the train station I saw the remains of a brick building that had been bombed during the war. Only the exterior walls were standing. The interior was a huge pile of rubble. I pointed to the building and said we could go there and not be noticed. He shrugged his shoulders and agreed. We began walking toward the deserted ruin, when I pretended to lose my balance and stumble. The Ukrainian stepped to one side, and as I stood up, I clutched a brick in my hand. It was as if I had concentrated all my fear into the arm holding the brick. With every ounce of strength, I swung that arm, thrusting the brick squarely into his face. I hit him as hard as I could. I hit him so hard that he crumpled and fell to the ground. Blood was shooting from his face. I did not stop to look or to see what happened once he fell. I simply ran. I ran as if the entire Nazi army were at my back. Sweat was pouring off my body, my legs felt weak and shaky, but I did not stop running.

I went up one street and down another. I did not know where I was, and I had no idea where I could go. I wasn't a young kid anymore. I was almost thirty, and I had lived through many frightening moments, but still this time, I was

very frightened. Finally, panting, with my lungs feeling as if they were about
to burst, I asked a man on the street where I might find a Jewish organization. He looked at me and gave me some directions. I turned down a series of
streets, until I reached the place. It was not at all what I had expected. The
man had given me directions to a convent, a convent filled with Catholic nuns.
I looked at the chapel bell tower and the heavy wooden doors, and I wanted
to cry. But I also knew I had no choice. It was getting close to dusk, and I had
no money for food or a place to stay. Raising my hand, I knocked on the door.

I told the nuns that I was a refugee, and they gave me food, a blanket, and
a bed. In the morning, they asked me if I would take other blankets to the
refugee camps, give them out, and talk to the Jews in the camps about con-
verting to Catholicism. They told me to think about it, they told me there
would be more blankets and money. But I wanted none of it. I thanked them
and left.

Outside, I wandered the streets, looking for anyone who resembled a Jew.
Finally, I saw a man dressed in the traditional long, dark jacket and dark pants
and wearing a hat. I went up to him and told him everything that had happened. The man took my arm and said he could help. We went to a main street,
where he summoned a taxi. He paid the taxi driver to take me to a Jewish camp
on the German-Austrian border. There, I could slip across without the required documents and return to Salzburg. I thanked the man, but even then
I could not relax. Only many hours later, when the border guards had waved
me across, did I at last sigh in relief.

I returned to Salzburg at night, and the very next day my brother-in-law
Chaskiel appeared. The evening when I was supposed to have arrived at Genia's, their neighbor had come to reclaim his document. When he told Genia
and Chaskiel that he had met me on the train, a train that would have arrived
that afternoon, Genia was overcome with fear. They wondered if something
had happened at the border, and then they began to wonder if something had
happened to me, if I had been killed. Chaskiel had tried to trace me, and when
he discovered that I never made it to the border, he rode the train to Salzburg
on the chance that for some reason I had gone back. When he heard the story, he wanted me to return to Germany with him, perhaps for good. But I told
him after that train ride, I would not go back to Germany for anything. I felt
that I had been lucky just to get out of Germany alive. The war had been over
for almost three years, yet even in peacetime, this world was a very sinister
place.

The days and weeks now seemed endless. I had my routines. I clung to
Sylvia, falling deeper in love. But otherwise I was alone. Then, suddenly, on
a warm summer afternoon in 1948, I found my sister Serke.

Serke, her husband, and their children had survived the war years in the
Soviet Union working on farms and camps near the Ural mountains. After

years of waiting, they had finally been allowed to leave, and they had arrived in Salzburg on their way to a new home in Israel. I found them because I was still visiting the refugee camps each time a new transport arrived. After almost two years of looking, I was losing hope. But then I heard that this transport was from the Soviet Union. I asked for my sister, and I found her, thin and dazed but alive. Serke and her family were staying in Salzburg barely two weeks. I told her what had happened to our parents, to Srulke, Ytzel, and Esther. I told her about finding Genia in Łódź. I told her about me.

As I spoke, I realized almost nine years had passed in our lives. Serke was now about forty. Her hair was turning white, her face had become etched with lines. She had spent almost ten years of her life in the Soviet Union, and it had made her old. Her children had lost their youth to Soviet farms and work camps. As we spoke, we cried together, crying perhaps for our lost lives. Serke did not know what had happened to Luza or Moshe. We could only hope that they, too, were still alive.

Serke wanted me to come to Israel, but she agreed that my chance to go the United States was worth waiting for. What I could not explain to her was that some of my reluctance in leaving was also because I did not want to leave Sylvia. In what seemed like only days later, Serke and her family were gone. At least they were finally accounted for, but their leaving also reminded me that ultimately I was, as I had been for nearly the entire war, very much alone. Close to a decade of running, hiding, and separation, of loss and destruction had irrevocably pulled us apart. More than leading us to other towns, our lives were leading us to other continents. Never again would we be that same family, sleeping one on top of the other in a tiny room.

After Serke left, I intensified my efforts to get an answer from the U.S. consulate, to find out when I would be sent to the United States. I wrote the consulate almost every week searching for news. I had also convinced Sylvia to apply for a visa, hoping that she would be able to come with me. Sylvia's mother was angry and devastated at the news. She did not want Sylvia to leave, especially now, because that meant she would also be separated from her grandson, whom she loved. She pleaded with Sylvia not to go, reminding Sylvia how she had sacrificed her marriage to Sylvia's father for her children. Sylvia could not bring herself to hurt her mother, and so we let everything continue, completely unresolved. In our minds, my leaving was an abstraction, something the U.S. government did not yet seem about to make real.

I had, however, already begun to form ideas about Americans. I had met quite a number of U.S. military people in Salzburg, but none I was closer to than a lieutenant named Charlie Murdoch. Charlie Murdoch was a judge in the U.S. army, and he presided over the trials of lower-level war criminals. Almost every day, he traveled back and forth from Munich to Salzburg to gather information and receive orders. Several times, he invited me to his courtroom in Salzburg to watch some of the trials. But mostly we spent our time together as friends. We would go out dancing, go out to eat, or just sit and talk. Many times, I didn't want to go with him for dinner because I did not have money to pay my part of the bill, but he would insist that I come and then pay for me. He was a very generous man, full of good humor.

Gradually, I even became a source for Charlie. Sylvia passed on to me the names of former Nazis from Linz and the area, names she had come across while she worked as a secretary during the war. She was upset that so many of them remained at large. I, in turn, passed those names along to Charlie. Once, I even went for fifteen minutes with Sylvia to one of the Nazi underground's meetings. We went in a different section of Salzburg so we would not be recognized, and yet the whole time I felt afraid. Nothing was said at the meeting while I was there. It was mostly just a collection of two dozen or so people, milling around. Yet I was certain the people there recognized me as a Jew, even if on the surface they were perfectly polite. Only when we had left and were several miles away did I begin to feel calm. Sylvia told me that some of the people at these meetings were also trying to figure out ways to retrieve boxes of Jewish jewelry that had been thrown into local lakes by the German SS at the end of the war.

Charlie and his good humor made me eager to see the United States, but when he left to return there at the beginning of 1949, I had almost given up on hearing from the embassy. I did not even get his address. It never occurred to me that I would actually be able to write to him or call him once I went to the United States. As the summer of 1949 arrived, I began to feel more anxious. There was no work to be found, not even as a laborer, and any money that I had saved from selling the handkerchiefs and other goods was all but gone. I did not know what I could do, and it seemed that all I could do was wait.

Then one day in the fall, without warning, it arrived, a notice from the U.S. consulate informing me that my visa had been granted and that my passage had been booked on the SS *Marina Plosche* out of Bremerhaven, West Germany, at the end of December. Sylvia cried when she saw the letter. There was no mention of Sylvia or her visa, and even more, now my departure seemed very real. I agonized over what to do. I had waited four years for this moment. This was my only chance. I had no future in Austria. But I loved Sylvia. Finally, we reached a decision, I would go to the United States and wait for Sylvia's visa to be approved. She would join me there. We would not be apart forever. Frau Pfeifer was heartbroken at the prospect, but at least she knew that Sylvia would, for now, not be leaving with me. I began making preparations for my departure.

When the day came, Sylvia went with me to the train station. From there, I would travel north through Germany to a waiting point near the port of Bremerhaven. At the station, we embraced, sobbing. In some ways, the entire moment felt unreal. I could not believe that I was truly leaving forever, that I was nearing my last moments on European soil. In a daze, I climbed onto the train. A number of other Jews from Salzburg, some of whom I had known in Parsch, were also leaving with me. We waved as the train pulled away, and within minutes, it seemed that years of our lives were also suddenly gone.

Waiting for the boat, I was both excited and despondent. The time seemed to pass with agonizing slowness, leaving me many hours to wonder if I was doing the right thing. Then, the messages started coming. Sylvia had been arrested trying to cross the border into Germany. She wanted to come with me or else she wanted me to return. I could not bear this. Perhaps the journey was not worth it. Perhaps I should go back. In my mind, I started preparing to return to Salzburg.

But many of the other refugees waiting to leave for the United States had heard my story and now knew what had happened. They were determined that I would not squander this chance, that I would board the boat. They almost considered me a traitor for falling in love with an Austrian woman. One of the refugees waiting to leave was a doctor, and he gave me an injection. I don't know whether he gave me a sedative or tranquilizers, but he and the other refugees stayed with me in my room, holding me almost prisoner so that I could not leave before we sailed. By the time the ship was ready for boarding, the injection had worn off, and my head had cleared. As we rode to the ship, I decided that I would board the ship. I would not go back, I would not return to Salzburg. As I looked up at the liner, I knew that this ship was what I had been waiting for, that this was my chance to go to the United States.

The voyage was horrendous. In the middle of the Atlantic, the ship was caught in a terrible storm. All around us, the ocean churned, and inside everything pitched and rolled. As I felt the waves batter the ship, I was afraid that it would sink and that we would all drown. The violent storm also caused almost everyone on the boat to become ill. People were just lying on the floor, groaning and holding their stomachs, as the boat listed from side to side. For days, it seemed we would be trapped on that ship and never reach land.

Our destination was New York City, but for some reason the ship was diverted to the port of Boston. We arrived at night. Every light in the city seemed to be ablaze. Thousands of bright lights were burning before us as we moved into the harbor. Never in my life had I seen anything like it, so much brilliant light fending off the darkness.

From the ship we were transferred to the train station. We would go to New York by rail the next morning. Right next to the station was a small diner, and several of us went inside. We had a bit of money, and we hoped to get something to eat. When the owner discovered that this was our first evening in the United States, that we had quite literally just stepped ashore, and that many of us, including me, could not even speak more than a word or two of English, he offered every person from the ship free coffee and Danish. People in the restaurant started talking in strange words I did not understand, but another passenger translated for me. "When the owner was told that he was doing 'too much,' he smiled and said, 'It's my pleasure,'" this passenger explained.

As I sipped my coffee and ate the sweet, sticky pastry, I thought, "This is America." This was like everything that I had ever been told.

When I arrived in New York, my aunt, several cousins, and their children were waiting. They carried signs, and as soon as the first passengers from the train began to appear, they started screaming and calling out my name. I remember blinding lights and hysterical voices as I stepped onto the platform and into a strange new world filled with things I had never seen and people I had never met.

We rode in a car back to their apartment in Brooklyn, and after some food, my aunt showed me to a room where I could sleep. Exhausted, I got into bed, and I saw a little girl, one of the children, about eleven years old, peering through a crack in the door, looking at me. A couple of the other kids opened the door to the room a tiny crack more to take a peak. I felt all these little eyes on me. I lay there on the bed, unable to sleep. My eyes began to fill, and then the tears came. I missed Sylvia. I missed everything I had known. I did not like this strange place with strange people and strange food. All I wanted at that moment was to be back with Sylvia. I sobbed the entire night. At dawn, my pillow was soaked with tears, and I was still in America.

Jack on his first trans-Atlantic boat trip to the United
States in 1949.

Jack returning to the United States with other refugees in 1951.

Jack Pomerantz and Nina Kibrick on their wedding day, August 1, 1953, in Newark, New Jersey.

Radzyń, Poland, in 1985, when Jack returned to visit.

Jack standing in front of the Obremskis' house in 1985. The Pomerantz family lived in a small, three-room shed in the back.

Jack standing alongside his family's former home, with Vladec Obremski (left)
and a Polish escort.

Jack Pomerantz with his family in November 1996. Front (left to right): Alexander Kasper, Nina Pomerantz, Francine Pomerantz, Hannah Kasper, Shaina Kasper; back: Arlene Pomerantz, Jack, Keith Kasper.

Epilogue

Nine months later, I went back to Europe. I missed Sylvia terribly and was desperately lonely in New York. I did not speak English. I did not like the food. I worked long hours at terrible jobs, and still I could not even make enough money to live on. One of my cousins owned a pipe factory, and he put me to work there, in front of the furnace for eight hours a day. The heat was so intense it burned my hands and singed my eyebrows. I could never work fast enough in the heat to suit him. Many days, I felt as if I were back in Siberia at the wood splitter. From there, I went to work in a chocolate factory and finally to a garment company on Sixth Avenue and Twenty-ninth Street. I wheeled huge barrels of material, and when I finally asked for a two-dollar-a-week raise, my boss kept telling me how he could get a Puerto Rican to do my job for two dollars less a week. This was not the America I had imagined. This was not the place I had dreamed of.

I was also living with relatives I did not know, relatives who knew nothing of Europe or the war other than what little they had read in the papers. I did meet other immigrants and spent my time with them, but being around other lost people offered little consolation.

It was, however, in New York that I discovered Moshe and Luza had survived the war. Having made it out of the Soviet Union, they were now safe in Israel. I located them through the Radzyń Society. Jewish immigrants from little towns throughout eastern Europe established societies named after their hometowns in the United States and also in Israel. Through these societies, they could keep in touch with their roots and with each other. After the war, these societies tried to keep track of residents who had survived and emigrated. It was through the Radzyń Society in New York that I received word of my brothers in Israel. I was overjoyed. I wrote to them and waited for their replies. Three of my brothers and sisters had perished, but four had survived. Even though they were almost halfway around the world, I felt as if a bit of our family had been reconnected.

In New York, however, I still felt terribly isolated and alone. One of the brightest spots in my life was a cab driver I met only once in my first week in the city. Since I did not know my way even around the block in Brooklyn, I took a cab to visit another cousin only a mile away. I was carrying with me every bit of money I had in the world, including a hundred dollar bill, which the Jewish relief agency had given me when I left Bremerhaven. By mistake, I gave the driver my hundred dollars when I got out of the cab. I did not even realize my error. Five minutes later, the cabbie knocked on my cousin's door. He had come to return the money. I do not know when he realized that I had given him the hundred dollars, but he returned it. That was the America I had envisioned. That was the spirit of generosity I searched for but seldom found in the rough-and-tumble world of postwar New York.

My relatives could not convince me to stay, but they did convince me to go to Washington and get a reentry visa, so that I could return if I wanted. By the fall of 1950, I was once again on ship, this time bound for Europe and for Sylvia.

When I returned, Sylvia and I were married. Life in Salzburg, however, had not improved. There was no work, and we started selling pieces of furniture from Hans Miedel's and Frau Pfeifer's just to survive. I soon realized that even if New York had been difficult, we faced nothing but poverty in Salzburg. Sylvia reapplied for a visa as my wife, and I decided to return to the United States to work and make money and send her whatever I could.

Returning was a lengthy, bureaucratic process. It took me almost another year to make it back to New York. But I knew that this time I would stay. I went back to Brooklyn and began sleeping on the couch of a couple I had met in Salzburg, Shepsil and Sara Stubinski. I worked hard to learn English, and I found a new job.

Months passed, and still there was no word about Sylvia's visa. I was settling into my life. In Salzburg, Waldamir was starting school. Our letters became less frequent, and then came the official ruling: Sylvia's visa application had been denied. The government had answered any lingering questions for us. Unless I returned to Austria, we were destined to spend years apart. I cared deeply for Sylvia and she for me, but the time had come to let go. We had to get on with our lives, each on different continents, in different worlds.

I had landed a job as a furniture finisher, and Stubinski's wife was trying very hard to find me a girlfriend. She knew about Sylvia, but she believed quite strongly that I needed a wife and a home in the United States. Perhaps she had an eye toward moving me off her couch and into someone else's house. Week after week, she would come home with the telephone numbers of women for me to call. One number belonged to Nina Kibrick, who lived all the way across the river in Irvington, New Jersey. I rode the bus for two hours to see her one Saturday night. And then I rode the bus two hours back again. Nina was a quiet, slender, dark-eyed woman. Her father's family came from a small village called Kusnitz in Russia and her mother's side from the adjacent territory of Moldavia. A few weeks passed, and I saw her again. Soon, I was seeing her every week. Nina reminded me of my first fiancée, the young woman in Brest, the sweet, gentle, caring person I had lost when I was very young and unknowing, so many years ago. But Nina was her own person, with her own generous heart and goodness. Without even realizing it, I had fallen in love. I wanted to marry Nina.

Sylvia and I finalized our divorce, and Nina and I were married. In the beginning, life was not easy. We lived in a one-room apartment. Nina worked full-time in a bank. I worked three jobs, seven days a week. We saved every penny we could for children and for a house of our own. We were lucky. We have two wonderful daughters, Francine and Arlene, and we have our own home. I am proud of my children. Whether it is a plant, an animal, or a person, they care for every living thing. I am also very proud of my wife. She is filled with extraordinary compassion and love. She is my partner. She is the person I turn to throughout the day. She has made my life whole.

I have my family, and I have a profession I love. When my children were little, I started to build houses, places people could turn into homes. On blank strips of land, I see beams and doors and windows, joined together to welcome someone in. Down to the smallest doorknob, I believe a home can be a place of beauty, a beauty that can surround us all our lives.

I am lucky. I survived. I prospered. I have the joys of a wonderful wife and family, children and three grandchildren, Alexander, Shaina, and Hannah. Along with the joy, we have also faced our share of heartache, but still I am lucky. Life does not always reward the survivors. My sister Serke lived a relatively peaceful life, dying in her early sixties in Israel. For my brother Moshe, things turned out very differently. Only about eight years after he had arrived in Israel, Moshe suffered a massive stroke. He spent the final thirty-five years of his life paralyzed and unable to speak. Moshe's story aches with tragedy because it follows so closely on a story with such joy, a story I learned years after it happened.

When Moshe and I met in the Soviet Union, he had been separated from his family for over a year. Once the war ended, he made his way south from Berozofka to look for them. At several points, he was joined by different Russian companions. Outside a train station near Taškent, or possibly in the city itself, while walking with a Russian friend, Moshe saw a group of children playing. He noticed one sandy-haired girl, about five or six years old, and said to his friend, "My little girl would now be just about the age of that little girl, running and playing."

At that same moment, the little girl looked up at the tall man walking along and stopped moving. She stared at him. Then she began to scream, "Tata, Tata," which in Yiddish means "father." She started running toward the man. As she ran, a group of women who had been sitting off to one side suddenly leapt up. One kept her gaze fastened on the child. Then she looked beyond to the pair of men, frozen in astonishment. She looked and she knew. Holding his arms open, with tears in his eyes, Moshe rushed toward his wife, Bransha, and daughter, Bella.

For years after his stroke, first Bransha and then Bella cared for Moshe, whose eyes flickered in recognition but who could make no sound. He passed away in the fall of 1992.

Luza also survived to be reunited with his family. But then they were torn apart. Only about four years after they arrived in Israel, Luza's wife, Haiya, died. Luza loved his wife so deeply that he was absolutely despondent over her loss and on the verge of suicide. He also was left with three small children to raise. Haiya had a sister in Israel, and she helped Luza care for the children, especially during the day, while Luza worked as a tailor. Haiya's sister would watch two of the children, and Luza would take his third child, little more than a baby, with him to the tailor shop. The child would play quietly at his feet while he cut and sewed. Eventually, Luza was able to find enough business that he could work out of his home and be around the children all the time. He would do anything for his children, and they grew up to be wonderful people. Luza succumbed to pneumonia in 1991. To the end, he was the kindest and gentlest of men.

My sister Genia died not long after Luza, but she had been suffering for years, her mind slowly deteriorating as she lived out her life in Germany. Her daughter, Yona, grew to be a strong, beautiful woman. Yet even now, she carries her mother's legacy. Throughout Europe, she searches crowds for women who might have her mother's face, for the sister who was lost in Poland almost fifty years ago. Even now, she is still looking. Life does not always reward survivors.

In the summer of 1985, I returned to Radzyń with my wife, Nina, and daughter, Francine. Almost fifty years had passed since I had fled. I expected to find nothing as I remembered it. Instead, I found nearly everything the same. Vladec Obremski still lived in the same house. And behind that house still stood the shed where my family had lived. Even the storage space where I had raised pigeons remained. The streets, the houses, and the old summer palace and bright stucco church in the center of town had barely changed in half a century. Time had made them older and shabbier. They had obviously suffered under years of poverty and neglect, under years of Communist rule. But nothing had replaced them as landmarks. The world had marched on, while Radzyń stood remarkably still.

There had been some changes, but they were more a result of age and life. Vladec was senile and a hunched, wizened old man. His brother, Romek, was dead and his sister, Yerke, had been married for years. He remembered just enough to tell me where she now lived, in another section of Radzyń. Many of the others I had known had already grown old and died. Yet in Radzyń, and also in the small village of Branica, people still remembered me and my father. They remembered us peddling, as if it were something we had been doing until only a few years ago.

We went to see Vladec's sister, Yerke, who had married the caretaker of the summer palace, and she proudly showed off its grounds. Then she invited us into her home for tea. But on the street, she also pointed to me and whispered to the cab driver who had driven us here all the way from Warsaw. She whispered and pointed, and I could not help feeling uneasy. What was she telling this man? Did Yerke tell him that I used to live in a shed that her family owned? Did she tell him that I was a Jew who had survived? Or that I had deserted the Polish military after the war? The last time Yerke had seen me, I was in my uniform. Would this cab driver, when I returned to his car, see me as a military deserter or a traitor? And what would he do? There was no way to know.

Inside her house, Yerke was pleasant. She showed us photographs of her grown children. She pointed to little knickknacks. In the back, she had a modest garden, some flowers and a few vegetables. When we asked to see it, she led us outside. As I walked through the plot, I felt hard stones under my feet, not pebbles, but slabs of stone. I looked down and saw that some slabs were in pieces, others were curved and cut like scrolls. I looked closer. There was writing on the stones.

I recognized the words, Hebrew words, Yiddish words, their outlines partly eroded by the elements. These were gravestones from the Jewish cemetery, now lying, cracked and broken, amid the dirt in the garden.

I asked Yerke about the stones, and she said that the Germans had taken them from the cemetery and brought them here during the war. Somehow, I could not imagine German soldiers hauling Jewish stones to a Polish garden plot to make a path. I looked down and said nothing. When the rainy seasons came, Yerke walked on these stones to keep her feet clear of mud. She walked over whole stones and half stones, stones for entire families and for firstborn sons, stones for babies who died before they ever spoke a word to the world, stones for parents whose children would one day die unspeakable deaths. I could not read the carved names, but I had my own: Abish, Freida, Esther, Ytzel, Srulke.

That fall, my wife and daughter sent Yerke packages of flower seeds for her garden, flowers to bloom among the stones.

Selected Bibliography

In addition to archival research in New York and Washington, D.C.—which covered a wide array of information, including highly detailed German bomber targeting maps at the New York Public Library that depicted Radzyń and surrounding towns, showing bridges, dirt and paved roads, and major buildings, and also including volumes of documents from the U.S. Army of Occupation in Europe now at the National Archives, which provided supporting information about Jack Pomerantz's years in Salzburg and immigration information—the following books and articles were especially helpful in preparing the manuscript.

I used the general histories cited below primarily to improve my own grasp of the salient issues, dimensions, and chronologies of the Holocaust. In addition, to help with the challenges of the collaboration and issues of memory and recollection, the selected articles and memoirs were useful. Finally, in a few instances, some material helped provide collaboration for Jack Pomerantz's recollections. This was especially true for the restricted training manuals from the U.S. Military Academy at West Point. I discovered them after I had completed the interviews for the section of the manuscript that covers the war on the eastern front and Jack Pomerantz's participation in it. His descriptions and recollections, down to the weather and road conditions during several campaigns, matched the content of the manuals with the exactness and clarity of two halves of a torn photograph, thus giving me great confidence in the accuracy and depth of his remembrances.

At no time, however, were details from any of these sources used to supplement details which Jack Pomerantz could not remember or of which he was unsure. In a few cases where there was conflict between other accounts and Jack Pomerantz's recollections, as, for example, in various accounts of the Jews of Lvov that differ from what his sister and brother-in-law had told him, I have always used Jack Pomerantz's version, while at the same time comparing it with other sources, with each ultimately acting as a check on the other. In most instances, however, his experiences lie well outside the scope of most of these works.

In the text, names also appear as Jack Pomerantz recalled, either in full or in part. Where individual names could not be recalled, that has been noted in the course of the text.

As a whole, the following books were most helpful in establishing an overall chronology for his experiences during the chaotic years of the war, and they helped guide me in my questions and in my organization of the manuscript. Always, my project has been to present Jack Pomerantz's story in its entirety, preserving its integrity and the language and power with which it was told.

L.W.W.

Selected Books and Articles

American Jewish Committee. *The Jewish Communities of Nazi-Occupied Europe*. New York: Howard Fertig, 1982.

Appleman-Jurman, Alicia. *My Story*. New York: Bantam Books, 1990.

Bauer, Yehuda. *A History of the Holocaust*. New York: Franklin Watts, 1982.

Bergman, Tamar. *Along the Tracks*. Translated by Michael Swirsky. Boston: Houghton Mifflin, 1991.

Boilles, Edmund B. *Remembering and Forgetting: An Inquiry into the Nature of Memory*. New York: Walker, 1988.

Clark, E. Culpepper, Michael J. Hyde, and Eva McMahan. "Communicating in the Oral History Interview: Investigating Problems of Interpreting Oral Data." *International Journal of Oral History* 1 (February 1980): 28–40.

Dawidowicz, Lucy. *From That Place and Time: A Memoir, 1938–1947*. New York: Bantam Books, 1989.

———. *The Holocaust and the Historians*. Cambridge, Mass.: Harvard University Press, 1981.

———. *The War against the Jews, 1933–1945*. New York: Bantam Books, 1986.

———, ed. *A Holocaust Reader,* New York: Behrman House, 1976.

Dwork, Deborah. *Children with a Star: Jewish Youth in Nazi Europe*. New Haven, Conn.: Yale University Press, 1991.

Encyclopedia Judaica. 16 vols. Jerusalem, Israel: Keter Publishing House, 1972.

Epstein, Helen. *Children of the Holocaust: Conversations with Sons and Daughters of Survivors*. New York: G. P. Putnam, 1979.

Farris, David. "Narrative Form and Oral History: Some Problems and Possibilities." *International Journal of Oral History* 2 (February 1980): 159–80.

Gilbert, Martin. *Final Journey: The Fate of the Jews in Nazi Europe*. Boston: George Allen and Unwin, 1979.

———. *The Holocaust: A History of the Jews of Europe during the Second World War*. New York: Holt, Rinehart and Winston, 1985.

———. *The Holocaust: Maps and Photographs*. New York: Hill and Wang, 1978.

———. *The Macmillan Atlas of the Holocaust*. New York: DaCapo, 1984.

Grade, Chaim. *My Mother's Sabbath Days*. Translated by Channa Kleinerman Goldstein and Inna Hecker Grade. New York: Alfred A. Knopf, 1986.

Gutman, Yisrael, and Shumel Krakowski. *Unequal Victims: Poles and Jews during World War II*. New York: Holocaust Library, 1986.

Heller, Celia S. *On the Edge of Destruction: Jews of Poland between Two World Wars.* New York: Schocken Books, 1980.

Kuper, Jack. *Child of the Holocaust.* New York: New American Library, 1980.

Langer, Lawrence. *Holocaust Testimonies: The Ruins of Memory.* New Haven, Conn.: Yale University Press, 1991.

Levi, Primo. *The Drowned and the Saved.* New York: Summit, 1988.

———. *If Not Now, When?* New York: Penguin Books, 1985.

———. *Survival in Auschwitz.* New York: Collier's, 1961.

Levin, Nora. *The Holocaust: The Destruction of European Jewery, 1933–1945.* New York: Schocken Books, 1973.

Markovna, Nina. *Nina's Journey: A Memoir of Stalin's Russia and the Second World War.* Washington, D.C.: Regnery Gateway, 1989.

Marrus, Michael R. *The Holocaust in History.* New York: Penguin Books, 1987.

———. *The Unwanted: European Refugees in the Twentieth Century.* New York: Schocken Books, 1985.

Marshall, Robert. *In The Sewers of Lvov: A Heroic Story of Survival from the Holocaust.* New York: Charles Scribner's Sons, 1989.

Mendelsohn, Ezra. *The Jews of East Central Europe between the World Wars.* Bloomington: University of Indiana Press, 1983.

Miller, Judith. *One by One by One: Facing the Holocaust.* New York: Simon and Schuster, 1990.

Mosse, Gerald L. *Toward the Final Solution: A History of European Racism.* London: Praeger, 1978.

Murphy, H. B. M. *Flight and Resettlement.* Paris: UNESCO, 1955.

Nir, Yehuda. *The Lost Childhood: A Memoir.* San Diego: Harcourt Brace Jovanovich, 1989.

Rothchild, Sylvia, ed. *Voices from the Holocaust.* New York: New American Library, 1981.

Salsitz, Norman, and Amalie Petranker. *Against All Odds: A Tale of Two Survivors.* New York: Holocaust Library, 1990.

Szwajger, Adina Blady. *I Remember Nothing More: The Warsaw Children's Hospital and the Jewish Resistance.* Translated by Tasja Darowska and Danusia Stok. New York: Pantheon Books, 1990.

The War in Eastern Europe, June 1941 to May 1945. Restricted Manuals. West Point, N.Y.: Department of Military Art and Engineering, United States Military Academy, 1949.

Werner, Harold. *Fighting Back: A Memoir of Jewish Resistance in World War II.* New York: Columbia University Press, 1992.

Wiesel, Elie. *Night.* New York: Bantam Books, 1982.

Index

JACK POMERANTZ was born in Radzyń, Poland. A retired housebuilder, he is the father of two daughters, Francine and Arlene, and grandfather of Alexander, Shaina, and Hannah Kasper. He lives in Short Hills, New Jersey, with his wife of over forty years, Nina.

LYRIC WALLWORK WINIK is a graduate of Princeton University and holds a master's degree in history from Johns Hopkins University. A regular contributor to *Parade* magazine, her articles have also appeared in such publications as the *New York Times,* the *Washingtonian* magazine, and *Forbes FYI.* A recipient of the Academy of American Poets e. e. cummings society prize, she is currently working on a novel. She lives in Chevy Chase, Maryland, with her husband, Jay Winik.